El Salvador
a country study

Federal Research Division
Library of Congress
Edited by
Richard A. Haggerty
Research Completed
November 1988

On the cover: Vendors and customers at a produce market

Second Edition, 1990; First Printing, 1990.

Library of Congress Cataloging-in-Publication Data

El Salvador: A Country Study.

  Area handbook series, DA Pam 550-150
  Research completed November 1988.
  Bibliography: pp. 269-83.
  Includes index.
  1. El Salvador I. Haggerty, Richard A., 1954-   . II. Library of Congress. Federal Research Division. III. Area handbook for El Salvador. IV. Series. V. Series: DA Pam : 550-150.

F1483.B55   1990
972.84—dc20   —dc20

                                           89-48948
                                                CIP

Headquarters, Department of the Army
DA Pam 550-150

For sale by the Superintendent of Documents, U.S. Government Printing Office
Washington, D.C. 20402

Foreword

This volume is one in a continuing series of books now being prepared by the Federal Research Division of the Library of Congress under the Country Studies—Area Handbook Program. The last page of this book lists the other published studies.

Most books in the series deal with a particular foreign country, describing and analyzing its political, economic, social, and national security systems and institutions, and examining the interrelationships of those systems and the ways they are shaped by cultural factors. Each study is written by a multidisciplinary team of social scientists. The authors seek to provide a basic understanding of the observed society, striving for a dynamic rather than a static portrayal. Particular attention is devoted to the people who make up the society, their origins, dominant beliefs and values, their common interests and the issues on which they are divided, the nature and extent of their involvement with national institutions, and their attitudes toward each other and toward their social system and political order.

The books represent the analysis of the authors and should not be construed as an expression of an official United States government position, policy, or decision. The authors have sought to adhere to accepted standards of scholarly objectivity. Corrections, additions, and suggestions for changes from readers will be welcomed for use in future editions.

Louis R. Mortimer
Acting Chief
Federal Research Division
Library of Congress
Washington, D.C. 20540

Acknowledgments

The authors wish to acknowledge the contributions of Howard I. Blutstein, Elinor C. Betters, John Cobb, Jr., Jonathan A. Leonard, and Charles M. Townsend, who wrote the 1970 edition of *El Salvador: A Country Study*. Their work lent perspective to several chapters of the present volume. The authors also are grateful to individuals in various agencies of the United States government and international and private institutions who gave of their time, research materials, and special knowledge to provide information and perspective.

The authors also wish to thank those who contributed directly to the preparation of the manuscript. These include Richard F. Nyrop, who reviewed all drafts and served as liaison with the sponsoring agency; Sandra W. Meditz, who reviewed drafts and provided valuable advice on all aspects of production; Dennis M. Hanratty, who contributed useful and substantive comments on several chapter drafts; Martha E. Hopkins, Patricia Mollela, Ruth Nieland, and Michael Pleasants, who edited portions of the manuscript; Marilyn Majeska, who also edited portions of the manuscript and managed production; Barbara Edgerton, Janie L. Gilchrist, and Izella Watson, who did the word processing; Andrea T. Merrill, who performed the final prepublication editorial review; Shirley Kessel, who compiled the index; and Malinda B. Neale of the Printing and Processing Section, Library of Congress, who prepared the camera-ready copy under the supervision of Peggy Pixley.

David P. Cabitto, Sandra K. Ferrell, and Kimberly A. Lord provided invaluable graphics support. David P. Cabitto also designed the cover and illustrations for the title page of each chapter. Susan M. Lender reviewed the map drafts, which were prepared by Harriett R. Blood, David P. Cabitto, and Kimberly A. Lord. Various individuals, libraries, and public agencies provided photographs.

Finally, the authors would like to thank several individuals who provided research support. Arvies J. Staton supplied information on ranks and insignia, and Timothy L. Merrill wrote the geography section in Chapter 2.

Contents

Chapter 3. The Economy 99
Donald E. Jacobson and David B. Ehrenthal

Chapter 4. Government and Politics 141
Richard A. Haggerty

List of Figures

Preface

Like its predecessor, this study is an attempt to treat in a compact and objective manner the dominant social, political, economic, and military aspects of contemporary El Salvador. Sources of information included scholarly books, journals, and monographs; official reports of governments and international organizations; numerous periodicals; and interviews with individuals having special competence in Salvadoran and Latin American affairs. Chapter bibliographies appear at the end of the book; brief comments on sources recommended for further reading appear at the end of each chapter. Measurements are given in the metric system; a conversion table is provided to assist readers unfamiliar with metric measurements (see table 1, Appendix). A glossary is also included.

Although there are numerous variations, Spanish surnames generally consist of two parts: the patrilineal name followed by the matrilineal. In the instance of José Napoleón Duarte Fuentes, for example, Duarte is his father's name and Fuentes his mother's maiden name. In nonformal use, the matrilineal name is often dropped. Thus, after the first mention, just Duarte is used. A minority of individuals use only the patrilineal name. El Salvador also abounds in political and other organizational acronyms. Where discrepancies existed, the form most frequently employed in the country itself has been used.

Country

Formal Name: Republic of El Salvador.

Short Form: El Salvador.

Term for Citizens: Salvadoran(s).

Capital: San Salvador.

Geography

Size: Approximately 21,041 square kilometers.

Topography: Two parallel mountain ranges running east to west divide country into two regions: mountains and central plateau, and coastal plains (Pacific lowlands). Southern mountain range made up of more than twenty volcanoes. Eruptions rare, but earthquakes frequent because of location at conjunction of three geologic plates. Río Lempa only navigable river. Numerous volcanic lakes in interior highlands.

Climate: Tropical climate with pronounced wet and dry seasons; rainy season (winter) from May to October, dry season (summer) from November through April. Temperatures vary with elevation and show little seasonal change. Pacific lowlands uniformly hot; central plateau and mountain areas more moderate.

Society

Population: Population estimated at 5.4 million in 1988. Rate of annual growth estimated at 2.4 percent in 1980s.

Language: Spanish official language and spoken by virtually all Salvadorans. Some traces of Indian languages, but no segment of population linguistically distinct.

Ethnic Groups: In late 1980s, about 89 percent of population mestizo (Spanish and Indian), 10 percent Indian, and 1 percent unmixed Caucasian.

Education and Literacy: Approximately 69 percent of population ten years or older considered literate in early 1980s. Higher rate of literacy in urban than in rural areas. Public education system included one year of preschool, nine years of basic education, and three years secondary education. Major universities National University of El Salvador and Jesuit-run Central American University José Simeón Cañas.

Health: Serious malnutrition, particularly among young children. Malaria, enteritis, and pneumonia most serious diseases. Medical attention to general population inadequate, especially in rural areas.

Religion: Overwhelmingly Roman Catholic, although Protestant missionary groups, especially evangelicals, active and continued to make significant number of converts.

Economy

Gross Domestic Product (GDP): Approximately US$4.6 billion in 1986, or US$938 per capita. Growth extremely modest from 1983 through 1986, averaging about 1.5 percent annually.

Agriculture: Accounted for about 24 percent of GDP in 1986. Production of export commodities predominated. Coffee major crop, accounting for half of export earnings in 1987. Sugar and cotton other major exports. Agriculture adversely affected during 1980s by insurgent conflict, uneven implementation of agrarian reform, and inconsistent government policies.

Industry: Accounted for over 20 percent of GDP in 1986, with manufacturing accounting for most sectoral activity (17.4 percent of GDP). Also included construction (3.1 percent of GDP) and some mining (0.1 percent of GDP). Manufacturing concentrated in food processing, tobacco products, textiles, and clothing. Output declined seriously during 1980s as result of guerrilla sabotage (mainly attacks on electrical grid), capital flight, and labor unrest.

Services: Almost 50 percent of GDP in 1986. Services tended to follow prevailing trends in economy as a whole. Included transportation, commerce, insurance, health care, utilities, and other public services.

Currency: Colón, consisting of 100 centavos. Unified exchange rate of ¢5 to US$1 established in November 1986.

Imports: Approximately US$975 million in 1987. Raw materials accounted for over 50 percent of imports, followed by consumer goods (24 percent) and capital goods (23 percent).

Exports: Approximately US$591 million in 1987, representing decline of over 21 percent compared with 1986 figures, mostly because of drop in coffee prices. Agricultural commodities (coffee, sugar, and cotton) made up bulk of exports.

Balance of Payments: Overall positive balance maintained during late 1980s despite significant trade deficit. Major compensating factors large inflows of foreign aid—mostly from United States—and remittances from Salvadorans living abroad (again, mainly in United States).

Fiscal Year: Calendar year.

Fiscal Policy: Although government expenditures in mid-1980s remained fairly stable relative to GDP, overall budget deficit reached 5.4 percent of GDP in 1986. Deficit financing accomplished primarily through Central Reserve Bank of El Salvador, although public enterprises and development programs relied heavily on foreign aid and international loans.

Transportation and Communications

Roads: Over 10,000 kilometers, of which about 1,500 paved. Major arteries Pan American Highway and Carretera Litoral.

Railroads: Total system just over 600 kilometers, 380 kilometers of which owned by Salvador Railways, nationalized by government in mid-1960s.

Ports: Two major ports—Acajutla and La Unión. Minor ports at La Libertad and Puerto El Triunfo.

Airports: Ilopango International Airport only airport capable of accommodating jet aircraft in late 1980s. Ninety-five usable airfields throughout country, although only five paved.

Telecommunications: System not highly developed despite significant growth during 1960s and 1970s. Internal and external systems suffered regular and significant damage from guerrilla sabotage throughout 1980s. All services provided by National Telecommunications Administration (Administración Nacional de Telecomunicaciones—Antel), a public enterprise.

Government and Politics

Government: Under 1983 Constitution, elected representative government divided into three branches. President, vice president, and Council of Ministers (cabinet) comprise executive branch. President directly elected for five-year term and may not be reelected; also serves as constitutional commander in chief of armed forces. Unicameral, sixty-member Legislative Assembly constitutes legislative branch. Judicial branch headed by Supreme Court of Justice; below Supreme Court are chambers of second instance, courts of first instance, and justice of the peace courts. Magistrates appointed by Legislative Assembly to fixed terms. Governors of departments (states) appointed by president; mayors and municipal council members directly elected. Military exerts political influence, particularly on issues relating to national security, but active-duty military personnel constitutionally prohibited from seeking office.

Politics: Long characterized by military rule supporting dominance of economic elite, in late 1980s political system still adapting to demands for free elections, representative democracy, and more open public discourse. Civil conflict between government forces and Marxist guerrillas greatly exacerbated political polarization rooted in historical dichotomy between wealthy elite and impoverished and excluded majority. In late 1980s, the two major political parties were the moderate, center-left Christian Democratic Party (Partido Demócrata Cristiano—PDC) and the right-wing Nationalist Republican Alliance (Alianza Republicana Nacionalista—Arena). As of late 1988, PDC held presidency, but Arena had one-seat majority in Legislative Assembly.

International Relations: Mainly limited to Central American region until 1980s, when civil conflict made El Salvador focus of international attention. Relations with United States became increasingly important during 1980s because of critical contribution of United States economic and military aid to survival of elected government, bolstering of war-ravaged economy, and improved performance of armed forces. Government of José Napoleón Duarte Fuentes participated actively in Contadora process, a joint Latin American mediating effort seeking to ease Central American tensions through diplomatic negotiations. Duarte signed Central American Peace Agreement, product of unmediated talks among the Central American states, in August 1987.

International Agreements and Membership: Party to Inter-American Treaty of Reciprocal Assistance (Rio Treaty). Also member of Organization of American States, Central American Common Market, United Nations, and several of its specialized agencies: World Bank, International Monetary Fund, and Inter-American Development Bank.

National Security

Armed Forces: Salvadoran armed forces included army, air force, navy, and security forces (National Guard, National Police, and Treasury Police). Total strength about 59,000 in late 1980s—47,000 regular armed forces and 12,600 security forces.

Organization: Country divided into six military zones and fourteen subordinate military regions. In 1980s army consisted of six infantry brigades, nine cadre infantry regiments, one mechanized cavalry regiment, one artillery brigade, one engineer battalion, six independent immediate-reaction battalions, and seven detachments. Air force made up of four squadrons of fixed-wing aircraft and one helicopter squadron. Air force antiaircraft artillery battalion and paratrooper battalion manned by army personnel. Navy, in addition to coastal patrol units based mainly at La Unión, included Marine Infantry Battalion and commando unit.

Equipment: Most weaponry, especially after 1980, supplied by United States, although some aircraft of Brazilian and French manufacture.

Police: Responsibilities divided among components of security forces: National Police handled urban security; National Guard, rural security; and Treasury Police (including customs and immigration), border control.

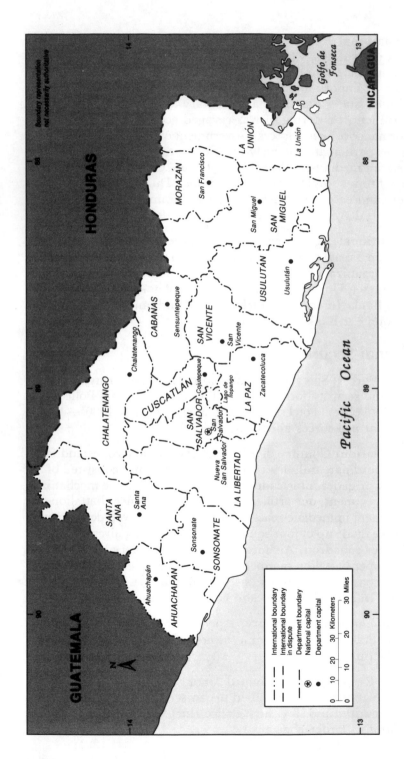

Figure 1. Administrative Divisions of El Salvador, 1988

Introduction

EVENTS IN EL SALVADOR assumed worldwide prominence in the late 1970s as political and social tensions fueled a violent civil conflict that persisted throughout the 1980s. The intense controversy and scrutiny accorded this diminutive nation ran counter to the relative obscurity that had characterized it during its colonial and national history. A backwater of the Spanish Empire, El Salvador passed through the turbulent era of the Central American Federation (1823–41) to separate independence as a liberal state dominated both politically and economically by a landed oligarchy (see The Coffee Republic, ch. 1). The roots of this elite-dominated system lie in Spanish colonial structures; the system bequeathed to modern El Salvador a legacy of economic and social inequality and political authoritarianism—not a promising base on which to build a democratic state.

For many Salvadorans, land tenure crystallizes the inequality of their society. Historically, the elite held title to most of the productive arable land. This was especially true by the late nineteenth century after the abolition of Indian communal lands known as *ejidos* and the consequent seizure of the bulk of those lands by private owners. Although the desire for land reform has been strong throughout Salvadoran history, no effective change in the concentration of land took place until 1980, when a military-civilian junta government decreed a three-phase program (see The Reformist Coup of 1979, ch. 1). The impact of the 1980 reforms is undeniable; their scope and significance for the future of the country, however, are matters of continuing controversy. This volume attempts to synthesize divergent opinions on this question, noting both the accomplishments and the limitations of the reforms (see Agrarian Reform, ch. 2; The Land Tenure System, ch. 3; The Constitution of 1983, ch. 4). Although the term *agrarian reform* is commonly applied to the Salvadoran effort, the term *land reform* more correctly describes the program because it failed to follow up the transfer of ownership with credit and other forms of support.

El Salvador's history of dependence on the export of a single agricultural commodity—first cacao, then indigo, then coffee—locked the country into a "boom and bust" economic cycle that persists to this day (see Growth and Structure of the Economy, ch. 3). Apart from its purely economic effects, such as wide fluctuations in foreign exchange, domestic income, and employment, this system also weakened the country's security. Failure to diversify and the consequent heavy reliance on exports of coffee and the other two leading commodities, cotton and sugar, made producers, processors, and distributors of those products the targets of attacks by antigovernment guerrilla forces that sought to topple the national economy by chipping away at its broad underpinnings (see Major Crops and Commodities, ch. 3). The economic burden of the civil conflict—estimated at approximately US$2 billion in the 1979–88 period—inhibited any effective restructuring and further enhanced the importance of coffee exports as the major source of foreign exchange and the only viable short-term alternative to continued infusions of economic aid from the United States.

Throughout most of El Salvador's history, traditions of political authoritarianism accompanied by repression by the military and the security forces had led to a generally exclusionary political process that only occasionally produced limited reforms in areas such as education and public welfare (see Repression and Reform under Military Rule, ch. 1). As was the case in other aspects of Salvadoran life, however, the cycle of change initiated by the reformist military coup of 1979 and driven by the civil conflict also transformed governmental and political institutions. With encouragement and support from Washington, the Salvadorans promulgated a new constitution in 1983 that allowed for the free election of a president, members of a Legislative Assembly, and municipal representatives. From March 1982 to March 1989, voters cast their ballots in six free and fair elections. Although some commentators have rightly noted that elections alone do not constitute democracy, this record of popular participation in the face of consistent and violent efforts by the guerrillas to disrupt balloting should not be dismissed. To many observers the participation of the leftist Democratic Convergence (Convergencia Democrática—CD) in the 1989 presidential election suggested that the system was approaching a level of institutionalization that might allow it to incorporate all political sectors, even those associated with the previously rejectionist Farabundo Martí National Liberation Front-Revolutionary Democratic Front (Frente Farabundo Martí de Liberación Nacional-Frente Democrático Revolucionario—FMLN–FDR).

Although the connections were not as clear as FMLN–FDR propagandists asserted, the continuing civil conflict did have some precursors in such uprisings as Anastasio Aquino's rebellion in 1833 and the 1932 rural insurrection led by communist organizers such as Agustín Farabundo Martí. The latter incident, fed by severe economic distress provoked by the Great Depression, set off the military's bloody overreaction (*la matanza*), in which thousands of people, mainly Indian campesinos, perished (see Economic Crisis and Repression, ch. 1). Although an aberration in terms of its scope, *la matanza* also represented a warning of the extreme violence that lay beneath the surface of Salvadoran life. That warning rang out again, in a more complex social and political context, in the 1970s.

Most commentators agree that the refusal of the military to recognize the victory of José Napoleón Duarte Fuentes, one of the founders of the Christian Democratic Party (Partido Demócrata Cristiano—PDC), in the 1972 presidential elections set in motion a chain of events that led directly to the violent civil conflict that afflicted the country throughout the 1980s (see Dashed Hopes: The 1972 Elections, ch. 1). The failure of the system to respond to the legitimate political aspirations of an emerging middle class strengthened the arguments of those on the fringes of the political spectrum who preached a revolutionary doctrine. The diverse coalition that initially supported the violent overthrow of the military government included students, disillusioned politicians of a leftist or progressive stripe, "liberationist" Roman Catholic clergy and laymen, peasants, and guerrilla/terrorist groups with ties to Cuba and, after 1979, to the Sandinista government in Nicaragua (see The 1970s: The Road to Revolt, ch. 1; Revolutionary Groups, ch. 2; Left-Wing Extremism, ch. 5). The latter groups saw themselves as the vanguard of a revolution. The escalation of terrorism and paramilitary violence in the early 1980s by both rightist and leftist forces further restricted the range of political action in El Salvador; at the same time, the perception that the guerrilla forces sought to redress socioeconomic inequities brought them adherents at home and supporters abroad.

The reformist military coup of 1979 was an effort by concerned sectors of the armed forces to provide an alternative to leftist revolution and to prevent El Salvador from becoming "another Nicaragua." Although much of the original promise of the coup, e.g., significant agrarian reform, never materialized, the action by the armed forces altered the trend of events by reintroducing Duarte's PDC into the political arena and by providing an entrée for the United States government to play a major role in funding and fashioning a political and military response to the country's crisis. Without United States support, it is likely that the guerrilla forces, which united under the banner of the FMLN in 1980, would have taken power or forced a coalition government by 1983–84. With Washington's support and active involvement, the armed forces expanded both their force levels and their equipment inventory, forcing the FMLN to adopt the classic guerrilla tactics of hit-and-run attack, sabotage, intimidation, propaganda, and rural mobilization.

The nature and proper description of the conflict between government forces and adherents of the FMLN–FDR have been the subject of some debate. This volume has chosen to employ the term *civil conflict* for several reasons. Although the term *civil war* is frequently applied to the conflict in the North American press and elsewhere, the scope of the conflict and the estimated level of popular support for the FMLN–FDR were judged to be insufficient to justify that description. Other observers, particularly in the early 1980s, have described the "Salvadoran Revolution" as a movement similar to that which brought the Sandinista National Liberation Front (Frente Sandinista de Liberación Nacional—FSLN) to power in Nicaragua. The post-1983 narrowing of the Salvadoran conflict in both military and political terms, however, rendered it closer to an insurgency than to a true revolution; therefore, the term *insurgency* is also utilized throughout the volume, usually in a military context. In the broader sense, however, insurgency is too limited a description, given the level of social upheaval that accompanied the initiation of hostilities in the early 1980s, the support (however unquantifiable) for the FMLN–FDR among certain sectors of the population, the crippling economic impact of guerrilla attacks, the high number (some late 1988 estimates exceeded 60,000) of fatalities attributed to military engagements and politically motivated violence, and the unresolved social and political tensions that still prevail in El Salvador. The term *civil conflict* is thus a sort of compromise and is employed in a broad political-military sense.

The conflict raged on several fronts in 1989. In the field, a battle-hardened and politically indoctrinated corps of FMLN guerrillas frustrated the efforts of the armed forces to eliminate them militarily. A low-intensity conflict, marked by indecisive armed clashes and a constant struggle for the "hearts and minds" of the rural population, defined the efforts of both sides. On the political front, the electoral process represented only the most visible arena of competition. The judiciary, inefficient and biased in favor of the well-to-do, exemplified the need for institutional reform if El Salvador wished to emerge from the conflict as a functional society governed by the rule of law. The Duarte administration (1984–89) took several steps toward reforming the judiciary, but much remained to be accomplished in this area (see The Criminal Justice System, ch. 5).

As it drew to a close, the Duarte government appeared bereft of major accomplishments. Duarte's failure to end the civil conflict, to stabilize the economy, and to maintain his PDC as a viable alternative to the extremes of the right and the left disappointed many of his followers at home and his supporters abroad. Any fair assessment of Duarte's contribution, however, must take into account the extremely trying circumstances under which he governed. With the civil conflict as a constant backdrop, Duarte struggled to exert influence over a military institution with no history of obedience to civilian authority; to implement land and other reforms in the face of determined resistance by the elite; to maintain crucial economic and military support from the United States; and to negotiate an honorable settlement with the FMLN–FDR. The personal stresses of the 1985 kidnapping of his daughter by the FMLN and his 1988 diagnosis of terminal liver cancer also weighed heavily on him and may well have affected his decision making and weakened his influence over the armed forces, the government, and his party. Duarte himself admitted in May 1989 that his most significant achievement would be the transfer of power to his successor, Alfredo Cristiani Burkard. This would be the first transition in Salvadoran history from one elected civilian president to another.

The new president's party, the Nationalist Republican Alliance (Alianza Republicana Nacionalista—Arena), was a political enigma to most observers. Arena presented two faces to the world; one was Cristiani's, and the other belonged to party founder Roberto D'Aubuisson Arrieta. The image fostered by Cristiani and his followers was one of comparative political moderation, support for free enterprise, a desire to adjust but not completely repeal the previously enacted economic reforms, and a willingness to explore options for resolving the civil conflict, possibly through negotiations with the FMLN–FDR. Conversely, D'Aubuisson's faction of the party reportedly aspired to restore—to the extent possible—the economic order and landownership pattern that had prevailed before the 1980 reforms (see The Structure of Society, ch. 2). These hard-line *areneros* also reportedly favored a concept of "total war" against the guerrillas. Also referred to as the "Guatemalan solution" after a violent style of counterinsurgency waged in that country in the mid-1980s, such an approach would inevitably entail sharply increased civilian casualties. In the minds of some observers, D'Aubuisson's reputed ties to right-wing death squads in the early 1980s also called up the specter of sharply increased levels of human rights violations should his faction prove to be the dominant one within the party.

Cristiani garnered an absolute majority in the elections of March 19, 1989, taking 53 percent of the vote; the runner-up, PDC candidate Fidel Chávez Mena, drew 36 percent. The PDC's future was uncertain because of a lack of strong, credible leadership and the widespread popular disillusionment stemming from Duarte's seemingly ineffectual rule. The party enjoyed a firm organizational base, however, and almost certainly would survive as a viable opposition. As had been the case for Arena, the prospects for the PDC will depend to a great extent upon the performance of the party in power.

Cristiani's election arguably acquired a greater legitimacy than Duarte's 1984 victory as a result of the participation of the CD, which ran as its presidential candidate Guillermo Manuel Ungo Revelo, leader of the FMLN's political arm, the FDR. At the same time, the CD's poor electoral showing of less than 4 percent called into question the level of popular support for the FMLN–FDR and for the left in general after years of civil strife.

As his June 1, 1989, inauguration approached, Cristiani's political position was strong, based on the mandate of a first-round electoral victory, his party's effective control of all three branches of government (judicial appointments emanate from the Legislative Assembly), and the recent appointment of an aggressive chief of the Joint General Staff, Colonel René Emilio Ponce Torres. Although some members of the United States Congress expressed concern over the electoral outcome based on Arena's violent image and history, the consensus in that body in the immediate postelectoral period appeared to favor sustained levels of aid conditioned on continued efforts by the Salvadorans to stem human rights violations by military and paramilitary groups. Cristiani's intentions with regard to the future conduct of the civil conflict remained ambiguous during the interregnum. His position on negotiations with the FMLN paralleled that of outgoing President Duarte. "We are willing to talk," he was quoted as saying during the presidential campaign, "but not to negotiate any platform." From this viewpoint, the Salvadoran Constitution and government are established and inviolable, and the only basis for negotiations lies in the integration of the guerrillas into that system. The leaders of the FMLN showed few signs of accepting this course, which they had rejected several times in the past.

The FMLN appeared to show some flexibility in its negotiating stance in January 1989, however, when it announced a plan under which it would participate in and recognize the results of the presidential election under certain conditions. The stipulations included a six-month postponement of the balloting, enhanced security guarantees for the CD, the drafting of a revised Electoral Code, the establishment of provisions for absentee balloting, and the restriction of armed forces personnel to quarters on election day. The proposal dropped the previous FMLN demands for a power-sharing arrangement and the integration of guerrilla forces into a revamped national military organization. President Duarte initially rejected the proposal, citing the unconstitutionality of extending his term past June 1. Consideration of the offer was extended, however, after the United States Department of State announced that it was "worthy of serious and substantive consideration." During a late February meeting in Mexico, FMLN leaders Francisco Jovel ("Roberto Roca") and Jorge Shafik Handal and representatives of the major Salvadoran political parties agreed to curtail the postponement demand from six to four months, but the FMLN introduced new demands for the restructuring of the Salvadoran security forces and a reduction in the overall force level of the armed forces.

The new security-related demands effectively invalidated the proposal, given the lack of enthusiasm or incentive for the High Command to accept a unilateral drawdown of its forces. Duarte's final counteroffer, announced after consultation with the armed forces leadership, called for a six-week delay in balloting, an immediate cease-fire, and direct talks among the executive branch, leaders of the Legislative Assembly, and FMLN delegates. The offer drew an enthusiastic endorsement from the Department of State; the FMLN, however, rejected it.

Observers disagreed as to whether the proposal constituted a genuine effort to resolve the civil conflict or merely another in a series of tactical maneuvers by the rebels. The discussions failed to produce a cessation of hostilities inside El Salvador. FMLN forces continued their policy of assassinating elected mayors; a car bomb exploded on February 21 in San Salvador near the headquarters of the army's First Infantry Brigade; and attacks by guerrilla forces in Apopa and Zacatecoluca left more than two dozen soldiers and civilians dead. In a significant terrorist action, FMLN defector Napoleón Romero, also known as Miguel Castellanos, was assassinated in the capital on February 17. As the March 19 election approached, the rebels' radio broadcasts warned citizens of a nationwide transportation stoppage and an intensified campaign against military installations. Even the CD's Ungo was forced to flee from a March 16 attack on a National Guard barracks in San Salvador. Rebel efforts to disrupt the balloting were cited by some sources as a partial explanation for the comparatively low voter turnout of just over 50 percent.

The assassination of the country's attorney general by an FMLN terrorist on April 19, 1989, signaled the new administration that negotiation and conciliation no longer occupied a prominent position on the rebels' short-term agenda. A number of observers believed that the FMLN would deliberately escalate both rural attacks and urban terrorism in an effort to provoke the extremist wing of Arena into a backlash of repression against suspected leftist subversives, a tactic that presumably would diminish the authority and standing of the Cristiani administration and enhance the popular appeal of the guerrillas. No realistic or credible voices predicted a reduction in the prevailing level of violence or a short-term resolution of the conflict. As the 1980s drew to a close, El Salvador seemed to be locked into a state of chronic instability and conflict.

May 16, 1989

* * *

On November 11, 1989, the FMLN launched a major military offensive that brought heavy fighting to San Salvador for the first time in the civil conflict. The kickoff of the offensive followed a decision by the guerrilla leadership to suspend ongoing negotiations with the Cristiani administration. Although the rebels' communique announcing the abandonment of the peace talks cited the October 31 bombing of a union headquarters—presumably by a right-wing group—the offensive had clearly been in the planning stages for months prior to that event. The late October seizure by Honduran authorities of a weapons cache in a van en route to El Salvador from Nicaragua strengthened the claims of the Salvadoran armed forces that the Sandinista government continued to provide material aid to the FMLN despite numerous denials of such support from Managua.

Throughout October, spiraling acts of political violence had contributed to an extremely tense atmosphere throughout the country. FMLN personnel in late September attacked the home of the commander of the Third Infantry Brigade in San Miguel department and shot to death the daughter of another army colonel in mid-October. In response, right-wing groups bombed the homes of leftist politicians, including that of Rubén Zamora Rivas, the vice presidential candidate of the CD in the 1989 elections. Some observers likewise viewed the bombing of the union headquarters, which killed ten people and wounded thirty, as a response to an unsuccessful rebel mortar attack on the San Salvador headquarters of the Joint General Staff.

The November offensive focused on San Salvador, although the rebels also launched simultaneous attacks in the departments of San Miguel, Usulután, Santa Ana, La Paz, and Morazán. For more than a week, FMLN guerrillas held positions in poor neighborhoods of the capital. Some civilians joined the combatants in erecting fortifications; others acquired weapons and joined in the fighting.

According to most reports, the majority of the former group were pressed into service, while most of the latter were members of "popular organizations" (also known as mass organizations)—labor, human rights, and other groups that had served as legal fronts for the FMLN. Heavy fighting went on for more than a week; casualties were high. The Salvadoran armed forces, trained in rural counterinsurgency, not urban house-to-house combat, relied on aerial fire support from both helicopters and fixed-wing gunships to root out the guerrillas. Although this tactic may have spared the lives of some soldiers, it greatly increased the toll on the civilian population. Estimates of those killed in the fighting exceeded 1,000, with more than 30,000 displaced from their battle-damaged homes. Toward the end of the offensive, the rebels briefly occupied positions in the Escalón section of the city, a bastion of the Salvadoran upper class that had never experienced at first hand the violence of the conflict.

On November 16, six Jesuit priests and two women were murdered on the campus of the Central American University José Simeón Cañas in San Salvador. The six, including the rector and vice rector of the university, were prominent leftist intellectuals who maintained contacts with members of the FMLN and were therefore branded as "communists" by the Salvadoran right wing. The circumstances of their deaths, which took place after curfew (imposed when President Cristiani declared a state of emergency on November 12) in an area controlled by the army, led most observers to blame military personnel. President Cristiani condemned the atrocity and attended the priests' funeral. Nevertheless, the blatant nature of the act and the probable involvement of some element of the armed forces raised doubts about the president's authority and prompted calls from some members of the United States Congress to either cut future aid or condition it on the progress of the investigation.

Under pressure from the United States government, Cristiani announced on January 7, 1990, that an investigation undertaken with the assistance of police officials from Britain, Spain, and the United States had determined that armed forces personnel had indeed been involved in the murder of the Jesuits. Subsequently, nine members of the army, including a colonel and four lieutenants, were arrested. The colonel, Guillermo Alfredo Benavides, commander of the Captain General Gerardo Barrios Military Academy, was also a member of the same graduating class (the so-called *tandona,* or big class) as the chief of the Joint General Staff, Colonel Ponce. Some reports claimed that certain members of the officer corps resented Ponce's willingness to "betray" a classmate by acquiescing in Benavides's detention, in contravention of the established tradition of solidarity among members of a *tanda*. If ultimately brought to trial, Colonel Benavides and the lieutenants would be the first Salvadoran officers prosecuted for human rights abuses.

Intensified controversy and political polarization all but guaranteed the prolongation of the civil conflict. The leadership of the FMLN, who had never favored the incorporation of leftist parties such as the CD into the existing political framework, undoubtedly undertook the offensive with this goal in mind. One major result of the offensive appeared to be a rededication of the guerrilla forces to a strategy of revolutionary struggle devoid of the political involvement represented by the CD and the popular organizations. The resumption of hostilities on a large scale, particularly in the capital, may also have been intended to provoke the kind of right-wing backlash represented by the murder of the Jesuits.

El Salvador's foreign relations, aside from the imperative of maintaining aid from the United States, continued to focus on Central America. On November 26, 1989, Cristiani indefinitely suspended diplomatic and trade relations with Nicaragua in response to strong evidence of Sandinista involvement in providing surface-to-air missiles and other weapons to the FMLN. One day earlier, a light plane carrying such missiles crashed in eastern El Salvador; piloted by a Nicaraguan and with Cuban nationals on board, the plane apparently had experienced mechanical trouble sometime after takeoff from Montelimar, near Managua. The introduction of surface-to-air missiles threatened to restrict the Salvadoran armed forces' use of helicopters in transport, fire support, and medivac roles; the involvement of the Nicaraguan and Cuban governments in supplying such weapons indicated support for the FMLN strategy of prolonging the conflict through military escalation.

The suspension of relations cast a cloud over the summit of the five Central American presidents, held in San José, Costa Rica, on December 10–12, 1989, as part of the ongoing peace process under the terms of the Esquipulas II agreement. Despite several heated rhetorical exchanges between the Salvadoran and Nicaraguan governments prior to the summit, Nicaraguan president Daniel Ortega Saavedra endorsed the presidents' final declaration, which asserted "solid support for Salvadoran president Alfredo Cristiani and for his government." The declaration further urged a cessation of hostilities in El Salvador and the resumption of a dialogue between the government and the FMLN. To that end, the presidents called on the secretary general of the United Nations to act as a mediator between the two sides. The presidents had previously requested that the UN establish an Observer Group in Central America in order to facilitate the demobilization of the Nicaraguan Resistance forces (the *contras*). The December declaration expanded that request to include the FMLN.

For its part, the FMLN initially condemned the presidents' declaration as "neither realistic nor viable." In mid-January, however, the guerrilla leadership announced its acceptance of UN mediation and expressed its willingness to resume negotiations within thirty days. Neither the rebels nor the government, however, gave any public indication of a willingness to alter their previous negotiating positions.

January 23, 1990 Richard A. Haggerty

Chapter 1. Historical Setting

Pedro de Alvarado, Spanish conqueror of El Salvador

THE HISTORY OF EL SALVADOR revolves around one central issue—land. In this, the smallest country in Central America, land always has been a scarce commodity whose importance has been amplified by the comparative absence of precious metals or lucrative mineral deposits. Agriculture defined the economic life of the country well before the arrival of the Spanish conquistadors in the early 1500s, and, despite some modest advances in industrial capacity, agriculture has continued to dominate the nation's wealth, social structure, and political dynamics.

The unequal distribution of land in El Salvador can be traced directly to the Spanish colonial system, under which land title was vested in the crown. Those select individuals granted control of specified areas acted, at least in theory, only as stewards over the lands and peoples under their control. Although private property rights eventually were established, the functional structure put in place by the Spanish was perpetuated well into the twentieth century by the landed oligarchy, with the assistance of the military.

Although the indigenous, or Indian, population gradually was diminished through disease and abuse and eventually subsumed into a growing mestizo (mixed Caucasian and Indian) population, its position at the base of society was assumed by the rural lower class. Until the mid-twentieth century, the patterns of landownership and income distribution ran unrelentingly against this segment of the population. As elsewhere in Latin America, those with more got more, those with less got less. Under the model of monoculture export that came to prevail in El Salvador, the concentration of land into large units, or haciendas, made for greater overall efficiency of production. The other side of the economic coin, however, was engraved with images of worsening poverty, deprivation, illiteracy, and disease as the single-minded pursuit of wealth by a minuscule percentage of the population denied the vast majority of Salvadorans access to more than a subsistence level of income.

Although slow to develop, the political ramifications of this process of skewed distribution were inevitable. Unfortunately for the marginalized campesinos (farmers or farm laborers), however, the landowners were prepared to protect their gains by force against any effort to improve the lot of the lower class. A rural uprising in 1833, led by Indian leader Anastasio Aquino, was put down by forces hired by the landowners. A century later, another insurrection, this time led by the Marxist Agustín Farabundo Martí, provoked a now-legendary reprisal known as *la matanza* (the massacre). The troops that carried out this action, in which by some estimates as many as 30,000 Salvadorans were killed, belonged to the Salvadoran armed forces. Institutionalized and nominally independent from the landed oligarchy, the armed forces proceeded from that point to assume control of the political process in El Salvador.

The Salvadoran officer corps was not altogether unsympathetic to popular sentiment for reform of the oligarchic system. In the Salvadoran political equation, however, the economic elite's resistance to change remained a given. Therefore, efforts by the military to institute gradual, guided reforms—land reform chief among them—repeatedly ran into the brick wall of elite opposition and influence. It was not until 1980, when the officer corps allied itself publicly with the middle-class Christian Democratic Party, that substantive reform appeared achievable. By that time, however, El Salvador stood on the threshold of a major civil conflict between government forces backed by the United States and guerrillas supported by Nicaragua, Cuba, and the Soviet Union. This conflict catapulted the country's internal conflicts onto the world stage. The future course of reform in El Salvador was thus uncertain, as the nation entered the 1980s burdened with the legacies of economic and social inequality and political exclusion of the middle and lower classes by the elite.

Spanish Conquest and Colonization

When the Spanish first ventured into Central America from the colony of New Spain (Mexico) in the early sixteenth century, the area that would become El Salvador was populated primarily by Indians of the Pipil tribe. The Pipil were a subgroup of a nomadic people known as the Nahua, who had migrated into Central America about 3000 B.C. The Nahua eventually fell under the sway of the Maya Empire, which dominated the Mesoamerican region until its decline in the ninth century A.D. Pipil culture did not reach the advanced level achieved by the Maya; it has been compared, albeit on a smaller scale, to that of the Aztecs in Mexico. The Pipil nation, believed to have been founded in the eleventh century, was organized into two major federated states subdivided into smaller principalities. Although primarily an agricultural people, the Pipil built a number of large urban centers, some of which developed into present-day cities, such as Sonsonate and Ahuachapán (see fig. 1).

Ruins at Tazumal

The Pipil were a determined people who stoutly resisted Spanish efforts to extend their dominion southward. The first such effort by Spanish forces was led by Pedro de Alvarado, a lieutenant of Hernán Cortés in the conquest of Mexico. It met with stiff resistance from the indigenous population. Alvarado's expeditionary force entered El Salvador—or Cuscatlán, as it was known by the Pipil—in June 1524. The Spaniards were defeated in a major engagement shortly thereafter and were forced to withdraw to Guatemala. Two subsequent expeditions were required—in 1525 and 1528—to bring the Pipil under Spanish control. It is noteworthy that the name of the supposed leader of the Indian resistance, Atlacatl, has been perpetuated and honored among the Salvadorans to the relative exclusion of that of Alvarado. In this sense, the Salvadoran ambivalence toward the conquest bears a resemblance to the prevailing opinion in Mexico, where Cortés is more reviled than celebrated.

The Spanish had come to Central America seeking, at least in part, to add to the store of precious metals that constituted the most immediate spoils of the Mexican conquest. In the small colony that they dubbed El Salvador ("the savior"), they were severely disappointed in this regard. What little gold was available was accessible only through the laborious and time-consuming method of panning, a process that consumed the effort of numerous impressed Indian laborers for a number of years. Denied the opportunity for

5

quick riches, the conquistadors and later the Spanish settlers eventually came to realize that the sole exploitable resource of El Salvador was the land.

El Salvador thus was relegated to the status of a backwater of the Spanish Empire. In this state of neglect and isolation, the seeds of the country's politico-economic structure were planted. Large tracts of land were granted by the crown, initially under the terms of the *encomienda* (see Glossary) system, whereby the grantee was invested with the right to collect tribute from the native inhabitants of a designated area. The manifest abuse of the Indian population that resulted from the *encomienda* system contributed to its replacement in the mid-sixteenth century by the *repartimiento* (see Glossary) system. Under *repartimiento,* representatives of the crown were empowered to regulate the work allotment and treatment of Indian laborers. Although more humane in theory, it was a system that was extremely vulnerable to abuse. The colony's distance from the mother country, the ease with which royal officials could be corrupted, and the prevailing disregard among the elite—made up of *peninsulares,* born in Spain, and criollos born in the New World of Spanish parentage—for the plight of the Indians militated against any substantive improvement in living conditions for the indigenous population.

Although landholders in El Salvador exercised nearly absolute power within their fiefdoms, they did not begin to realize the full economic potential of their holdings until they instituted the system of widespread cultivation of a single lucrative export commodity. The first of these commodities was cacao, which flourished during the latter half of the sixteenth century. Cultivation of indigo followed and produced tremendous profits during the eighteenth century. Largely as a result of the importance of the indigo trade, the colonial capital of San Salvador eventually came to be considered the second city of the Captaincy General of Guatemala, the Spanish administrative unit that encompassed most of Central America during the colonial period. The indigo boom effectively played itself out by the mid-nineteenth century, however, after the discovery in Germany of a synthetic dye that could be produced much more economically.

The fortunes of the Spanish Empire waned throughout the eighteenth century and were dashed completely by the Napoleonic conquest of the Iberian Peninsula in 1808. As the Salvadorans moved toward independence, the legacies of their progenitors, both Indian and Spanish, were firmly fixed. The predominance of agriculture was a fact of life well before the Conquest; the Spanish contributed to this basic system by emphasizing production for export versus cultivation for subsistence. Individual loyalties under the pre-Conquest civilization were given primarily to one's family and to one's village; Spanish rule did little or nothing to change this attitude or to build any substantial sense of national identity among the common people. Religious influence on daily life was strong in both pre-Conquest and colonial societies. The simple animistic nature of the Indians' beliefs allowed for the ready assimilation of Roman Catholic dogma. As elsewhere in Latin America, the hierarchical structure of the church complemented the rigid stratification of colonial society. In many ways, independence would serve only to exacerbate the inequities inherent in that society.

El Salvador and the United Provinces of Central America

The colonies comprising the Captaincy General of Guatemala declared their independence from Spain on September 15, 1821. It was not long before the new states, particularly El Salvador, had to contend with attempted annexation by another large power in the form of an independent Mexico under self-proclaimed Emperor Agustín de Iturbide. A Mexican force dispatched by Iturbide succeeded in bringing to heel the uncooperative Salvadorans, but only briefly. When the emperor himself fell from power in 1823, his dream of a Central American empire died with him. The five states of El Salvador, Guatemala, Honduras, Nicaragua, and Costa Rica went on to establish themselves as the United Provinces of Central America on July 1, 1823 (see fig. 2).

The United Provinces, unworkable though they proved to be, constituted the only successful political union of the Central American states in the postcolonial era. Many optimistic residents of the region no doubt held high hopes for this new nation at its inception. Their sentiments were expressed elegantly, though ironically— given the subsequent course of events—by the liberator of South America, Simón Bolívar, who expounded in 1815 on the prospects for such a federation: "This magnificent location between the two great oceans could in time become the emporium of the world. Its canals will shorten the distances throughout the world, strengthen commercial ties with Europe, America, and Asia, and bring that happy region tribute from the four quarters of the globe. Perhaps some day the capital of the world may be located there, just as Constantine claimed Byzantium was the capital of the ancient world."

Unfortunately for those of Bolívar's idealistic inclinations, the Central American Federation was not immune to the conflict between liberals and conservatives that afflicted nineteenth-century Latin America as a whole. Generally speaking, the liberals were

7

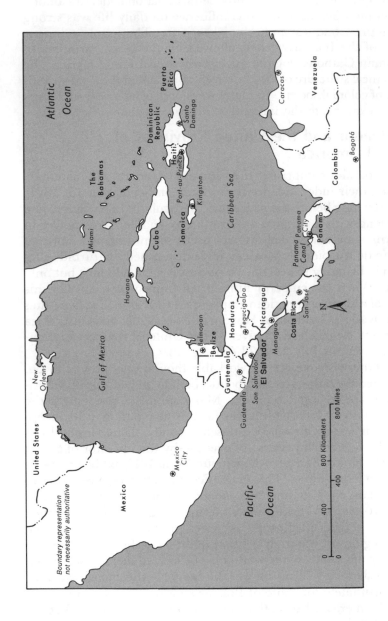

Figure 2. Middle America, 1988

more open to foreign ideas (particularly from the United States, France, and Britain); they welcomed foreign investment and participation in a laissez-faire process of economic development; and they sought to limit the influence of the Roman Catholic Church over the lives of the people. The conservatives' inclinations were almost diametrically opposed to those of the liberals. Conservatives were generally more xenophobic; they advocated more protectionist economic policies; and they championed the traditional role of the church as the predominant moral arbiter and preserver of the social and political status quo.

Split by the dichotomy between liberals and conservatives, the United Provinces never functioned as the unified national unit envisioned by its founders. Control of the federal government passed from liberal to conservative hands in 1826, only to be restored to the liberal faction under the leadership of the Honduran Francisco Morazán in 1829. Neither faction, however, was able to assert federal control over all five Central American states. Therefore, although the liberal governments enacted political, economic, and social reforms, they were never able to implement them effectively. The period of the United Provinces was thus one of Central American polarization impelled by deep divisions among the populace, not the unification originally anticipated by idealists.

El Salvador was a stronghold of liberal sentiment. Most Salvadorans, therefore, supported the rule of Morazán, who served as president of the federation from 1829 to 1840 when he was not leading forces in the field against the conservative followers of Rafael Carrera of Guatemala. In the waning days of liberal rule, San Salvador served as Morazán's last bastion. Unable to stem the tide of conservative backlash, the liberal forces fell to those of Carrera in March 1840. Morazán died before a firing squad in September 1842.

The almost unceasing violence that attended the effort to unite Central America into one federated nation led the leaders of the five states to abandon that effort and declare their independence as separate political entities. El Salvador did so in January 1841. Although their destinies would remain intertwined and they would intervene in each other's affairs routinely in the years to come, the countries of Central America would from that time function as fragmented and competitive ministates readily exploitable by foreign powers.

The Coffee Republic

The Oligarchy and the Liberal State

Coffee would become the last of the great monoculture export commodities in El Salvador. Its widespread cultivation began in the mid-nineteenth century as the world demand for indigo dried up. The huge profits that it yielded served as a further impetus for the process whereby land became concentrated in the hands of an oligarchy. Although legend and radical propaganda have quantified the oligarchy at the level of fourteen families, a figure of several hundred families lies much closer to the truth. A succession of presidents, nominally both conservative and liberal, throughout the last half of the nineteenth century supported the seizure of land from individual smallholders and communal owners.

Despite the continued participation of conservatives, however, the period of the establishment of the coffee republic (roughly 1871 to 1927) is described commonly as the era of the liberal state in El Salvador. The church was not as powerful in El Salvador as in other Latin American states at the time; therefore, the economic aspects of liberalism—an adherence to the principles of free-market capitalism—dominated the conduct of the state. Anticlericalism was a distinctly secondary theme, expressed primarily through social legislation (such as the establishment of secular marriage and education) rather than though the kind of direct action, e.g., repression and expropriation, taken against the church in nineteenth- and early twentieth-century Mexico.

Despite some differences over the degree of emphasis of political versus economic issues, Salvadoran liberals generally agreed on the promotion of coffee as the predominant cash crop, on the development of infrastructure (railroads and port facilities) primarily in support of the coffee trade, on the elimination of communal landholdings to facilitate further coffee production, on the passage of antivagrancy laws to ensure that displaced campesinos and other rural residents provided sufficient labor for the coffee *fincas* (plantations), and on the suppression of rural discontent.

The coffee industry grew inexorably in El Salvador, after a somewhat tentative start in the mid-1800s. Between 1880 and 1914, the value of coffee exports rose by more than 1,100 percent. Although the coffee industry itself was not taxed by the government, tremendous revenue was raised indirectly through import duties on goods imported with the foreign currencies that coffee sales earned (goods intended for the consumption of the small coffee-producing elite). From 1870 to 1914, an average of 58.7 percent of government revenue derived from this source. Even if the coffee elite did not run the government directly (and many scholars argue that they did), the elite certainly provided the bulk of the government's financial support. This support, coupled with the humbler and more mundane mechanisms of corruption, ensured the coffee growers of overwhelming influence within the government and the military.

The priorities of the coffee industry dictated a shift in the mission of the embryonic Salvadoran armed forces from external defense of the national territory to the maintenance of internal order. The creation of the National Guard (Guardia Nacional—GN) in 1912 epitomizes this change (see The Security Forces, ch. 5). The duties of the GN differed from those of the National Police (Policía Nacional—PN), mainly in that GN personnel were specifically responsible for providing security on the coffee *fincas*. Most *fincas* enjoyed the services of their own GN units posted on the grounds; regional GN commanders routinely were compensated by the *finca* owners to ensure the continued loyalty of the guardsmen.

Suppression of rural dissent was subtle and institutionalized; campesinos generally accepted the status quo because of the implied threat of retaliation from the GN or other military units. One exception to this pattern was Aquino's rebellion. Although it predated the coffee boom, its reverberations were felt throughout Salvadoran society for decades.

Aquino was a laborer on an indigo hacienda in the region of Los Nonualcos in the central part of the country. He led a brief but violent uprising in 1833. The Indian participants aimed to end their impressment into the army and effect the return of tribute paid to the government under false pretenses after 1811, when tribute requirements were discontinued by the Spanish parliament (but payments were still collected by the local authorities). In the initial uprising, several thousand rebels, mainly Indians, successfully captured several army posts between Santiago Nonualco and San Vicente, where Aquino's forces won a battle against government troops only to be defeated the next day by reinforcements mustered during the rebels' march. Had Aquino chosen to proceed directly to San Salvador after his early victories, the capital would have been largely undefended. As it was, the defeat at San Vicente effectively ended the rebellion, reestablished governmental control over the rural areas, led to Aquino's capture and execution some months later, and deterred any comparable act of violent dissent for approximately 100 years.

From the time of its declaration of independence from Spain as a part of the United Provinces of Central America, El Salvador was governed under a succession of constitutions. A number of these documents were produced during the era of the liberal state. The constitution of 1871 attempted to increase the power of the legislature relative to that of the president; it specified a two-year term for the chief executive with no immediate reelection. The constitutions of 1872 and 1880 were drafted as little more than legal circumventions of that two-year restriction. The constitution of 1885 never went into effect because the body that drafted it, the National Assembly, was dissolved four days after its adoption. The last constitution of the liberal era, the constitution of 1886, was the longest lived of all Salvadoran charters, governing the country until 1939 and serving as the basis of a post-World War II document as well (see The Constitutions of El Salvador, 1824–1962, ch. 4).

The men who served as presidents of the liberal state in El Salvador came to power through a limited array of means. Santiago González, who assumed the office in 1871, apparently sought to establish a personalist dictatorship. He never successfully consolidated his rule, however, and was defeated by Andrés Valle in the elections of 1876. Valle fell victim to one of the chronic afflictions of Salvadoran political history—intervention from Guatemala. He was replaced less than a year after his election by Rafael Zaldívar, who was more to the liking of the Guatemalan dictator Justo Rufino Barrios. Zaldívar proved exceptionally durable; he was twice elected president after his initial violent installation, serving as the country's leader from 1876 until his overthrow in 1885 by forces led by Francisco Menéndez, who was ousted and executed by his army commander, General Carlos Erzeta, in 1890. Erzeta is the only president during the period of the liberal state who is reputed to have made some effort to improve the lot of the lower classes by attempting to enforce an agricultural minimum wage, though the evidence for even this small gesture is sketchy.

Another confrontation with Guatemala contributed to the downfall of Erzeta, who was ousted in 1894 by Rafael Gutiérrez; he, in turn, was replaced four years later in a bloodless coup led by General Tomás Regalado. His term took El Salvador rather uneventfully into the twentieth century. Regalado's peaceful transfer of power in 1903 to his handpicked successor, Pedro José Escalón, ushered in a period of comparative stability that extended until the depression-provoked upheaval of 1931–32. The only exception to this pattern of peaceful succession was the assassination of President Manuel Enrique Araujo in 1913. Araujo was reputed to have held somewhat reformist views toward some of the policies of the liberal state, in particular the notion of financing development through foreign loans. His assassination may have sprung from this sort of policy dispute, although the full motive has never been established satisfactorily.

Araujo's death ushered in a brief period of modified dynastic rule, whereby President Carlos Meléndez named his brother Jorge as his successor; Jorge in turn tapped his brother-in-law, Alfonso Quiñónez Molina, to succeed him. The Meléndez and Quiñónez clans were two of the most powerful among the ranks of the Salvadoran oligarchy.

Throughout the period of the liberal state in El Salvador, the preeminent position of the oligarchy was never threatened by the actions of the government. Some have attributed this to the pervasive influence of the organization that has been described as the "invisible government" of the country, the Coffee Growers Association (Asociación Cafetalera). The direct (in the case of the Meléndez-Quiñónez minidynasty) and indirect connections of the presidents of the period with the country's powerful families undoubtedly came into play as well. Generally speaking, however, the system continued to function without adjustment because it worked well from the perspective of the small percentage of Salvadorans who benefited from it, namely the economic elite, upper-echelon government officials, and the military High Command.

Although society in general appeared to be static under the liberal state, the same truly cannot be said for the Salvadoran oligarchy. The introduction of coffee production in itself changed the composition of that group, as the new coffee barons joined the ranks of the old plantation owners (who in many cases were slow to recognize the potential of coffee and lost some wealth and standing by delaying their switch from indigo production). New blood also was introduced into the oligarchy by way of foreign immigration. These immigrants, who would eventually come to constitute the bulk of the Salvadoran merchant class, frequently married into the land-owning oligarchic families, further diversifying the composition of the elite stratum of society (see The Upper Sector, ch. 2).

Another process worthy of note during this period despite its lack of tangible results was the ongoing series of unification efforts by the Central American states. El Salvador was a prime mover in most of these attempts to reestablish an isthmian federation. In 1872 El Salvador signed a pact of union with Guatemala, Honduras, and Costa Rica, but the union was never implemented. In 1876 a congress of all five Central American states failed to achieve agreement on federation. A provisional pact signed by the five states in 1889 technically created the "Republic of Central America"; that effort too never was realized. Undaunted, the governments of El Salvador, Honduras, and Nicaragua formed the "Greater Republic of Central America" (República Mayor de Centroamérica) via the Pact of Amapala (1895). Although Guatemala and Costa Rica considered joining the Greater Republic (which was rechristened "the United States of Central America" when its constitution went into effect in 1898), neither country joined. This union, which had planned to establish its capital city at Amapala on the Golfo de

Fonseca, did not survive Regalado's seizure of power in El Salvador in 1898. Although the Central American spirit seemed willing, the commitment was weak. The notion of unification was another manifestation of the idealistic liberal ethos, and it proved durable and quite resistant to political realities.

Economic Crisis and Repression

The presidency of Pío Romero Bosque (1927–31) was a transitional period in Salvadoran history that ended the relatively stable functioning of the coffee republic and the liberal economic system that sustained it. The world depression of the 1930s, which precipitated a sharp fall in world coffee prices, hit hard in El Salvador. The loss of income reverberated throughout the society; as always, those on the lower end of the economic scale felt the deprivation most keenly, as wages were reduced and employment levels cut back. The government first responded with limited reform to ease this situation and the popular unrest it produced. The subsequent response was brutal repression.

President Romero was the designated successor of President Quiñónez, who apparently expected Don Pío, as he came to be known, to carry on the noninterventionist political tradition of his predecessors. Romero, however, for reasons of his own, decided to open up the Salvadoran system to a limited but still significant degree. He turned on Quiñónez, exiling him from the country, and sought to exclude other members of the elite from the government. He is best remembered for allowing the presidential and municipal elections of 1931, the freest held in El Salvador up to that time. These elections still excluded any radical party that might have sought to overturn the existing governmental system; nevertheless, they resulted in the election of Arturo Araujo, who enjoyed a mildly reformist reputation despite his oligarchic family background.

Araujo assumed the presidency at a time of severe economic crisis. Between 1928 and 1931, the coffee export price had dropped by 54 percent. The wages paid agricultural workers were cut by an equal or greater extent. Food supplies, dependent on imports because of the crowding out of subsistence cultivation by coffee production, likewise fell sharply. Privation among the rural labor force, long a tolerated fact of life, sank to previously unknown depths. Desperate campesinos began to listen more attentively to the exhortations of radicals such as Agustín Farabundo Martí.

Martí came from a relatively well-to-do landowning family. He was educated at the University of El Salvador (commonly referred to as the National University), where his political attitudes were influenced by the writings of Karl Marx and other communist theorists. He was an original member of the Central American Socialist Party (founded in Guatemala in 1925) and a propagandist for the Regional Federation of Salvadoran Workers. He also spent a few months in Nicaragua with that country's noted guerrilla leader, Augusto César Sandino. Martí and Sandino parted ways over the Nicaraguan's refusal to add Marxist flourishes to his nationalistic battle against a United States occupation force. Jailed or expelled several times by Salvadoran authorities, Martí kept up his efforts to organize popular rebellion against the government with the goal of establishing a communist system in its place. The widespread discontent provoked by the coffee crisis brought ever-increasing numbers of Salvadorans under the banner of such Marxist organizations as the Communist Party of El Salvador (Partido Comunista de El Salvador—PCES), the Anti-Imperialist League, and the Red Aid International (Socorro Rojo Internacional—SRI). Martí was the Salvadoran representative of the SRI, which was closely associated with the other two groups.

Most dissatisfied Salvadorans were driven more by hunger and frustration than by ideology. Araujo, a product of the economic elite, was burdened by loyalty to his class, by the unyielding opposition of that class to political reform, by the increasing polarization between the elite and the masses, and by the suspicions of the military. Araujo's initial response to popular unrest, perhaps a conditioned one, was to quell disturbances by force. When demonstrations persisted, the president decided to offer a concession instead of a club. He scheduled municipal elections for December 1931; furthermore, he offered the unprecedented gesture of allowing the PCES to participate in those elections.

In the tense political atmosphere of the time, this last concession aroused both the landholding elite and, more important, the military. A December coup staged against Araujo drew support from a large number of military officers, who cited Araujo's ineptitude to justify their action. This rationalization did not match the portentous significance of the event, however. The 1931 coup represented the first instance when the Salvadoran military took direct action as an institution to curtail a potential political drift to the left. This watershed event ushered in a period of direct and indirect military rule that would last for fifty years.

The rebellious officers shortly installed as the country's leader General Maximiliano Hernández Martínez (known in El Salvador by his matronymic, Martínez), who had been Araujo's vice president and minister of war. Surprisingly, Martínez allowed the promised elections to take place only a month later than originally scheduled, and with the participation of the PCES. The general's motivations in this regard, however, seem to have run more toward drawing his enemy into the open than toward the furthering of democratic government, for the communist candidates who won municipal offices in the western part of the country subsequently were barred from assuming those offices.

The denial of the municipal posts has been cited as the catalyst for the launching of a rural insurrection that had been in the planning stages for some time. Unfortunately for the rebels, the military obtained advance warning of their intentions. Martí and other rebel leaders were arrested on January 18, 1932. Confusion and poor communications led the insurgents to go ahead with their action as planned four days later. The rebels succeeded in capturing government buildings in the towns of Izalco, Sonzacate, Nahuizalco, Juayúa, and Tacuba. They were repulsed by the local garrisons in Sonsonate, Santa Tecla, and Ahuachapán. Even the small successes of the insurgents were short lived, however, as GN and army units were dispatched to relieve local forces or to retake areas held by the rebels. Less than seventy-two hours after the initial uprising, the government was again firmly in control. It was then that reprisals began.

The military's action would come to be known as *la matanza*. Some estimates of the total number of campesinos killed run as high as 30,000. Although the true number never will be known, historian Alastair White has cited 15,000 to 20,000 as the best approximation. No matter what figure one accepts, the reprisals were highly disproportionate to the effects of the communist-inspired insurgency, which produced no more than thirty civilian fatalities. The widespread executions of campesinos, mainly Indians, apparently were intended to demonstrate to the rural population that the military was now in control in El Salvador and that it would brook no challenges to its rule or to the prevailing system. That blunt message was received, much as it had been after the failure of Aquino's rebellion a century earlier. The memory of *la matanza* would linger over Salvadoran political life for decades, deterring dissent and maintaining a sort of coerced conformity.

Repression and Reform under Military Rule

The assumption of power by Martínez initiated an extended period of rule by a military institution that continued to struggle with its own conception of its role as director of the country's political process. Older, more conservative officers were pushed by their younger subordinates to loosen up the system and institute at least some limited reforms in order to minimize the likelihood of another violent disruption like that of 1932. The notion of guided reform, instituted and controlled from above, generally came to be accepted as the best course for the military to steer between the twin shoals of heavy-handed repression and radical revolution. That is not to say, however, that repression was abandoned as a tool of political control. In fact, it alternated with guided reform depending on the prevailing socioeconomic pressures of the time. This process of limited liberalization combined with firm control characterized the political order of El Salvador for some five decades.

The first of many military presidents to come, Martínez was an autocrat who enjoyed the longest tenure in office of any Salvadoran president. His anticommunist fervor, so amply demonstrated by *la matanza*, has made him an enduring hero of the political right (a right-wing death squad of the 1970s would bear his name). His personal quirks are also legendary. A believer in spiritualism and other mystic creeds, he is most frequently remembered for having strung colored lights throughout San Salvador in an effort to ward off a smallpox epidemic.

Martínez was confirmed as president by the legislature in 1932. He was elected to a four-year term of office in 1935 and a six-year term in 1939. Although it was marked by institutionalized repression of dissent, Martínez's tenure was not altogether a negative period for the country. It provided a stability and continuity that contributed to a general improvement in the national economy. Like other Salvadoran presidents before him, Martínez did not interfere greatly with the elite-dominated economic system. He did, however, make some minor concessions to the poor, establishing a government welfare institution known as Social Improvement (Mejoramiento Social), continuing a very limited land redistribution program begun under Araujo, and attempting to protect the domestic handicraft industry. Although he was personally drawn to the fascist movements in Mussolini's Italy and Nazi Germany, Martínez committed El Salvador to the Allied effort during World War II. This pragmatic move apparently bought El Salvador a fair amount of goodwill in Washington. Despite the length of his rule, relations between the general and the oligarchy were uneasy, in part because of Martínez's humble origins, but also because of his personal eccentricities and the unpredictability that they seemed to reflect. This vague distrust of Martínez was transformed into active elite opposition by his decision in 1943 to raise more revenue through an increase in the export tax.

The last straw for the general's detractors was his effort to extend his term beyond 1944 by means of legislative fiat rather than direct election. The coalition that united in support of his overthrow was a somewhat eclectic one: civilian politicians, pro-Axis military officers, businessmen and bankers (who objected to the government's limited economic restrictions), and irate coffee producers. An initial attempt to oust Martínez by force was unsuccessful, but subsequent unrest in the capital, including a general strike, moved him to resign his office in May 1944. His successor, General Andrés Ignacio Menéndez, called for political liberalization and free elections; the sincerity of his appeal was never tested, however, as he was turned out of office by the military in October.

Menéndez's replacement was Colonel Osmín Aguirre y Salinas, the director of the PN and a former follower of the deposed Martínez. The Aguirre regime went ahead with elections scheduled for January 1945 but manipulated the results to ensure the victory of its candidate, General Salvador Castaneda Castro.

Castaneda's rule was unremarkable. The events of 1944 had left the country in an unresolved state of political uncertainty. Fearing some action against him and his conservative followers, Castaneda sought to weed out young reform-minded officers by dispatching them abroad for training. This sector of the officer corps, however, was substantial, and its members could not be excluded indefinitely from the political process. They made their influence felt in 1948, when Castaneda made his own attempt to extend his term in office by way of legislative maneuvering without recourse to the ballot box. The movement that ousted him from power on December 14, 1948, referred to itself as the Military Youth (Juventud Militar). For as long as its members exerted control in El Salvador, they would refer to their action as the Revolution of 1948.

The coup leaders established a junta, which was referred to as the Revolutionary Council; it included three mid-level officers and two civilian professionals. The council ruled for some twenty-one months and guided the country toward comparatively open elections in March 1950. During this period, it became clear that Major Oscar Osorio was the dominant force within the junta and among the officer corps. Osorio was so sure of his support that he resigned from the junta in order to run in the elections as the candidate of the Revolutionary Party of Democratic Unification (Partido Revolucionario de Unificación Democrática—PRUD).

Osorio eked out a victory over Colonel José Asencio Menéndez of the Renovating Action Party (Partido Acción Renovadora—PAR) and went on to establish the PRUD as a quasi-official party modeled roughly on the Institutional Revolutionary Party (Partido Revolucionario Institucional—PRI) of Mexico. Although the PRUD enjoyed some measure of support, it was never able to

Revolution Monument, San Salvador

replicate the broad base of the PRI, mainly because the process
that produced the PRUD—the so-called Revolution of 1948—was
not itself a mass movement.

The policies of Osorio and his successor, Lieutenant Colonel José
María Lemus, were distinctly different from those of previous Salvadoran leaders. They emphasized economic development, public works, the diversification of agriculture, the establishment of

such programs as social security (including medical and hospital care), and improvements in sanitation and housing. Union organization was encouraged, and collective bargaining was instituted. All this was accomplished within the boundaries of guided reform; no measures were taken that might have threatened the elite-dominated system (agrarian reform, for example, was never attempted), and radical elements were discouraged or eliminated through repressive means.

The election of Lemus in 1956 did much to discourage the notion of possible political pluralism in El Salvador. As the candidate of the PRUD, Lemus initially was challenged by the standard-bearers of three other ad hoc parties. The most popular of the three appeared to be Roberto Canessa, a civilian who had served as Osorio's foreign minister. A month before the election, however, Canessa was disqualified by the government-controlled Central Electoral Council on a technicality. Another opposition candidate was barred from the race because of allegations of fiscal impropriety during his tenure as ambassador to Guatemala. Although the opposition attempted to unite behind the remaining candidate, Lemus topped the official election returns with an improbable 93 percent of the vote.

Perhaps in an effort to make amends for the means by which he came to office, Lemus initially took some conciliatory steps, such as declaring a general amnesty for political prisoners and exiles, voiding a number of repressive laws left over from previous regimes, and selecting men of recognized probity and ability for his cabinet. The course of his administration, however, was dominated by economic events. A decline in the export prices of coffee and cotton and the resultant drop in income and revenue exposed the weakness of the PRUD's limited reforms. Heavy-handed political manipulations by the government and the party, in particular the approval of a new electoral law that all but precluded an effective opposition, exacerbated widespread dissatisfaction with the Lemus government. After 1959 the influence of what then appeared to be a popular, nationalistic revolutionary movement in Cuba was felt in El Salvador as it was throughout Latin America. Student groups were particularly inspired by the example of Fidel Castro Ruz and his revolutionaries. Public demonstrations in San Salvador called for Lemus's removal and the imposition of a truly democratic system. The president responded by abandoning his earlier efforts at reform in favor of heightened repression. Free expression and assembly were banned, and political dissidents were detained arbitrarily.

This instability provoked concern among important political actors in El Salvador. For the elite, the government's emphasis on economic development was pointless under such a climate; the emerging middle class likewise felt a threat to its gains from the specter of revolution; and the military reacted almost reflexively to the spectacle of a president who had lost control. Lemus was deposed in a bloodless coup on October 26, 1960.

Governmental authority again passed into the hands of a military-civilian junta. The ranking military representative was Lieutenant Colonel Julio Adalberto Rivera. Aside from Rivera, the junta member who drew the most attention was Fabio Castillo, a university professor and known sympathizer with the Cuban Revolution. Castillo's presence, along with the renewed reformist policies of the junta, convinced the elite and the conservative military officers that the government was influenced by communism. Again, it was the military that acted to head off this perceived threat to stability. A coup by young officers overthrew the junta on January 25, 1961. The officers affirmed their anticommunist and anti-Castro convictions, retained Rivera as part of a new junta, and promised elections.

The Christian Democrats: A Centrist Alternative?

The electoral preparations that had begun under the 1960 junta stimulated the mobilization of political parties of moderate and leftist inclinations. These opposition parties were unable to establish their organizations and followings sufficiently to present any effective challenge to the 1962 election of Rivera to the presidency. Rivera ran as the candidate of the National Conciliation Party (Partido de Conciliación Nacional—PCN), which would succeed the PRUD as the official party in El Salvador. The PCN began as a splinter group from the Christian Democratic Party (Partido Demócrata Cristiano—PDC), which eventually became the leading opponent of the PCN and a major force for peaceful change in the Salvadoran system.

The PDC had been founded in November 1960. The party grew out of informal meetings among middle- and upper-class activists who sought to devise a vehicle to represent their interests in the political arena. The concerns of the Salvadoran middle class by and large revolved around economic progress and political stability. It saw the prospects for both concerns threatened from the political right and from the left. The Salvadoran right stifled popular aspirations through its adamant opposition to reform and its support for the elite-dominated economic system. The left promised to abandon the capitalist model that had created the middle class

21

in favor of a communistic system. Fidel Castro's communist leanings were confirmed in 1961 when he declared that he was, and had been since his student days, a Marxist-Leninist. From the perspective of the PDC's founders, the only way to protect their gains and ensure their future and that of the middle-class sectors as a whole was to achieve representation within the governmental system. To reach this goal, they saw the need to follow a centrist path that would incorporate more Salvadorans into the political process without exerting undue pressure on the prevailing economic order.

The ideologists of this new party, principally lawyers Abraham Rodríguez and Roberto Lara Velado, saw Christian democracy as the path they were seeking. The roots of Christian democratic ideology extended back as far as Pope Leo XIII's encyclical *Rerum Novarum* (1891), which called on Christians to work for social and economic reform. Its more immediate influences, however, were found in the works of Pope John XXIII and the French philosopher Jacques Maritain. The Christian democratic movements in Chile and Venezuela also served as role models. The founders of the PDC, including the civil engineer José Napoleón Duarte Fuentes, emphasized the ideological basis of the party—its support for reform, its call for the application of moral principles to political and economic life, and its rejection of extremist solutions such as those advocated by Marxism—as a new development in Salvadoran politics. This was true, but only to the extent that party members accepted that ideology and acted upon it. Duarte himself came to the PDC without a strong ideological grounding, but his belief in the possibility of peaceful democratic change, as well as his personal magnetism, made up for that initial shortcoming.

Duarte's practical political skills eventually made him the PDC's leading figure. He was elected to the post of secretary general at the party's first convention in May 1961. At the time, his selection was a victory for those party members who referred to themselves as "purists," eschewing collaboration with nonelected governments. In order to legitimize its rule, the ruling junta had approached the PDC membership about participation in the government, and some early PDC adherents responded favorably to this idea. After Duarte's election to party leadership, this collaborationist faction split off to form the PCN. Tied into the system, the PCN went on to sweep all the available seats in the December 1961 Constituent Assembly (see Glossary) elections and to serve as the vehicle for Rivera's election to the presidency in April 1962.

Rivera was a proponent of the sort of guided reforms initiated by the military's revolution of 1948. His developmentalist economic policies received a boost from the United States in the form of generous aid allocations under the banner of United States president John F. Kennedy's Alliance for Progress. Although he discussed publicly the need for economic reforms, including agrarian reform, Rivera did nothing to further them. Perhaps his major contribution to Salvadoran political life was the decision to allow the participation of opposition parties through a liberalized electoral system that called for proportional representation in the country's Legislative Assembly. Previously, the party that won the most votes in each department (the equivalent of states under the Salvadoran system) was awarded all the legislative seats allocated to that department. The proportional allocation of seats based on each party's departmental electoral showing represented a significant step forward for the opposition, which obtained some voice in government even if it was still denied any real power.

In March 1964, the first elections were held under the new system. Although the PCN retained an unchallenged majority in the Legislative Assembly, the PDC won fourteen seats in that body, along with thirty-seven mayoralties. Perhaps the most significant victory was Duarte's election as mayor of San Salvador. He built a strong base of popular support in this post through improvements in municipal services and the organization of local self-help groups to promote small-scale civic improvements such as school renovations, establishment and maintenance of parks, and adult education programs. He was reelected in 1966 and 1968. Leadership of the populous capital city heightened Duarte's political profile and made him a national figure.

Strong economic growth in the early 1960s solidified the position of the PCN as the official party. The leadership of the party was drawn mainly from the ranks of middle-class professionals. It cannot be said to have represented the interests of that class, however. The most important constituency of the PCN was the military; without its support and cooperation, the party could not have governed. PCN governments protected the political power and social and economic perquisites that the officer corps had long enjoyed. They also preserved, at least for a time, the domestic stability required for economic growth within the prevailing elite-dominated system. Like many other Latin American militaries, the Salvadoran armed forces saw the maintenance of the societal status quo as serving their best interests. The PCN shared this conservative viewpoint and worked closely with the military leadership, seeking its advice and support on policy initiatives and political issues. In essence, under the PCN the military continued to rule El Salvador from behind the scenes. The electoral base of the PCN was found among the peasantry. Latin American peasants are on the whole a politically conservative group; in rural El Salvador, this natural tendency was reinforced by the ubiquitous presence of the armed forces.

The political perceptions of certain Salvadoran sectors, particularly agricultural and business interests, led them to oppose the PDC and favor the PCN. Although it was a moderate party by Latin American standards, the PDC was seen by the Salvadoran right as a dangerously left-wing organization. The Christian Democrats' occasional use of the words *revolution* or *revolutionary* to describe their vision of social reform invoked in the minds of large landowners and businessmen images of Castro's Cuba, a prospect they would go to any lengths to avoid in El Salvador.

The leading contenders in the elections of 1967 were the PCN, the PDC, and the PAR. The PCN's candidate was Rivera's interior minister, Colonel Fidel Sánchez Hernández. The PDC nominated Abraham Rodríguez, who proved to be a lackluster campaigner. The PAR had undergone an internal dispute that led its more conservative members to bolt and form a new party, the Salvadoran Popular Party (Partido Popular Salvadoreño—PPS). The PPS chose as its candidate a retired army major, Alvaro Martínez. The remaining leftist members of the PAR nominated Fabio Castillo, who had served on the 1960 junta. By the standards of the Salvadoran right, Castillo was a communist.

The issue of the supposed communist nature of the PAR came to dominate the 1967 campaign. By election day, the PAR had been denied media access by broadcasters who either disagreed with the party's political line or feared some retaliation from the government if they granted air time to the PAR. The PDC condemned the red-baiting engaged in by Sánchez and the PCN, even though many Christian Democrats differed with some of the proposals made by Castillo, such as establishing relations with Cuba and broadening ties with other communist countries. In the balloting on March 5, the PAR actually garnered more votes in San Salvador than did the PDC, although the Christian Democrats had a better showing in rural areas than they had anticipated. All of this was academic in terms of the presidential race, however, since Sánchez won an absolute majority. In general terms, though, the 1967 elections demonstrated increased voter participation and a growing acceptance of the political process as a legitimate means of popular expression.

The 1969 War with Honduras

Like many other conflicts in Salvadoran history, the 1969 war with Honduras, sometimes referred to as the Soccer War, was rooted in economic disparity. El Salvador is a small country with a large and rapidly growing population and a severely limited amount of available land. Honduras is a larger country with a smaller population and a less-developed economy. By 1969 some 300,000 Salvadorans had drifted over the border and taken up residence in more sparsely populated Honduras. The vast majority of these Salvadorans were squatters, technically illegal immigrants whose sole claim to the land they worked was their physical presence on it. For Hondurans, the land itself was not so much the issue. What rankled them was the image of being pushed and potentially enveloped by the Salvadorans. Throughout the 1960s, the mechanisms of the Central American Common Market (see Glossary) worked to the advantage of the more developed economies of the region, particularly those of Guatemala and El Salvador. The growth of Salvadoran-owned businesses in Honduras—shoe stores were the most visible of these enterprises—underscored for Hondurans the relative economic disparity between the two countries. The issue of the Salvadoran squatters, despite its lack of real economic significance, became a nationalistic sore point for Honduras, a question of adding territorial insult to perceived economic injury.

The border situation became increasingly tense during the two years preceding the outbreak of hostilities. In early 1969, the regime of Honduran president Oswaldo López Arellano (1963–71) invoked a dormant agrarian reform law as a pretext to evict Salvadoran squatters and expel them from the country. The López government was experiencing economic and political difficulties and saw the Salvadorans as convenient scapegoats. Stories and images of displaced refugees filled the Salvadoran press and the airwaves. Tales of violent displacement by the Honduran military began to circulate throughout El Salvador. Tension between the two countries continued to build. The incident that provoked active hostilities—and lent the conflict its popular designation as the Soccer War—took place in San Salvador in June 1969. During and after a soccer match between the Honduran and Salvadoran national teams, the Honduran team members were vilified and harassed by Salvadoran fans. The reportage of this incident brought matters to a fever pitch.

Beyond national pride and jingoism—which was expressed by Duarte and the PDC with a fervor equal to that of Sánchez and the PCN—the Salvadorans had other motivations for launching a military strike against Honduras on July 14, 1969. The influx of displaced Salvadoran squatters was placing a burden on services and threatening to provoke widespread social unrest. The situation was undermining the political support of the Sánchez

25

government; action against Honduras became the most expedient option to turn this situation around. Although war with Honduras almost certainly would lead to the breakdown of the CACM, the Salvadorans were willing to pay that price. In their estimation, the CACM was already close to a breakdown over the issues of comparative advantage; war with Honduras would only hasten that outcome.

The actual fighting was brief. Despite early Salvadoran air strikes, the Hondurans eventually dominated in that area, destroying most of the Salvadoran Air Force. The Salvadoran Army, however, clearly bested the Hondurans on the ground. The Salvadorans pushed rapidly into Honduran territory before fuel and ammunition shortages and diplomatic efforts by representatives of the Organization of American States (OAS) curtailed their progress. As many as 2,000 people, mainly civilians, were killed in the action.

The war had a number of immediate repercussions. The Salvadorans had expended large quantities of ordnance, necessitating heavy military expenditures to replenish depleted stocks. Trade between the two countries was disrupted completely, and the CACM ceased to function as anything more than a paper entity. El Salvador lost the economic "safety valve" formerly provided by illegal emigration to Honduras; land-based pressures again began to build. Although the vast majority of Salvadorans, including all the legal political parties, had united in support of the war, this unity did not last long.

Dashed Hopes: The 1972 Elections

In the wake of the Soccer War, the PDC sought to turn the issue of unequal land distribution to its political advantage. The war had not only highlighted this issue, it had exacerbated it. Returning refugees were unable to resume the kind of farming they had practiced in Honduras; their employment opportunities as coffee laborers, always limited and seasonal in nature, were restricted still further by the scale of the war-induced influx. Pressure intensified for some kind of land reform.

The PDC was the first political party to drop out of the so-called National Unity Front that had been formed to support the war effort against Honduras. Party spokesmen began to push the issue of full agrarian reform, including credit and technical assistance, as a major platform plank for the 1972 presidential elections. The thinking of the Christian Democrats on this question was as much practical as idealistic. Agrarian reform was not just a popular rallying point for them; it was also seen as a way to establish a new class of small- to medium-sized landholders who would presumably demonstrate some loyalty to the party and government that granted them that status. This was a common strategy for Latin American Christian democratic parties, in keeping with their advocacy of free-enterprise reformism.

The Legislative Assembly provided a tangible demonstration of the appeal of agrarian reform in January 1970 when it convened the National Agrarian Reform Congress in San Salvador. The congress included representatives from the government, the opposition, labor, and business groups. Its convocation was an unprecedented event in Salvadoran history, even though it was charged only with making recommendations, not policy. Moreover, those recommendations turned out to be, by Salvadoran standards, revolutionary. They included a call for massive land expropriation by the government in order to achieve a more equitable and productive distribution of national resources. The delegates judged that landholdings above a certain size could be characterized as fulfilling no legitimate "social function" and were thus legally liable to expropriation under the constitution. This call for expropriation actually exceeded what had been called for in the PDC's reform program. By agreeing to the resolutions of the congress, however, the PDC effectively incorporated expropriation into its political agenda. By so doing, it provoked further misgivings among the elite and conservative sectors of the military with regard to the party's intentions should it achieve power.

The legislative and municipal elections of March 1970 were discouraging for the PDC, as it dropped three seats in the Legislative Assembly and lost control of seventy municipalities. Electoral fraud was alleged against the PCN by the PDC and other opposition parties, but fraud never was proved. Nevertheless, the Christian Democrats confidently looked toward the 1972 presidential balloting. Duarte, the party's most popular figure, had agreed to resign the mayoralty of San Salvador and head the national ticket. Despite the 1970 results, there were signs of weakening popular support for the PCN stemming from economic decline. Agrarian reform provided a strong issue for a national campaign. One problem that confronted the PDC was internal in nature and concerned a dispute over tactics. One faction of the party advocated a direct organizational challenge to the PCN in its rural strongholds, whereas another faction stressed the need to radicalize PDC doctrine and programs in an effort to draw a sharper contrast between it and the ruling party. Duarte, not wishing to become embroiled in this potentially divisive debate, resigned as party secretary general and generally sought to remain above the fray.

The 1972 elections took place in an uneasy political atmosphere. The 1970 election of socialist Salvador Allende Gossens as president of Chile had resurrected anxieties over communist gains in Latin America. This concern was shared not only by the political right and the military but also by the majority of Christian Democrats. In El Salvador, organizational efforts by leftist parties such as the PCES and by activist Roman Catholic clergy were viewed with alarm by conservative sectors. The fears of the economic elite in particular were provoked by the 1971 kidnapping and murder of Ernesto Regalado Dueñas, the son of a prominent family, by a leftist terrorist organization calling itself "the Group" (see Left-Wing Extremism, ch. 5). A protracted teachers' strike in 1971 only added to the unsettled climate prevailing in the country.

The PDC opted to participate in the elections as the leading party of a coalition designated the United National Opposition (Unión Nacional Opositora—UNO). The other members of the coalition were smaller and more radical than the PDC. The National Revolutionary Movement (Movimiento Nacional Revolucionario—MNR) was originally a social democratic party. The MNR was pushed farther to the left, however, as former PAR supporters joined its ranks after their party was legally proscribed in 1967. The National Democratic Union (Unión Democrática Nacional—UDN) was an even smaller grouping that had once described itself as the party of the noncommunist left in El Salvador. By this time, however, the UDN had been infiltrated by the PCES and was functioning as a communist front group. Despite the leftist leanings of the MNR and UDN and the lingering effect of the agrarian reform congress, the UNO platform was moderate in tone, calling for measured reform, respect for private property, and the protection of private investment. As expected, Duarte was tapped as the presidential candidate. He in turn chose the MNR's Guillermo Manuel Ungo Revelo as his running mate.

President Sánchez chose Colonel Arturo Armando Molina as the PCN candidate. The PPS also entered the contest, led by José Antonio Rodríguez Porth. A small PCN splinter party calling itself the United Democratic Independent Front, funded by some leading oligarchic families, rounded out the field. The campaign was a violent and dangerous one for the opposition. UNO's leaders decried numerous incidents of harassment, kidnapping, and assault against their activists. The leading perpetrators of these actions, according to the opposition, were troops of the GN. Further roadblocks were thrown in the way of UNO by the PCN-controlled Central Electoral Council, which disqualified the opposition coalition's candidate slates for the Legislative Assembly in the departments of San Salvador, San Miguel, Usulután, Sonsonate, La Unión, and San Vicente.

The actual vote count in the presidential balloting of February 20, 1972, probably will never be known. As expected, Duarte ran strongly in San Salvador, offsetting the traditional PCN advantage in the countryside. Poll watchers for UNO claimed that the final tally nationwide was 327,000 for Duarte and 318,000 for Molina. Tabulations were suspended by the government, however, and a recount was initiated. The official results of that count placed Molina ahead of Duarte by 10,000 votes. The selection of the president thus was relegated to the assembly, where the PCN majority affirmed Molina's tainted victory after a walkout by opposition deputies. An appeal by Duarte and Ungo for new balloting was denied by the Central Electoral Council.

The blatancy of the fraud employed to maintain the PCN in power outraged and disillusioned many Salvadorans, including members of the armed forces. One faction of the officer corps, a new Military Youth, attempted to take direct action to redress the official exploitation of a system that had until that point shown some promise of evolving in a genuinely democratic direction. This group of young army officers, led by Colonel Benjamín Mejía, launched a coup on March 25, 1972. Their immediate goal was the establishment of a "revolutionary junta." It seemed clear, however, that the officers favored the installation of Duarte as president.

Mejía and his followers initiated their action by seizing the presidential residence and taking Sánchez and some of his family members hostage. From that point on, however, events ran against the insurgents. The thunder of aerial bombing over the capital soon announced the loyalty of the air force to the government. The coup attempt never gained the support of more than a minority within the officer corps, and that only in the army. Some residents of the capital took to the streets in support of the young officers, but they were no match for the loyalist military forces. In desperation, Mejía turned to Duarte, urging him to deliver a radio address in support of the rebels. Despite some misgivings, Duarte agreed. His address was broadcast shortly after noon and may have saved some lives by warning civilians to evacuate areas targeted for rebel artillery strikes. Its overall impact, however, was insufficient to reverse the tide of action in the streets. Loyalist forces regained effective control of San Salvador by early that evening.

Like many other government opponents, Duarte sought refuge within the foreign diplomatic community. He was taken in by the first secretary of the Venezuelan embassy but was soon tracked down by government security forces, who broke into the diplomat's house and dragged Duarte away amidst kicks and blows from rifle butts. The Christian democratic leader was detained briefly, beaten, and interrogated, then dispatched to Guatemala. From there, he flew to exile in Venezuela. He left behind a country where aspirations for change had been dashed and where repression was once again the official antidote to dissent.

The 1970s: The Road to Revolt

The government of President Molina attempted to exert old-fashioned coercive control over the country, using a relatively new instrument, a peasant organization known as the Nationalist Democratic Organization (Organización Democrática Nacionalista—Orden). Orden was established partially in secret in the early 1960s by then President Rivera and General José Alberto "Chele" Medrano in association with the GN, which provided some level of counterinsurgent training to peasant cells throughout the countryside. The counterinsurgent orientation of Orden was in keeping with the anticommunist tenor of the times and the general intent of military training and assistance provided to the armed forces of the region by the United States. Orden, however, never became a military force per se but functioned as a paramilitary adjunct and an important part of the rural intelligence network for the security forces. By the late 1970s, its membership reportedly totaled 100,000.

While Orden served as the eyes and ears of the security forces in rural areas, the military was confronted with a growing new phenomenon in the urban setting, that of left-wing terrorism. Soon after the failed coup attempt of 1972, kidnappings for ransom and hit-and-run attacks on government buildings and other targets became increasingly common in San Salvador. The groups claiming credit for the majority of these actions were the People's Revolutionary Army (Ejército Revolucionario del Pueblo—ERP) and the Farabundo Martí Popular Liberation Forces (Fuerzas Populares de Liberación Farabundo Martí—FPL), both radical offshoots of the PCES (the ERP was the new designation of "the Group" that had killed Regalado in 1971).

In 1969 the initial split took place between the followers of party leader Salvador Cayetano Carpio ("Marcial"), a Maoist advocate of a revolutionary "prolonged popular war" strategy for achieving power, and those of Jorge Shafik Handal, who held to the prevailing Moscow-line strategy of electoral participation. By the end of the 1970s, however, political violence and instability had increased markedly, strengthening the position of those who advocated a violent path to power. The success of the 1979 Nicaraguan revolution led by the Marxist Sandinista National Liberation Front (Frente Sandinista de Liberación Nacional—FSLN) apparently served to alter the thinking of policymakers in the Soviet Union, leading them to endorse the strategy of "armed struggle" long advocated by Cuba. By the end of the decade, no less than five Marxist guerrilla groups, including one directly affiliated with the PCES, were recruiting members for military and terrorist action against the government (see Left-Wing Extremism, ch. 5).

Popular support for radical leftist groups appeared to expand rapidly in El Salvador in the mid-1970s, although the ideological uniformity of that support was suspect. The vehicles for the mobilization of the "masses" behind a revolutionary program of radical reform were the so-called mass organizations (also known as popular organizations). Established and run clandestinely by the guerrilla groups, these organizations drew much of their leadership from radical Roman Catholic groups known as Christian Base Communities (Comunidades Eclesiásticas de Base—CEBs) that had been established by activist clergy throughout the country. The largest of the mass organizations was the FPL-affiliated Revolutionary Popular Bloc (Bloque Popular Revolucionario—BPR), with nine constituent peasant groups and an estimated 60,000 members. Other mass organizations included urban trade unions among their ranks. Through public demonstrations, strikes, seizures of buildings, and propaganda campaigns, these organizations sought to undermine the government and create conditions conducive to a revolutionary assumption of power by the left.

Right-wing reaction to the rise of the radical left took several forms. The Molina government made a belated and feeble attempt to appease rural demands for land by passing a law in 1974 calling for the forced rental or possible expropriation of unexploited or inefficiently used land, but the law was not enforced. The government, however, took another step toward reform in 1976, when it declared an agrarian transformation zone of some 60,000 hectares in San Miguel and Usulután departments that was to be divided among 12,000 peasant families. Large landowners, incensed by this prospect, sent a delegation to meet with the president, who subsequently agreed to exempt from redistribution all lands fulfilling a "social function." This euphemism effectively encompassed all the land in question, and the redistribution never was effected.

Although efforts at small-scale reform were unsuccessful in the 1970s, the other side of the reform-repression coin was much in evidence. A new development was the rise in nonofficial repression from the shadowy right-wing bands that came to be known as the "death squads." Apparently bankrolled by the oligarchy and drawing on active-duty and former military personnel for their members, the squads assassinated "subversives" in an effort to discourage further antigovernment activities and to deter potential expansion of the ranks of the mass organizations and other protest groups. From the perspective of the Salvadoran right, the most urgent threat emanated from the CEBs, which by the mid-1970s had incorporated large numbers of people into politicized Bible study and self-help groups. The death squads targeted both religious and lay members of these groups.

The first of the squads to make itself known publicly was the Wars of Elimination Anti-Communist Liberation Armed Forces (Fuerzas Armadas de Liberación Anti-comunista de Guerras de Eliminación—FALANGE), a title obviously concocted more for its acronym than for its coherence. Others, such as the White Warriors Union (Unión de Guerreros Blancos—UGB), would follow. These organizations found their inspiration in the severe anticommunist tactics of the military regimes in Guatemala (many Salvadoran death squad members had direct ties to the Guatemalan right) and Brazil. The example of extreme military reprisals against the left in Chile after the 1973 coup against Allende also was influential.

Official repression also prevailed during the 1970s. Crowds of antigovernment demonstrators that had assembled in the capital were fired on by the military in July 1975 and February 1977. The passage of the Law for the Defense and Guarantee of Public Order in November 1977 eliminated almost all legal restrictions on violence against civilians. Political scientist Enrique A. Baloyra has compiled statistics for the 1972–79 period showing a tenfold increase in political assassinations, a tripling in the prosecution of "subversives," and a doubling in the number of "disappeared."

The government's record in the electoral arena was equally discouraging for the opposition. The UNO coalition participated in the Legislative Assembly and municipal elections of 1974. Duarte even managed to slip back into the country to campaign briefly on behalf of coalition candidates. His efforts were wasted, though, as the balloting was manipulated even more flagrantly than that of 1972. In 1976 the opposition parties decided that electoral participation was pointless and declined to run candidates. Presidential elections in 1977 were too important to pass up, however. The atmosphere was too volatile to allow another run by Duarte, so UNO nominated retired Colonel Ernesto Claramount Rozeville to head its ticket. He was opposed by the official PCN candidate,

General Carlos Humberto Romero Mena. Once again, electoral fraud was clumsy and poorly disguised. Claramount, his running mate José Antonio Morales Ehrlich, and a crowd of thousands gathered in the Plaza Libertad in San Salvador to protest Romero's election. Their assembly was the occasion for the February 1977 attack that left as many as fifty protesters dead. As he was taken from the scene in a Red Cross ambulance, Claramount declared, "This is not the end. It is only the beginning."

The Reformist Coup of 1979

The tenure of President Romero was characterized by the abandonment of any official pretense of reform and a precipitous rise in politically motivated violence. The leftist guerrilla groups stepped up their operations—assassinations, kidnappings, and bombings—as a form of self-defense, as retaliation against government forces, and as part of a larger strategy of impelling the country further toward political anarchy, a state perceived by the left as one of the "objective conditions" necessary for a broad-based antigovernment insurrection. This process of extreme polarization alarmed those political actors who saw the old system of domination by the military and the elite as no longer workable, but who feared the consequences of a successful communist-led revolt. This loose coalition included young military officers, Christian democratic and social democratic politicians, and more progressive Salvadoran industrialists.

Many of these groups, with the exception of private sector representatives, came together in August 1979 to establish a political pressure group known as the Popular Forum (Foro Popular). The Popular Forum issued a call for an end to official and unofficial repression, the establishment of political pluralism, short-term and long-term economic reforms (including agrarian reform), and the incorporation of the mass organizations into the government. This last demand, coupled with the participation in the Popular Forum of the 28 of February Popular Leagues (Ligas Populares 28 febrero—LP-28), the most radical of the mass organizations (it was affiliated with the ERP), convinced many young military officers that some action was necessary to head off a leftist political victory in El Salvador. The government of Anastasio Somoza Debayle in Nicaragua had fallen only the month before, and, from the point of view of the Salvadoran military, the Popular Forum bore a suspicious resemblance to the Broad Opposition Front that had brought the FSLN to power in that country. Although the final form and nature of the new Nicaraguan government was not yet in evidence, the dissolution of Somoza's National Guard was seen in El Salvador as a precedent and a direct threat to the military institution.

Thus, in a climate of extreme violence, sharp political polarization, and potential revolution, yet another generation of young officers staged a coup in an effort to restore order and address popular frustrations. This new Military Youth deposed President Romero on October 15, 1979, issuing a proclamation decrying the violent, corrupt, and exclusionary nature of the regime. Beyond their concern with preventing ''another Nicaragua,'' the young officers also were motivated by a desire to address the country's critical economic situation. Their vague aspirations in this regard apparently revolved around the achievement of an acceptable level of political stability that would staunch the flight of capital out of the country and restore to some degree the smooth functioning of the economy. In this regard, the 1979 coup resembled those of 1948 and 1960. Where it differed, however, was in the realization that effective and radical (by Salvadoran standards) reforms would have to be included in their program even at the risk of alienating the economic elite.

The first junta established by the coup leaders included the officer who headed the reformist faction within the officer corps, Colonel Adolfo Arnoldo Majano Ramos, along with another officer of more uncertain political inclinations, Colonel Jaime Abdul Gutiérrez. The other junta members were Ungo from the MNR, Román Mayorga (a former president of the Jesuit-run Central American University José Simeón Cañas), and Mario Andino, a representative of the private sector. This junta wasted little time in announcing and attempting to implement a reformist program. It enacted decrees to freeze landholdings over ninety-eight hectares and to nationalize the coffee export trade. It did not move immediately to effect agrarian reform, but it promised that such a reform would be forthcoming. Another decree officially disbanded Orden. The implementation of that decree, like that of many others during the period of the reformist juntas, was hampered seriously by the limited influence of the reformist faction over the more conservative security force apparatus. Perhaps the best indication of this limitation was the fact that the level of violence carried out by the security forces against members of the mass organizations increased after the installation of the junta.

The upswing in repression against the left reflected not only the resistance of conservative military and security force commanders but also the outrage expressed by elite landowners and the majority of the private sector over the reform decrees and the prospect of even more wide-ranging actions to come. Some observers have alleged that the campaign of terror waged by the death squads was organized and coordinated by conservative officers under the leadership of Major Roberto D'Aubuisson Arrieta, a member of the country's executive intelligence agency, with the financial backing of the oligarchy. Although the evidence for this sort of sweeping conspiratorial concept is inconclusive, the existence of ties between the economic elite and security force personnel seems undeniable.

The military's reaction in general to the junta's reformism was mixed. The reformists sought to incorporate new sectors into the political system but stopped short of including the mass organizations in that effort because of the radical ties of those organizations. Conservative officers, led by the defense minister, Colonel Guillermo García, saw the reformists as playing into the hands of the left, weakening the military institution, and increasing the likelihood of a seizure of power by "extremist" elements. García, abetted by Gutiérrez, worked to undermine the reformists by excluding Majano's followers from key commands and positions through transfer or denial of promotion. The majority of Salvadoran officers seemed to fall into neither the reformist nor the conservative camp. Although they shared a generalized anticommunism and a strong commitment to the military institution, they were not sufficiently convinced that the kind of radical reform advocated by the junta was necessary. They opted for a sort of concerned neutrality and inaction that ultimately worked in favor of the aggressive conservative faction.

The first reformist junta eventually failed because of its inability to curb the increasing violence against the left. It was replaced on January 10, 1980, by a second junta. Majano and Gutiérrez remained as the military representatives, but the civilian members now included two prominent Christian Democrats—the party's 1977 vice presidential candidate, Morales, and Héctor Dada. José Avalos was the third civilian, replacing Andino, whose departure left the government without significant ties to the private sector. Direct participation in the government by the Christian Democrats was by no means universally accepted among the party membership. It was viewed as a bad precedent by those who still clung idealistically to their commitment to the democratic process. Moreover, the actual commitment of the government to effective reform was still questioned by the more progressive members of the party. On a practical political level, some felt that casting the lot of the PDC with that of the junta represented too great a risk of the party's prestige (admittedly somewhat eroded at that point anyway) for too little possible gain. On the other side of the ledger, however, proponents of participation (including Duarte, who had by this time returned from Venezuela) saw it as an opportunity to effect the kind of reforms that the party had long advocated, to establish a political center in El Salvador, and to make a transition to a genuinely democratic system.

The second junta was dogged by the human rights issue no less than its predecessor. The continued high level of political violence was attributable not only to the actions of the death squads and the security forces but also to the decision by the left to shun cooperation with the junta in favor of a call for armed insurrection. The three major mass organizations, along with the UDN, issued such a call on January 11, 1980. They established an umbrella front designated the National Coordinator, subsequently amended to Revolutionary Coordinator of the Masses (Coordinadora Revolucionaria de las Masas—CRM), to advance "the struggle." The MNR endorsed the manifesto of the CRM, further undermining the legitimacy of the junta government. The heightened militancy of the CRM was manifested in stepped-up demonstrations, occupations of churches and buildings, and strikes. On January 22, a mass rally held in San Salvador was fired on by the police, and twenty-four demonstrators were killed. On February 25, PDC activist Mario Zamora and others were murdered, apparently because they had been denounced publicly as subversives by now ex-Major D'Aubuisson. Zamora's killing led directly to the resignation of his brother, Rubén, from the government. Rubén Zamora established his own political party, the Popular Social Christian Movement (Movimiento Popular Social Cristiano—MPSC), taking a number of other disillusioned Christian Democrats with him. Reflecting the intense renewed debate within the PDC over participation in the government, Dada resigned from the junta. His place was taken in a third junta by Duarte, who finally decided to take a direct role in the process that he had supported previously from behind the scenes.

In an effort to display its commitment to change and to exert its authority within the country, the third junta decreed the most sweeping reforms enacted to that time, expropriating landholdings above 500 hectares and nationalizing commercial banks and savings and loan institutions. At the same time, it declared a state of siege in an apparent effort to back up its reforms with a show of force against the insurrectionist left. There were some paradoxical aspects to this policy of coupling reform with a hard military line toward the mass organizations and incipient guerrilla forces. For one thing, it strengthened the hand of military conservatives led by García and undercut efforts by Majano and others to reach an accommodation with wavering non-Marxist labor and peasant

Colonial church at Panchimalco, south of San Salvador

groups. It also helped frustrate the implementation of the agrarian reform program by facilitating reprisals by security force personnel or paramilitary groups (the now "unofficial" remnants of Orden) against the recipients of the expropriated acreage, much of which was distributed on a cooperative basis. Ultimately, the policies of the third junta seemed to do little to expand its popular base or enhance its legitimacy. As was the case with its predecessors, it also failed to rein in political violence, official or unofficial, originating from either side of the political spectrum.

That violence reached a dramatic apex in March 1980 with the murder of the archbishop of San Salvador, Oscar Arnulfo Romero y Galdámez, on March 24, 1980. Romero, who had been selected as archbishop in part because of his moderate political views, was influenced strongly by the liberation theology (see Glossary) movement, and he was appalled by the brutality employed with increasing frequency by government forces against the populace and particularly against the clergy. In his weekly radio homilies, he related statistics on political assassination and excesses committed by the military. He frequently urged soldiers to refuse to carry out what he characterized as immoral orders. His high profile made him an important political figure, and he had used his influence to urge the PDC to pull out of the junta and to argue against United States military aid to El Salvador. Despite his stature as the country's Catholic primate, he was targeted for assassination; all indications are that the killing was carried out by the right wing.

37

Romero's funeral on March 30 produced a dramatic clash between demonstrators and security forces. The BPR, seeking to capitalize politically on the archbishop's assassination, organized an antigovernment rally in San Salvador's Plaza of the Cathedral. What had been billed as a peaceful protest, however, turned violent. Responsibility for the melee that followed never has been firmly placed. Shooting erupted, apparently from both sides, and the police opened fire on the crowd. The resultant news footage of unarmed demonstrators being gunned down on the steps of the National Cathedral had a strong impact abroad, especially in the United States. El Salvador became almost overnight a focus of international debate and scrutiny.

Another high-impact incident was the murder of four churchwomen from the United States in December 1980. The murders themselves drew the ire of the United States government and public and prompted the administration of Jimmy Carter to suspend a program of limited military aid it had granted to the junta government (United States military aid had been rejected by the Romero government in 1977 when the Carter administration sought to link disbursement to human rights compliance). The subsequent investigation frustrated United States officials, angered the American public, and enhanced the suspicion that high-ranking officers in the security forces were orchestrating a cover-up of the affair.

The violent incidents that drew foreign attention to the chaotic situation in El Salvador were played out against a backdrop of a continuing power struggle within the military. While García continued to undermine the position of the reformist faction led by Majano from within the institution, other conservative commanders were plotting to stage a coup to force out the Majanistas once and for all. What at first appeared to be a preemptive strike against these conspirators on May 7, 1980, later proved to be the last nail in Majano's political coffin. A number of plotters, including D'Aubuisson, were captured by Majano loyalists during a planning session; incriminating documents also were seized at the site. The Majanistas, backed by the PDC members of the junta, demanded that D'Aubuisson and the others be tried for treason. The ex-major's release on May 13 and the subsequent failure of efforts to bring him to trial demonstrated the power shift within the military and the almost complete lack of PDC influence outside the reformist faction.

Majano's personal fall from power began with the announcement by Colonel García on May 10 that Colonel Gutiérrez was to function as sole commander in chief of the armed forces, a responsibility previously shared with Majano. The reassignment of Majanista officers, usually to foreign diplomatic positions, continued until September, when almost all remaining reformist officers were removed from their posts. Colonel Majano himself survived an assassination attempt by right-wing gunmen in November, only to be ousted from the junta on December 6 while on a visit to Panama. Majano returned in a vain effort to shore up his support among the ranks. By this time, however, he was practically bereft of support within the officer corps, the focus of real power in El Salvador at the time. Majano eventually fled into foreign exile rather than risk further attempts on his life. Many observers believed at the time that he took with him the last hopes of averting a major civil conflict through effective social and economic reform.

The Civil Conflict Begins

The early reaction of the Salvadoran radical left to the progression of reformist junta governments was characteristically fractious. The PCES expressed initial support for the first junta. Other groups, such as the ERP, condemned such impulses as collaborationist and renewed their call for an insurrection. Although some dialogue apparently took place between Colonel Majano and his supporters and some members of the radical left, the erosion of Majano's position within the military and the inability of the junta governments to stem the tide of right-wing violence, not to mention a certain suspicion among the Majanistas themselves of the leftists' ultimate goals, worked against any effort to incorporate them into the governmental structure. Some observers have noted this failure to bring the left into the political process as a major shortcoming of the reformist juntas. It appears, however, that the political will to do so was lacking on both sides. This was particularly true of the Marxist guerrilla groups that had expanded their membership and their aspirations since their establishment as urban terrorist cells in the mid-1970s.

Foreign influences on these Salvadoran guerrilla groups served in large part to convince their leadership of the need to sublimate old ideological quarrels in favor of a coordinated and cooperative effort to arouse the Salvadoran masses. The example of the Nicaraguan revolution served as both an inspiration and a loose blueprint for the Salvadorans. Nicaragua demonstrated the importance of incorporating as many sectors of society as possible into a revolutionary movement while still ensuring the predominance of a Marxist-Leninist "vanguard" group within the coalition. In Nicaragua the vanguard role was played by the FSLN, a group that had represented singlehandedly the pro-Cuban insurrectionist left in that country since the early 1960s. In El Salvador, the situation was more complicated. Clearly, several ideologically diverse (Maoist, pro-Soviet, and pro-Cuban) guerrilla groups could not fulfill simultaneously the role of revolutionary vanguard. Salvadorans recognized a need for unity that was not achieved until Cuba's Fidel Castro took a direct hand in the matter. The negotiating process began in Havana in December 1979, some two months after the reformist coup in El Salvador, and was concluded by May 1980, when the major guerrilla groups announced their unity under the banner of the Unified Revolutionary Directorate (Dirección Revolucionaria Unificada—DRU). Despite some continued infighting, the DRU succeeded in coordinating the groups' efforts to organize and equip their forces.

While the military strategy of the left was proceeding along one path, some opposition parties and the mass organizations were following a similar and eventually convergent course. On April 1, 1980, the Revolutionary Democratic Front (Frente Democrático Revolucionario—FDR) was established by the CRM, the umbrella group of the mass organizations. It brought together all five of the mass organizations associated with the DRU guerrilla groups as well as Ungo's MNR, Zamora's MPSC, another party known as the Popular Liberation Movement (Movimiento de Liberación Popular—MLP), forty-nine labor unions, and several student groups. FDR political leaders such as Ungo and Zamora began to travel abroad, where they found political and moral support, particularly in Mexico and among the social democratic parties of Western Europe. Meanwhile, the mass organizations began a campaign of general strikes in an effort to pave the way for a full or partial leftist assumption of power, either through insurrection or through negotiations.

In November 1980, the FDR was struck a traumatic blow when one of its leaders, Enrique Alvarez, was killed along with five other members of the front by a right-wing death squad. This incident underscored the danger of the FDR's strategy of open organization and opposition and contributed to its formal unification with the DRU. Although the leadership of the mass organizations had long been cooperating with the guerrilla groups, the politicians of the MNR and MPSC had sought to steer a slightly more independent path. After the Alvarez murder, however, they felt compelled to make common cause with the DRU; they took this action not only for their own protection but also because they believed that the prevailing level of violence in the country legitimized a violent response. By 1981 the FDR had been united formally with the Farabundo Martí National Liberation Front (Frente Farabundo Martí de Liberación Nacional—FMLN), the successor organization to the DRU. The first public announcement of the FMLN–FDR was made in Mexico City in January 1981, some four days after the FMLN guerrillas initiated an operation that they dubbed, prematurely and inaccurately, the "final offensive."

The guerrillas offensive began on January 10, 1981. From the perspective of the FMLN, its timing proved to be premature in a number of respects. The guerrillas' logistics network was not prepared to support an operation on an almost countrywide level; the rebels generally were not well armed and clearly were not well trained. The Salvadoran armed forces, although initially taken by surprise, were sufficiently cohesive to rally and beat back the guerrilla attacks. The FMLN hoped to establish operational control over Morazán Department and to declare it a "liberated territory." This major objective never was achieved. On a basic level, the final offensive demonstrated the limited extent of the guerrillas' support among the Salvadoran population. The anticipated countrywide insurrection on which the FMLN had staked so much of its hopes for victory never materialized.

The final offensive was not a total loss for the FMLN, however. It retained military strongholds, especially in Chalatenango Department, where its forces settled in for a protracted guerrilla conflict. The offensive focused further international attention on El Salvador and established the FMLN–FDR as a formidable force both politically and militarily; in August 1981, the governments of France and Mexico recognized the front as a "representative political force" and called for a negotiated settlement between the rebels and the government. Seeking to capitalize on such support, FDR representatives carried on a "political offensive" abroad while the FMLN forces dug in, resupplied, and continued their organizational and operational efforts in the field (see Left-Wing Extremism, ch. 5).

On the down side for the guerrillas, however, the armed forces continued to repulse their assaults with relative ease, even without the benefit of United States military aid. The timing of the final offensive had in large part reflected the desire of the FMLN to take power before the inauguration of United States president Ronald Reagan. Although it failed militarily, the offensive still drew considerable attention from observers and policymakers in Washington.

The United States Takes a Hand

The Carter administration had lost considerable leverage in El Salvador when the Romero government renounced United States aid in 1977. The United States therefore welcomed the October 1979 coup and backed up its approval with an economic aid package that by 1980 had become the largest among Western Hemisphere recipients. A small amount of military aid also was provided. United States advisers contributed to the third junta's agrarian reform program, particularly Phase III of the reform, the so-called Land to the Tiller decree of April 28, 1980, granting title to smallholders. Phase II, expropriating holdings between 100 and 500 hectares, was decreed in March 1980, but implementation was postponed. The government cited lack of administrative and financial resources for its inaction; many observers believed that political considerations were equally influential.

United States policy and influence in El Salvador, however, was fitful and inconsistent from 1979 through 1981. It was driven by two conflicting motivations in the complex and shifting political prism of El Salvador. The first motivation was the prevention of a leftist takeover. Both economic and military aid for the junta governments seemed to be intended to promote a centrist alternative to either a Marxist-led revolution or a conservative military regime. The assumption of power by the FSLN in Nicaragua increased the pressure on the United States to prevent a similar result in El Salvador; this pressure grew by 1981 as the Sandinistas consolidated their dominant role in the Nicaraguan government.

The second motivation was human rights. The Carter administration had established the promotion of human rights as a cornerstone of its foreign policy, particularly in Latin America. Like many Salvadorans, United States officials were frustrated by the inability of the junta governments to contain political violence. Nevertheless, Carter's policy was sufficiently flexible to allow increased aid levels despite a generalized upswing in human rights violations in El Salvador, as long as the government there appeared to be making good faith efforts at reform. It was not merely the general level of violence, however, but the specific murders of United States citizens that most affected dealings with El Salvador. As previously mentioned, the December 1980 murder of the four churchwomen produced a complete cutoff of aid pending an investigation of the case. On January 4, 1981, two American land reform advisers from the American Institute for Free Labor Development (AIFLD) were gunned down along with a Salvadoran in the Sheraton Hotel in San Salvador. This action alarmed not only the White House but also the United States Congress, and it added fuel to the effort to disburse aid based on improvements in the Salvadoran human rights situation.

The launching of the "final offensive" lent a new urgency to Washington's approach. On January 14, 1981, four days after the offensive began, Carter announced the approval of US$5 million in "nonlethal" military aid; an additional US$5 million was authorized four days later. The low level of the aid and the impediments to its rapid disbursement meant that it had little direct impact on the Salvadoran armed forces' response to the guerrilla offensive; the renewal of military aid, however, established a trend that President Reagan would build on when he assumed office on January 20, 1981.

The Reagan administration initially appeared to stress the need to shore up El Salvador as a barrier against communist expansion in Central America. The United States Department of State issued a special report on February 23, 1981, entitled *Communist Interference in El Salvador,* which emphasized Nicaraguan, Cuban, and Soviet support for the FMLN. The report was widely criticized in the American media and the United States Congress. Nevertheless, the administration succeeded in increasing substantially the levels of United States military and economic aid to El Salvador, first by executive order, then by legislative appropriation. Although Reagan downplayed the importance of human rights considerations, Congress voted in January 1982 to require certification by the executive every six months of Salvadoran progress in such areas as the curbing of abuses by the armed forces, the implementation of economic and political reforms (particularly agrarian reform), and the demonstration of a commitment to hold free elections with the participation of all political factions (all those that would renounce further military or paramilitary activity). The administration accepted the certification requirement, albeit reluctantly, and proceeded with a policy that emphasized economic maintenance in the face of guerrilla attacks on the country's infrastructure, military buildup to contain the insurgency, and low-key efforts in the human rights area.

The "Democratic Process"

As the FMLN guerrillas settled in for a protracted conflict marked by economic sabotage, the seizure of lightly defended towns and other targets, and the establishment of rural zones of influence, events in El Salvador increasingly began to be driven by decisions made in Washington. One area in which a consensus was reached among the Reagan administration, Congress, and Salvadoran moderates (mainly the PDC) was the desirability of establishing a legitimate government through a process of free elections. The Salvadoran right reluctantly joined this process after it became clear that the administration did not favor a conservative military coup. Duarte, who had been named provisional president on December 13, 1980, under a fourth junta government, announced on September 15, 1981, that elections for a Constituent Assembly would be held in March 1982. The Constituent Assembly would draft a constitution that would lay the groundwork for a presidential election. It also was hoped that the assembly would incorporate all or most of the reforms decreed by the junta governments into the new document.

The Constituent Assembly elections were participated in by six parties, but only three were of major significance. Two of these were familiar actors in El Salvador, the PDC and PCN. The third was a new party—the Nationalist Republican Alliance (Alianza Republicana Nacionalista—Arena)—led by D'Aubuisson, which represented the interests of the right. The FDR refused to participate in the elections, citing fears for the safety of possible candidates, the lack of proper political conditions, and the inordinate influence of the United States. It maintained that negotiations between the FMLN–FDR and the government should precede the holding of elections.

In the three-way contest that developed, the PDC was at a disadvantage in several respects. Its grass-roots organization had suffered from inactivity and the crippling impact of death squad assassinations. Ideologically, its appeal among the conservative rural population was limited in comparison to that of the center-right PCN and the rightist Arena, which also benefited from D'Aubuisson's image as a strong, virile man of action, or caudillo. The PDC also lacked the funds available to the other parties, especially Arena.

Despite a clear preference for Duarte and the PDC in Washington, the Christian Democrats captured only a plurality (35.5 percent, equating to twenty-four seats) of the balloting for the sixty-member Constituent Assembly. Although this was the largest total of any single party, it left the PDC facing a conservative majority in that body as Arena garnered nineteen seats and 25.8 percent of the vote and the PCN won fourteen seats with its 16.8 percent of the total ballots. This result took policymakers in Washington somewhat by surprise. Advocates of reform suddenly were faced with the prospect of a new constitution drafted by a conservative, and presumably antireform, Constituent Assembly. An even more worrisome eventuality for the United States was the possible election of D'Aubuisson as the country's provisional president. D'Aubuisson had been elected speaker of the Constituent Assembly, and many observers expected him to win the provisional presidency as well. The fact that he was passed over for this post in favor of the moderate independent Alvaro Magaña Borja reportedly reflected pressure both from the United States government, which did not wish to be put in the position of requesting increased levels of aid for a D'Aubuisson-led government, and the Salvadoran armed forces, which shared the Reagan administration's interest in raising the level of military aid.

Although it had initiated a democratic process of sorts, El Salvador was still volatile as 1983 approached. The FMLN–FDR had strengthened itself militarily and continued to press for a negotiated "power-sharing" agreement that would grant it a role in a revamped governmental structure. After their successful response to the poorly coordinated "final offensive," the armed forces bogged down and seemed unwilling or unable to respond effectively to the guerrilla threat. Political violence continued at high levels. The increasing involvement of the United States prompted comparisons with the early days of the Vietnam conflict. The ambiguity of the Salvadoran situation from the American perspective was not improved by the conservative victory in the 1982 elections. As seen from both San Salvador and Washington, the future for El Salvador appeared uncertain at best (see Relations with the United States, ch. 4).

*　　*　　*

Comprehensive studies of Salvadoran history are few. Alastair White's *El Salvador,* published in 1973 and reissued in 1982, remains the major general work on the subject. Other authors have produced useful volumes of more limited scope. Thomas P. Anderson's *Matanza: El Salvador's Communist Revolt of 1932* is a detailed account of a critical event. Twentieth-century political history is addressed effectively in Stephen Webre's *José Napoleón Duarte and the Christian Democratic Party in Salvadoran Politics, 1960–1972.* El Salvador's political prominence after 1979 drew increased attention to the subject; the results, however, are mixed. The majority of recent works are excessively polemicized, mainly as a result of the polarized atmosphere prevailing in the country throughout the early 1980s. One exception is Enrique A. Baloyra's *El Salvador in Transition,* an illuminating study of Salvadoran politics after 1948. Duarte's autobiography, aptly titled *Duarte: My Story,* is interesting in an anecdotal sense but of relatively limited value to the historian. (For further information and complete citations, see Bibliography.)

Chapter 2. The Society and Its Environment

Girl selling fruit

IN THE LATE 1980s, El Salvador was a country with major social, economic, and political problems that had reached crisis proportions on a national level. These problems reflected a basic pattern of social, economic, and political inequality that has persisted since the colonial era and grown in intensity during the twentieth century.

El Salvador is the smallest country in Central America in land area; it is also the most densely populated. These conditions have combined with marked imbalances in income distribution to create sharp contrasts in standards of living and general quality of life between the powerful and wealthy elite and the poverty-stricken masses. Limited productive territory, continuing high rates of population growth, and restricted ownership of land have led to a high level of unemployment and underemployment among the still largely rural and agrarian population. This population has lost much of its subsistence land base and therefore has had to rely for survival on participation in the cash economy, to which, however, most of its members were distinctly marginal.

The socioeconomic plight of the rural population, largely ignored by military dominated governments, contributed to the development of an armed insurgent movement by the early 1980s. Pressure for economic reforms also played a part in the dialogue over political change as El Salvador's rigidly controlled oligarchic system enforced by the military confronted pressures for a more open form of participatory democracy. Meanwhile, the turmoil and destruction caused by civil conflict exacerbated the problems of an already seriously stressed population.

Geography

El Salvador, the smallest Spanish-speaking nation in the Western Hemisphere, is located on the western side of the Central American isthmus. With an area of 21,041 square kilometers, the country is only slightly larger than Massachusetts. It is roughly rectangular in shape with 515 kilometers of land boundaries and 307 kilometers of coastline on the Pacific Ocean. El Salvador is bounded by Guatemala to the west and Honduras to the north and east, and it is separated from Nicaragua on the southeast by the Golfo de Fonseca (see fig. 1; fig. 2).

Geology

El Salvador, along with the rest of Middle America (a region comprising mainly Mexico and Central America), is one of the most seismologically active regions on earth, situated atop three of the large tectonic plates that constitute the earth's surface. The motion of these plates causes the area's earthquake and volcanic activity.

Most of Central America and the Caribbean Basin rests on the relatively motionless Caribbean Plate. The Pacific Ocean floor, however, is being carried northeast by the underlying motion of the Cocos Plate. Ocean floor material is relatively dense; when it strikes the lighter granite rocks of Central America, the ocean floor is forced down under the land mass, creating the deep Middle America Trench that lies off the coast of El Salvador. The subduction of the Cocos Plate accounts for the frequency of earthquakes near the coast. As the rocks constituting the ocean floor are forced down, they melt, and the molten material pours up through weaknesses in the surface rock, producing volcanoes and geysers.

North of El Salvador, Mexico and most of Guatemala are riding on the westward-moving North American Plate that butts against the northern edge of the stationary Caribbean Plate in southern Guatemala. The grinding action of these two plates creates a fault, similar to the San Andreas in California, that runs the length of the valley of the Río Motagua in Guatemala. Motion along this fault is the source of earthquakes in northernmost El Salvador.

El Salvador has a long history of destructive earthquakes and volcanic eruptions. San Salvador was destroyed in 1756 and 1854, and it suffered heavy damage in the 1919, 1982, and 1986 tremors. The country has over twenty volcanoes, although only two, San Miguel and Izalco, have been active in recent years. Violent eruptions are rare. From the early nineteenth century to the mid-1950s, Izalco erupted with a regularity that earned it the name "Lighthouse of the Pacific." Its brilliant flares were clearly visible for great distances at sea, and at night its glowing lava turned it into a brilliant luminous cone.

Physical Features

Two parallel mountain ranges cross El Salvador east to west with a central plateau between them and a narrow coastal plain hugging the Pacific (see fig. 3). These physical features divide the country into two physiographic regions. The mountain ranges and central plateau covering 85 percent of the land comprise the interior highlands. The remaining coastal plains are referred to as the Pacific lowlands.

The northern range of mountains, the Sierra Madre, forms a continuous chain along the border with Honduras. Elevations in this region range from 1,600 to 2,200 meters. The area was once heavily forested, but overexploitation led to extensive erosion, and it has become semibarren. As a result, it is the country's most sparsely populated zone, with little farming or other development.

The southern range of mountains is actually a discontinuous chain of more than twenty volcanoes, clustered into five groups. The westernmost group, near the Guatemalan border, contains Izalco and Santa Ana, which at 2,365 meters is the highest point in El Salvador. Between the cones lie alluvial basins and rolling hills eroded from ash deposits. The volcanic soil is rich, and much of El Salvador's coffee is planted on these slopes.

The central plateau constitutes only 25 percent of the land area but contains the heaviest concentration of population and the country's largest cities. This plain is about 50 kilometers wide and has an average elevation of 600 meters. Terrain here is rolling, with occasional escarpments, lava fields, and geysers.

A narrow plain extends from the coastal volcanic range to the Pacific Ocean. This region has a width ranging from one to thirty-two kilometers with the widest section in the east, adjacent to the Golfo de Fonseca. Near La Libertad, however, the mountains pinch the lowlands out; the slopes of adjacent volcanoes come down directly to the sea. Surfaces in the Pacific lowlands are generally flat or gently rolling and result from alluvial deposits from nearby slopes.

El Salvador has over 300 rivers, the most important of which is the Río Lempa. Originating in Guatemala, the Río Lempa cuts across the northern range of mountains, flows along much of the central plateau, and finally cuts through the southern volcanic range to empty into the Pacific. It is El Salvador's only navigable river, and it and its tributaries drain about half the country. Other rivers are generally short and drain the Pacific lowlands or flow from the central plateau through gaps in the southern mountain range to the Pacific.

Numerous lakes of volcanic origin are found in the interior highlands; many of these lakes are surrounded by mountains and have high, steep banks. The largest lake, the Lago de Ilopango, lies just to the east of the capital. Other large lakes include the Lago de Coatepeque in the west and the Lago de Güija on the Guatemalan border. The Cerrón Grande Dam on the Río Lempa has created a large reservoir, the Embalse Cerrón Grande, in northern El Salvador.

Climate

El Salvador has a tropical climate with pronounced wet and dry seasons. Temperatures vary primarily with elevation and show little

51

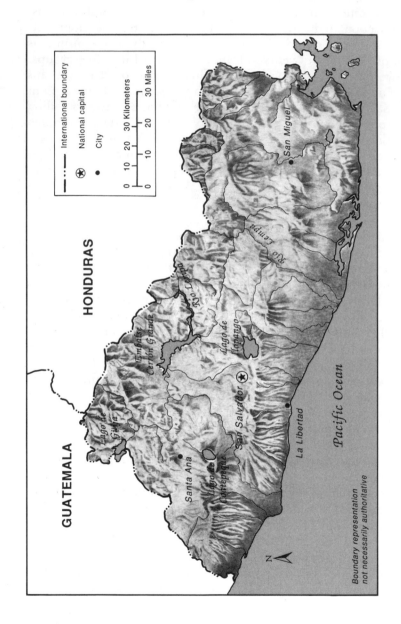

Figure 3. Topography and Drainage

seasonal change. The Pacific lowlands are uniformly hot; the central plateau and mountain areas are more moderate.

The rainy season, known locally as *invierno,* or winter, extends from May to October. Almost all the annual rainfall occurs during this time, and yearly totals, particularly on southern-facing mountain slopes, can be as high as 200 centimeters. Protected areas and the central plateau receive lesser, although still significant, amounts. Rainfall during this season generally comes from low pressure over the Pacific and usually falls in heavy afternoon thunderstorms. Although hurricanes occasionally form in the Pacific, they seldom affect El Salvador.

From November through April, the northeast trade winds control weather patterns. During these months, air flowing from the Caribbean has had most of the precipitation wrung out of it passing over the mountains in Honduras. By the time this air reaches El Salvador, it is dry, hot, and hazy. This season is known locally as *verano,* or summer.

Temperatures vary little with season; elevation is the primary determinant. The Pacific lowlands are the hottest region, with annual averages ranging from 25°C to 29°C. San Salvador is representative of the central plateau, with an annual average temperature of 23°C and absolute high and low readings of 38°C and 7°C, respectively. Mountain areas are the coolest, with annual averages from 12°C to 23°C and minimum temperatures sometimes approaching freezing.

Population

Although historically El Salvador has been home to a culturally diverse mix of peoples including blacks, Indians, Hispanics, and North Europeans, by the 1980s the population of the country was essentially homogeneous in terms of ethnicity and basic cultural identity. Virtually all Salvadorans spoke Spanish, the official language, as their mother tongue, and the vast majority could be characterized as mestizos (or ladinos, a term more commonly used in Central America), meaning persons of mixed biological ancestry who follow a wide variety of indigenous and Hispanic customs and habits that over the centuries have come to constitute Spanish-American cultural patterns. In the late 1980s, the ethnic composition of the population was estimated as 89 percent mestizo, 10 percent Indian, and 1 percent white.

In contrast to most other Central American countries, El Salvador no longer possessed an ethnically or linguistically distinct Indian population, although persons of Indian racial or cultural heritage still lived in the western departments of the country (see

Indians, this ch.). During the twentieth century, this population was rapidly assimilated into the dominant Hispanic culture. Similarly, there was no ethnically or culturally distinct black population.

In spite of ethnic homogeneity, however, Salvadoran society in the 1980s exhibited strong contrasts in life-style based on extremes of great wealth and abject poverty. These contrasting life-styles, in turn, created serious rifts in Salvadoran society that effectively divided the population into distinctive subcultural groups.

Demographic Trends

The population of El Salvador at the time of the national census in 1971 was 3,549,000. According to estimates, population growth averaged 3.4 percent annually in the 1970s and 2.4 percent in the 1980s. One United States government estimate claimed a 1988 population figure of 5,389,000 (estimates vary). Although El Salvador's high rate of population growth was similar to that of other Central American countries, the social and political effects of this population increase were aggravated by the very limited national territory available for the population.

Consequently, El Salvador also consistently had very high population density. From a figure of 170 persons per square kilometer in 1970, density has been projected to rise to about 230 persons per square kilometer in 1980 and to an extremely high 420 persons by 2000. El Salvador is the most crowded country of Central America (indeed, of all Latin America), and that condition will continue into the foreseeable future. This demographic situation has further exacerbated the problems associated with the inequality of national resource distribution. But the consequences of these demographic pressures have not been limited to El Salvador. Historically, high Salvadoran population density has contributed to tensions with neighboring Honduras, as land-poor Salvadorans emigrated to less densely populated Honduras and established themselves as squatters on unused or underused land. This phenomenon was a major cause of the 1969 war between El Salvador and Honduras (see The 1969 War with Honduras, ch. 1).

The distribution of population in El Salvador also remained uneven. The least densely populated areas were the northern departments of Chalatenango, Morazán, and Cabañas, encompassing the marginal land and rugged terrain of the descending slopes of mountain ranges that peak in Honduras (see Physical Features, this ch.). In contrast, the areas of greatest settlement were in the fertile central zone, where there was a large rural population, and in the major urban areas, including the San Salvador metropolitan

Izalco Volcano, Sonsonate Department

area (which had 828 persons per square kilometer in 1971), Santa Ana, and San Miguel.

The department of San Salvador was the most populous of El Salvador's fourteen departments, with a population density in the mid-1970s of 825 persons per square kilometer. The second most densely populated department at that time was neighboring Cuscatlán, with 206 persons per square kilometer. All other departments had fewer than 200 persons per square kilometer.

Observers believed that significant population growth would continue in the capital, San Salvador, where the net increase in population for the decade of the 1960s (202,000 persons) and of the 1970s (327,000) almost equaled and exceeded, respectively, the city's total population in 1950 (213,000). The population of San Salvador in 1980 was estimated to be 858,000, a figure that represented 30 percent of the total national population. The capital accounted for approximately 60 percent of the total urban population during 1950–80; its growth rates ranged between 4.4 percent and 5 percent during that period. Projections placed the population of the capital at approximately 1 million by 1990 and 1.5 million by the end of the century.

The number of small urban centers under 50,000 inhabitants in El Salvador increased from five in 1950 to eighteen by 1980. Inhabitants of these centers comprised 24 percent of the total urban population in 1980. San Miguel and Santa Ana, the two secondary cities of the country, accounted for an estimated 15 percent of the total urban population in 1980 and had an estimated annual growth rate of 3 percent (Santa Ana) and 4 percent (San Miguel) for the decades between 1950 and 1980. Nevertheless, these two cities were unable to compete with San Salvador in growth and prosperity. San Salvador's urbanized area was 5.7 times as large as that of Santa Ana, the next largest city, by the mid-1970s.

The urban population has grown approximately 50 percent in each decade from 1950 to 1980 and was projected to increase 3.9 percent annually from 1971 to 2000, as compared with an approximate rural population increase of only 30 percent per decade and a projected annual rate of increase of 2.8 percent from 1971 to 2000. But the rural population has been and will continue to be significantly larger than the urban in absolute numbers. The net rural population in 1971 was over 2.6 million, but it was projected to reach an estimated 6 million persons by the end of the century.

This high rural population growth rate accounted for the relatively low share, only 30 percent, of the total national population found in the capital in 1980. In addition, relatively few "new cities," towns increasing from under to over 10,000 inhabitants, appeared in the three decades prior to 1980. Urban growth therefore was limited primarily to increases in existing cities. During the 1950–80 period, urban areas accounted for 35 to 40 percent of the national population increase; analysts projected, however, that between 1980 and 2000 the urban sector as a whole would probably have to absorb 48 to 57 percent of that increase. San Salvador was expected to receive the bulk of urban population growth, perhaps as much as 65 to 69 percent from 1980 to 2000, while the two secondary cities and the smaller urban centers would decline somewhat in percentage of total urban population.

Population Growth and Age Distribution

The population of El Salvador increased from 1.9 million inhabitants in 1950 to 4.1 million in 1975 and 4.7 million in 1984. It was projected to increase to 8.8 million by the year 2000. In other words, the population would have doubled in each quarter-century since 1950. This high growth rate was a result of three main factors characteristic not only of El Salvador but also of Central America as a whole: a rapidly falling death rate, a continued high birth rate, and a very young population, i.e., a high proportion of the national population under age twenty (see fig. 4).

Although there was some variance in figures between El Salvador's census reports and estimates by the United Nations Latin American Center for Demography (Centro Latinoamericano de Demografía—Celade), there was agreement on basic birth and death statistics. The crude birth rate (the annual number of births per 1,000 inhabitants) declined from a relatively stable 49 through the 1950s to 44.4 in the late 1960s. In the major industrial nations, the rate is commonly below 20. The annual death rate per 1,000 inhabitants, however, declined by approximately one-third during the same period, falling from 21.3 to 13, and this decline contributed to the high rate of national population increase.

From 1970 to 2000, a continuing decline in both birth rates and death rates was anticipated. Studies projected a gradual fall in the crude birth rate from 42.2 in 1970–75 to 33.5 in 1995–2000 and in the crude death rate from 11.1 in 1970–75 to 7.2 in 1985–90 and 5.6 in 1995–2000 (see table 2, Appendix). These two trends would operate more or less in tandem, however, so that the rate of natural increase, though declining, would still hover at around 3 percent. The overall population was very young; the median age in the country declined from nineteen in 1950 to seventeen in 1975, and 41.3 percent were projected to be under age fifteen by the year 2000. It is noteworthy here that life expectancy at birth improved from approximately forty-six years in the 1950s to fifty-nine years in 1977 and to sixty-five years in 1984 (sixty-three years for males and sixty-six for females), largely as a result of mass immunization schemes and control of disease-bearing insects. Life expectancy was expected to reach sixty-nine to seventy years in 1995–2000.

Birth rates showed that total fertility rates (the number of children a woman would bear in her lifetime if she experienced average fertility) ranged from approximately 6.1 to 6.3 in the mid-1970s, down from 6.7 in 1961. Analysts projected that this rate would drop to 4.4 in 1995–2000. The decrease in the level of fertility since 1961 was seen in the twenty- to thirty-nine-year-old age-group.

Family planning programs of both the privately organized Salvadoran Demographic Association, which was founded in 1962 and began operations in 1967, and (after 1971) government agencies under the Ministry of Public Health and Social Services probably contributed to this decline in fertility rates. The groups lobbied for family planning programs, provided family planning clinics, and dispensed birth control information and devices. Female sterilization was the most common birth control method because it is final and does not require frequent checkups or visits to clinics for additional supplies. The need for clinic visits has associated use of oral contraceptives in the popular mind with illness. In addition, there were fewer religious objections to sterilization. At the same time, abortions also were widely practiced. Abortion was illegal in El Salvador, and improperly performed abortions were

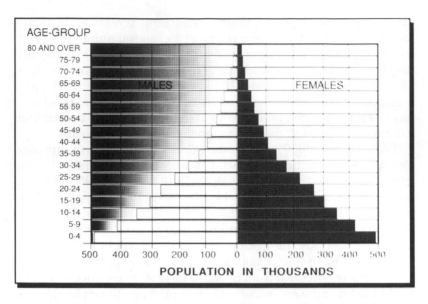

Source: Based on information from Robert W. Fox and Jerrold W. Huguet, *Population and Urban Trends in Central America and Panama,* Washington, 1977, 103–4.

Figure 4. Estimated Population Distribution by Age and Sex, 1985

common. They were the third leading cause of hospital admissions in 1975, constituting 24 of every 1,000 admissions, according to a sample survey.

Fertility rates showed significant contrasts between urban and rural settings. In 1975 the birth rate per 1,000 women in rural areas was estimated at 46 to 47, whereas in urban areas it stood at approximately 34 to 35 (31 to 33 for the San Salvador metropolitan area). On average, by age thirty-five, rural women had seven children while urban women had only five. By the end of their childbearing years, rural women, on average, had eight children, and urban women had six. Given the markedly inferior health conditions of the countryside, however, of the two additional children born to rural women, only one would survive. The number of children under age one per 1,000 women between ages fifteen and forty-four declined by 16.5 percent in urban areas from 1961 to 1971, while it remained essentially unchanged over that same time period in rural areas.

Disparate fertility rates underscored the point that El Salvador continued to be a rural country in the late 1980s, "rural" in this context including all population in towns of less than 20,000. In fact, El Salvador showed the highest rural population increase—82 percent from 1961 to 1980—in Latin America.

Metro Center shopping mall, a modern retail center in San Salvador

The Structure of Society

In the late 1980s, El Salvador was experiencing severe internal stress as a result of an ongoing insurgency, a severely debilitated economy, and persistent socioeconomic inequalities. Despite reform efforts begun under the post-1979 civilian-military junta governments, the country's longstanding division between rich and poor still represented a challenge to Salvadoran leaders and to the society as a whole.

The sharp contrast between those with great wealth and those living in extreme poverty had characterized Salvadoran society for more than a century and had roots in its colonial past (see Spanish Conquest and Colonization, ch. 1). When El Salvador became an independent republic in the early nineteenth century, this pattern did not change. Wealthy landowners, members of only a very few families, organized the national government to secure their positions and continued to dominate Salvadoran national life. Rural peasants and workers provided for their own subsistence needs and labored for the elite. Indeed, as the century progressed, this pattern was sharpened by the successful introduction of coffee as an export cash crop. As the landed elite, along with more recently arrived European banking and financial families interested in coffee, began to realize the wealth potential of this crop, they increased the size of their estates.

They did so by absorbing into their private holdings public lands (forests) and the communal lands of *municipios* (the Salvadoran equivalent of counties) and Indian communities, lands formerly cultivated in small subsistence plots by mestizo and Indian peasants. The government officially decreed these common lands out of existence in favor of private property ownership in 1881. Those dispossessed of their subsistence lands became permanent or seasonal laborers working for extremely low wages on coffee estates, which were labor-intensive enterprises. To protect their lands and their prosperity, the coffee elite formed a strong economic and political oligarchy. The army and the National Guard (Guardia Nacional—GN) were employed to control the unrest and occasional open rebellions among the many now landless and poorly paid laborers.

When coffee prices fell during the Great Depression of the 1930s, laborers' wages were reduced still further, and since much subsistence land had been converted to private coffee cultivation and the production of staple crops had declined accordingly, living conditions worsened (see Economic Crisis and Repression, ch. 1). Unemployment rose too, as many coffee growers decided not to harvest their crops. In addition, many small landowners, unable to survive the low coffee prices, lost their lands to those who were wealthier, and landownership became even more concentrated.

In the decades following the depression, export agriculture became somewhat diversified as cotton and, to a lesser extent, sugar also became important plantation cash crops, and some of the elite began to argue for industrial development. The upper class in general, however, strongly resisted any significant changes in the basic social, economic, and political order. After a rural uprising in 1932 and the brutal reprisals later referred to as *la matanza* (the massacre), in which about 30,000 were killed by troops, the dominance of the elite was preserved and defended by the Salvadoran military (see Economic Crisis and Repression, ch. 1).

The Upper Sector

In relation to the total population, the Salvadoran elite was very small; by the early 1980s it constituted approximately 2 percent of the population. This social sector, however, owned 60 percent of the nation's productive land, exercised direct or indirect control over all key productive sectors of the economy, and accounted for one-third of the national income.

The economic interests of the elite fell into three general categories: export-oriented agribusiness, including coffee, cotton, sugar, and cattle; commercial and financial enterprises, including insurance, financial investment, real estate, utilities, and banks;

and relatively newer retail and industrial interests, including distributorships and manufacturing. Given the continued dominance of export agriculture and of financial interests in the 1980s, this third category remained less significant overall.

Among the elite, there were divisions based on relative social status and prestige as determined by ancestry. The oldest and most prestigious families were those associated with the colonial "founding fathers" who had developed export agriculture. Next in the pecking order were the families, mainly involved in banking and finance, whose European ancestors had immigrated to El Salvador in the late nineteenth and early twentieth centuries with a useful knowledge of foreign markets. The newest elite families, on the lowest social rung of the upper echelon, included Lebanese, Palestinians, and Jews and were pejoratively referred to as "Turcos" by the "older" elites. These most recent immigrants constituted the bulk of the Salvadoran merchant class; they tended to socialize primarily within their own group.

Despite these social distinctions, the Salvadoran elite as a whole was interconnected through bonds of shared economic interest, direct business dealings, particularly between the agribusiness and financial sectors, and frequent intermarriage. The families of the oligarchy generally intermarried. Daughters anticipated lives as pampered mothers and wives, while sons expected a place in one of the family businesses. Generally, members of elite families tended to live in San Salvador, whence they traveled periodically to their plantations, which were usually directed on site by resident administrators, or to Western Europe or the United States for business or recreation. The elite educated their children in private schools and in United States universities, entertained at fashionable clubs, and enjoyed extravagant conspicuous consumption.

To reconcile their differences and represent their interests, the elite organized into associations. Most notable among these associations was the National Association of Private Enterprise (Asociación Nacional de la Empresa Privada—ANEP), which has expressed oligarchy views through various declarations in the media and before the government (see Political Dynamics, ch. 4).

The economic oligarchy, although traditionally the most influential sector of Salvadoran society, was not the most powerful in and of itself. The Salvadoran upper sector also included the officer ranks of the military. Active or retired military personnel headed the government from 1932 to 1982, and, as a result, ambitious individual military officers and officer factions also emerged as interest groups in their own right. Members of the military gradually became involved in the elite economic structure—managing and

61

directing banks, the social security institute, the national airline, and the census bureau, as well as owning large estates and becoming involved in export agriculture. This combination of the officer corps and the elite families constituted the most powerful political and economic force in the country.

Although their interests became closely interwoven, the economic oligarchy and the military remained separate entities. A few select military personnel were adopted into the oligarchy after their retirement, but few in the military were welcomed into the more exclusive San Salvador clubs frequented by the elite. For its own part, the officer corps was a closed and cliquish group; 90 percent of its members were graduates of the Captain General Gerardo Barrios Military Academy (Escuela Militar Capitán General Gerardo Barrios) and organized in mutually supportive networks based on graduating class membership. Each graduating class formed a group known as a *tanda,* whose members assisted each other and entered alliances with other *tandas* to broker the allocation of command and staff positions within the armed forces (see Officer Corps Dynamics, ch. 5). The military served as one of the few mechanisms of upward mobility in Salvadoran society. The expectation of power and prestige was a considerable motivator for cadets, most of whom typically came from a Salvadoran middle-class background.

The Lower Sector

The vast majority of Salvadorans were members of the lower sector of the population, which was composed of full- or part-time laborers, peasant smallholders, and the unemployed. Although there was considerable diversity within this large social sector, most of its members shared the common denominators of dependence on the cash economy and insufficient earning power for even a minimally adequate standard of living. The variation within this population reflected degrees of landlessness, types of employment, residence locations, and relationship with economic and military power holders.

In 1981 approximately 58 percent of Salvadorans lived in rural areas, some as full-time estate workers (*colonos*), others owning or more likely renting (*arrendatarios*) small plots of marginal land, and many, both those with small plots of land and the vast number who were landless, as seasonal wage laborers or unemployed. During the 1980s, the number of workers depending on agriculture for jobs increased, as a result of both population growth in the rural areas and the civil conflict, which eliminated more nonagricultural than agricultural jobs.

The extent of access to marginal subsistence plots varied according to the degree of plantation development in the various regions of El Salvador. The hilly northern departments of Chalatenango, Cabañas, and Morazán, adjacent to the Honduran border, contained relatively few large estates. Consequently, subsistence farms continued to exist there. But such farms, being small and with marginal soil quality, generally did not provide full self-sufficiency or year-round employment. Nor was much cash available from the sale of produce, for the government, concerned with providing affordable food for city dwellers, kept food prices low. Consequently, members of these peasant families migrated seasonally to cash crop (coffee) estates at harvest time, when they obtained temporary jobs at very low wages, or moved to San Salvador.

Peasants living in areas where coffee, cotton, and sugarcane were grown extensively were less likely to have access to subsistence plots, although valiant attempts were made to cultivate the rocky, marginal land on the steep hillsides of the volcanic ranges of central El Salvador, where coffee estates absorbed all good land in the central valleys and on the cultivable slopes. The development of cotton estates on the low-lying coastal plain and of sugarcane, grown between the coastal cotton and hilly coffee regions, also dislocated many peasants. In addition, large-scale mechanization in the 1970s eliminated the need for sizable labor forces on these estates. For example, one 6,000-hectare cotton estate employed a total regular work force of only thirty-five people. The development of grazing lands for export cattle on the coastal plain and in some interior valleys again reduced available subsistence land while requiring very few laborers. In the 1970s, more of El Salvador's land resources were used for cattle grazing than for production of food crops.

In addition, as social unrest grew among rural laborers, large estate owners preferred wherever possible to increase the use of seasonal rather than permanent workers. In the cotton-growing areas, for example, the number of *colonos* decreased by 60 to 95 percent during the 1960s. Overall, the number of landholdings with *colono* arrangements dropped from a high of 55,000 in 1961 to 17,000 in 1971. Permanent agricultural workers were thought to be more susceptible than temporary workers to political organization and therefore were believed to constitute more of a potential threat to elite land rights. This attitude further increased the number of underemployed and unemployed landless laborers in the countryside. A few statistics illustrate the situation in general. In 1961, about 12 percent of the rural population was landless; by 1971 the figure had reached 29 percent; in 1975 the number of landless was estimated at 41 percent. Similarly, from 1950 to 1970 rural

63

unemployment stood at 45 to 50 percent. By 1975 only 37 percent of rural workers worked full time, 14 percent worked an average of nine months, 19 percent worked an average of six months, and a full 30 percent worked for only two to three months annually. By 1980 an estimated 65 percent of the rural population was landless and dependent on wage employment.

The small percentage of the labor force employed in industry was somewhat better off than agricultural workers, but only about 12.8 percent of the labor force was employed in industry in 1961, and by 1971 that number had dropped to 9.8 percent (see Industry, ch. 3). Their low numbers in part reflected the use of capital-intensive technology, which made it unnecessary to hire a large work force. Jobs also were few because industry in general, and manufacturing in particular, remained limited as a result of capital flight caused by political instability, the unsettled economy, and damaging guerrilla attacks.

Enlisted military personnel, another component of the lower sector, were young peasant conscripts or volunteers who had joined the armed forces to enjoy three meals a day and a warm place to sleep; some of the conscripts had been impressed into service in response to manpower shortages. After discharge from active duty, some ex-servicemen signed on for further service and benefits as military reservists in the GN or in civil defense groups.

The Middle Sector

The small proportion of society constituting a middle class—about 8 percent in the early 1980s—included skilled workers, government employees, professionals, school teachers, smallholders, small businessmen, and commercial employees. These people were caught between the polar extremes of wealth and poverty. Not being members of the traditional oligarchy—although the great success of nineteenth-century coffee production had stimulated the development of the middle sector as well as of the elite—the middle sector traditionally had little direct influence in government affairs. Similarly, although profoundly influenced by the United States, members of this population sector did not have sufficient wealth to enjoy ready access to schooling or travel in that country. Instead, having only a tenuous toehold on property and limited power within the existing Salvadoran system, the middle sector found its position precarious and felt seriously threatened by El Salvador's political and economic crises.

After the depression of the 1930s, the middle sector hoped to improve the standard of living for all Salvadorans through agrarian reform and through legalized peasant organizing. In the 1960s

Village woman in Santa Inés, San Miguel Department
Courtesy Inter-American Development Bank

and early 1970s, various professionals and other members of the middle class tried to promote meaningful elections and called for a transition to more open and participatory democratic procedures. As economic and political crises deepened in the 1970s and 1980s, however, many members of the middle class became alienated by the rising tide of political violence. Many of these Salvadorans wished that the problem of "subversives" would simply go away so that order, stability, and economic growth could be restored. Others, however, chose to become increasingly active in political parties or popular organizations.

Indians

In contrast to most other Central American countries, El Salvador in the late 1980s did not contain an ethnically distinct Indian population. Native communities of Pipil and also Lenca, located mainly in the western departments, constituted perhaps 60 percent of the population throughout the colonial era and into the early decades of independence. But the development of coffee estates saw the dissolution of the communal lands of native villages and the slow but continual incorporation of Indians into the general cash economy, where they became peasants and wage laborers. By the late nineteenth century, this assimilation process was essentially complete. The 1930 census, the last census containing the category of "Indian," designated only 5.6 percent of the population, or some 80,000 persons, as Indian, although it is not clear what criteria were used in this determination. Other, possibly more accurate, independent estimates, however, placed the mid-twentieth-century Indian population at 20 percent, or close to 400,000 persons. The criteria used in these estimates to identify individuals as Indian included religious activities, distinctive women's dress, language, and involvement in various handicrafts. Still, the life-style of the majority of these people was no longer completely Indian. Most were ladinoized, Hispanic acculturated, monolingual Spanish speakers who did not wear distinctive Indian dress. The remaining Indian population was found primarily in southwestern El Salvador.

The abandonment of Indian language and customs was hastened by political repression after an abortive peasant/Indian uprising in 1932. The revolt centered in the western part of the country, around the former Indian towns of Ahuachapán, Santa Ana, and Sonsonate, where the growth of coffee estates since the late nineteenth century had absorbed subsistence lands of Indians and mestizos alike. The revolt was supported by a number of Indian community leaders (*caciques*). Even though most Indian communal lands had been lost, traditional community-centered religious-political organizations (*cofradías*) and their leaders remained sufficiently influential to organize and direct popular unrest. The harsh and bloody reprisal (*la matanza*) by government forces that ensued fell on the entire population of the region whether they had been combatants or not, and most had not. Perhaps as many as 30,000 were killed, including many who were culturally designated as Indian or who were deemed by government forces to have an Indian-like physical appearance. In the face of such racially motivated repression, most natives stopped wearing traditional dress, abandoned the Pipil language, and adopted ladino customs. In 1975 it was estimated that no more than 1 percent of the population wore distinctive Indian clothing or followed Indian customs.

Even though visible signs of ethnic identity were all but lost, many persons retained an interest in Salvadoran Indian heritage and worked to preserve it as best they could. During the 1970s, the Central American University José Simeón Cañas (Universidad Centroamericana José Simeón Cañas—UCA) in San Salvador began a systematic study of the surviving elements of the Pipil language; researchers found that about one-tenth of households in Sonsonate, Ahuachapán, and La Libertad contained at least one Pipil speaker. Various aspects of Indian tradition, including dance ceremonies that had been held in private for thirty years, were also rediscovered. As political tensions grew in the 1980s, however, access to Indian households became more difficult, and the Pipil language study was stopped.

In short, although observers have estimated that much of the Salvadoran population in the 1980s could be said to possess an Indian racial background, culturally there was no significant Indian ethnic sector in the country. Nonetheless, the concept of Indian ethnicity was still a rallying point. In the mid-1980s, thousands of persons nationwide supported a popular organization known as the National Association of Salvadoran Indians (Asociación Nacional Indígena Salvadoreña—ANIS) headquartered in Sonsonate.

Rural Life

As indicated, El Salvador remained a largely rural country despite the growth of San Salvador and its environs. For the vast majority of rural residents, however, land shortages, unemployment and underemployment, and extremely low wages combined to keep the standard of living low and the quality of life barely tolerable.

Standard of Living

In this largely agrarian society, land distribution continued to lie at the heart of the many problems afflicting the poor. In 1971, which as of 1988 was the date of the latest census, 92 percent of farms, some 250,500 in number, covered less than ten hectares each and together constituted only 27 percent of total farm area. These farms were the holdings of peasant laborers who planted basic foodstuffs such as corn, beans, rice, and sorghum on 95 percent of their holdings. They used rotational methods of agriculture in which individual plots were cultivated for about two years, then left fallow while another plot was tilled.

The 8 percent of the farms with an area greater than ten hectares occupied the remaining 73 percent of farm area. Within this category, 1,941 farms between 100 and 500 hectares in size, representing 0.8 percent of the total number of farms, accounted for 38.7 percent of all land under cultivation. Less than 20 percent of this land produced basic grains. Farms of more than 500 hectares accounted for more than 15 percent of the cultivated land. These farms included the agricultural estates of the elite. The data actually understated the extent of land concentration within the upper sector, however, since some elite individuals owned more than one farm and some large farms were registered in the names of various family members in an effort to conceal family holdings.

At the other end of the scale, there was a considerable increase during the 1970s in the number of farms composed of less than one hectare of land. These farms were on very poor soil, often on steep hillsides prone to erosion, and frequently were rented rather than owned. Such small rental farms were particularly common in the hilly northern departments of Chalatenango, Cuscatlán, Morazán, and Cabañas. In 1950 there were 70,400 such farms; in 1961 there were 107,000; in 1971 there were 132,000; and in 1975 there were 138,800. Stated somewhat differently, in 1975 an estimated 96.3 percent of the rural population had access to five hectares or less of generally marginal quality land per family; approximately seven hectares were judged necessary for a "typical" family of six people to produce enough food and income for its needs.

Wage labor was the alternative to agricultural self-sufficiency for the majority of rural Salvadorans. In fact, by 1980 approximately 65 percent of the rural work force was landless and dependent on temporary or full-time wage labor; more than half the rural families depended on wage work for over half their income. Given the lack of permanent jobs in the agricultural sector, the low wage scale, and the number of laborers seeking work, however, cash income was insufficient for many peasant laborers in the countryside. In 1975, for example, a typical family of six was estimated to need US$533 in annual income to buy the basic food needed to survive, yet 60 percent earned US$120 or less.

The effect of a declining national economy in the late 1970s and early 1980s, as evidenced by a decline in agricultural production of 7.4 percent in 1982 and 8.7 percent in 1983, restricted the number of available jobs (see The Labor Force, ch. 3). Unemployment and underemployment increased markedly during the late 1970s and early 1980s and reached such serious proportions that by 1986, according to Salvadoran government statistics, 30 percent of the work force was unemployed and another 20 percent was underemployed (unofficial sources claimed even higher figures). Of those working, a reported 80 percent worked only part time, often at jobs lasting only a few days, or received less than the minimum wage. Regular day labor on a cotton or sugar estate sometimes provided the equivalent of US$1.75 per day or less; seasonal jobs at harvest sometimes paid as little as US$0.60 a day.

In addition, even as the number of workers receiving less than the minimum wage increased, the buying power of that wage declined by 65 percent from 1979 to 1983, further aggravating the already serious economic problems of the poor. The minimum diet was very sparse, consisting of maize, beans, rice, sorghum, and, for a family of six, less than one kilogram of meat per month and a per capita caloric intake that was the lowest in the Western Hemisphere. Consumption levels in general fell by 27 percent between 1979 and 1981 and by a further 20 percent by 1984; the overall cost of living rose 98 percent during the 1979-84 period. Clothing and foodstuffs—items on which some 63 percent of all Salvadoran families spent 62 to 65 percent of their income—rose by 153 and 122 percent, respectively.

Poverty encouraged the additional hardship of broken families, a particularly acute problem among landless laborers who often had to move to find work. By 1980 about 25 percent of households were headed by women, partially as a result of men leaving the family unit in search of work. That over 60 percent of children were born out of wedlock was another indication of familial instability.

Health and Welfare

Insufficient income had a serious adverse effect on the general health and vitality of the rural population. In the mid-1980s, El Salvador was among the countries of the Western Hemisphere most seriously affected by malnutrition. During the 1970s, the poorer 50 percent of the population consumed, on average, only 63 percent of required calories and 56 percent of required protein according to accepted international guidelines for adequate nutrition; the overall population averaged 77.2 percent of the minimum standard for caloric consumption and 83.6 percent of the standard for protein consumption. Anemia, riboflavin deficiencies, and vitamin A and other vitamin deficiencies were widespread among the population.

Malnutrition was particularly prevalent among young children. Even before the upset caused by civil conflict during the 1980s, approximately 48.5 percent of children under five years of age suffered from mild malnutrition, 22.9 percent from moderate malnutrition requiring medical attention to cure, and 3.1 percent from severe malnutrition requiring hospitalization for adequate recovery. Stated differently, 80 percent of children suffered from at least first-degree malnutrition—10 to 24 percent underweight—and 5 percent suffered from third-degree malnutrition—over 40 percent underweight. Because pregnant women usually lacked proper nutrition as well, many children were born underweight and undernourished.

The poverty responsible for inadequate nourishment among campesinos was also reflected in substandard homes and living conditions. In some regions, land for housing and domestic life was limited to an absolute minimum by the expansion of private estates. Some closely crowded groups of huts were strung along the remaining narrow strips of public lands bordering highways and rivers or erected on narrow peripheries between the fenced boundaries of estates closed to resident laborers and the nearest public road, in an arrangement called "fence housing."

Rural homes typically sheltered four or more persons. They usually had one, sometimes two, rooms, dirt floors, walls of adobe brick or *bahareque* (wood frame with a mud or rubble fill) or of poles and straw, and thatched or tiled roofs. The kitchen commonly was in a separate shelter or located under an extension of the main roof. Even in the 1980s, almost none of the rural population had access to sewage systems. Some 12 percent had latrines or septic tanks, but 80 percent had no sanitation facilities. Surface water was seriously polluted by agriculture and industry, yet 60 percent of the rural population depended on rivers and streams and/or rainwater and 22 percent on wells for their water needs. Some 93 percent were without electricity and used kerosene lamps or candles for light and wood or charcoal for cooking and heat.

Conditions such as these, combined with malnutrition, produced high rates of chronic illness and high mortality, especially in infants and young children. Although families of three to four children were considered the most desirable size, rural women actually had an average of six to eight children and, given the high infant

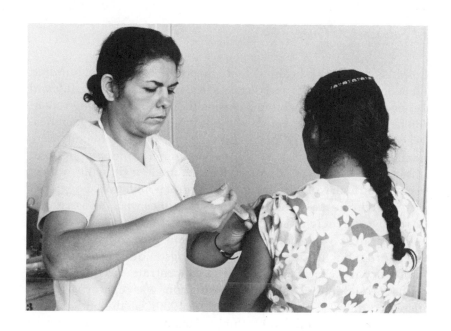

Nurse in rural health post administering an injection
Courtesy Inter-American Development Bank

death rate (about 120 to 125 per 1,000 live births) often had twice as many pregnancies. In general, about 30 percent of all deaths per year were of children under the age of one, and another 14 percent occurred in the age-group from one to four.

Several diseases posed particularly serious problems. Malaria was of major concern in rural departments, with morbidity ranges between 4,100 and 1,800 per 100,000 inhabitants in the 1980s. Water-borne diseases were also particularly common and one of the major factors affecting mortality. In the 1970s and 1980s, the leading causes of death included enteritis and other diarrheal diseases, as well as pneumonia and other respiratory diseases, such as bronchitis, emphysema, and asthma. Nutritional insufficiencies, perinatal complications, infections, and parasitic diseases also took a high toll, especially among children (see table 3, Appendix). As of 1987, El Salvador had reported sixteen cases of acquired immune deficiency syndrome (AIDS), the lowest total of any Central American country except Belize. Of the sixteen, six victims had died.

High mortality rates reflected the fact that health care itself was limited and medical facilities for the general population inadequate. This condition was aggravated by the civil disturbances of the 1980s. The 1971 census indicated that there were three doctors and seventeen hospital beds for every 10,000 persons. In 1984 ten general hospitals and twelve health centers, in addition to several hundred other community posts and dispensaries, provided between 0.5 and 1.5 beds per 1,000 inhabitants outside the San Salvador metropolitan area. Some rural regions did not have any hospital facilities. Where rural hospitals existed, health care personnel frequently were hampered in their work by limited equipment and supplies and unsanitary conditions. These conditions made it difficult to meet even the ordinary medical needs of the rural population. For example, most births took place at home, sometimes with the assistance of relatives or neighbors, but often unassisted.

Rural areas were deprived of sufficient government-financed social programs in part because of a longstanding governmental preference to keep taxes low and to concentrate the provision of services in San Salvador. The situation was exacerbated by increased military spending during the 1980s, as the budget allocations for the Ministry of Public Health and Social Services declined in real terms. Similarly, the number of medical personnel available to work in rural areas declined drastically after the Medical School of the National University was closed in 1980, ending the flow of interns, who had provided much of the medical care in the countryside. In addition, many doctors and other health workers in rural areas either relocated or abandoned their efforts as a result of the intensifying civil conflict in the 1980s.

The government, particularly through the Ministry of Public Health and Social Services, recognized as national priorities the need for improvement of health services, control of malaria, improved sanitation and drinking water quality, and increased child survival. It pledged to follow various lines of action toward these ends.

Social security was another government benefit to which rural Salvadorans had far less access than urban dwellers. The social security system was administered by the Salvadoran Social Security Institute, an autonomous institution first established in 1949. Its medical benefits and pension system, implemented in 1969, covered employees in industry and commerce but excluded agricultural workers, domestics, casual employees, and civil servants. The latter were covered by a different system. The institute also administered a number of hospitals throughout the country. Individuals (and their spouses) covered by the system were entitled to sickness and maternity benefits, care for work-related injuries, and pensions on the basis of old age or disability. The system was funded by payroll deductions from the insured, as well as by employer and government contributions.

Education

Public education was a higher priority than health care for government spending, and statistics reflected this disparity. School attendance and literacy in general increased notably in El Salvador as a whole during the twentieth century, particularly during the 1960s, when an ambitious program of school construction was carried out. Officially, literacy increased from 26.2 percent of the adult population in 1930 to 59.7 percent in 1971. By 1980 only 31 percent of the population aged ten years or older was considered illiterate.

The Salvadoran education system included one year of preschool, nine years of basic education, three years of secondary education, and higher education at two universities and several specialized postsecondary institutions. The curriculum at the basic and secondary levels, developed by the Ministry of Education, was uniform throughout the country. The provision of education, however, suffered from a rural-urban dichotomy. Countrywide statistics displayed the weakness of the school system on the secondary level; in a 1976 study, only 34 percent of students reached grade nine, and 15 percent reached grade twelve.

In the 1970s, primary-school enrollment increased by 90 percent. The benefit of such schooling, however, disproportionately favored urban areas, especially San Salvador, even though the majority of the illiterate population lived in rural areas. Stated differently, in 1980 about 40 percent of the rural population over age ten was illiterate, as compared with 25 percent of the urban dwellers. In the 1970s, fewer than two-thirds of school-age rural children attended primary schools, as compared with more than 90 percent of their urban counterparts. About 8 percent of the country's total enrollment in middle secondary education, grades seven through nine, were rural children; at the upper secondary level, grades ten through twelve, about 1 percent were rural children. In addition, illiteracy was twice as prevalent among women as among men; only about 30 percent of higher education students were female.

The high degree of rural illiteracy reflected several factors. At the most basic level, the number of teachers and schools provided for rural areas was seriously inadequate. In the 1970s, only 15 percent of the nation's schoolteachers served in rural areas; although 64 percent of primary schools were in rural areas, only 2 percent of secondary schools were. Existing rural schools were able to accommodate only 43 percent of the rural school-age population. Furthermore, of the primary schools available for rural children, approximately 70 percent offered education only below grade five.

By contrast, 90 percent of urban primary schools offered grade five or above. In rural areas, the 1976 student-to-teacher ratio was sixty to one, as compared with forty to one in urban areas.

In addition, there was a high attrition rate in school attendance in rural areas as students left school to earn incomes or work at home. It is significant that although school attendance generally began at about the age of eight or nine, about 70 percent of all male workers began work before the age of fifteen, many by age ten or earlier, thus permitting only one or two years of schooling. Many girls also dropped out of school at an early age to assume domestic responsibilities, such as caring for younger siblings, working in the fields, or tending animals. Therefore, in 1976 only about 20 percent of rural school-age children reached grade six, and only 5.7 percent reached grade nine.

Efforts to improve this situation in the rural agricultural areas were somewhat discouraging, in part because of the political tensions of the 1980s. In some situations, teachers, mainly women, faced threats if they were thought to be supporters of political change. Furthermore, many rural landowners seemed to prefer an uneducated rural population, on the grounds that better educated workers would expect better wages and be more likely to organize and lobby the government for reform, particularly land reform. A number of national education plans developed by the Ministry of Education had recognized the disparity between rural and urban education, but none had succeeded in bringing rural education up to the urban level.

Migration

Salvadoran migratory patterns have been shaped by socio-economic problems such as insufficient land, limited job opportunities, low wages, and persistent poverty. Some Salvadorans emigrated permanently from the country, some moved within the rural area itself, and some moved to urban areas in search of a better life. Internal and external migration levels were augmented by the civil conflict of the 1980s, although family and community fragmentation and dislocation were long-standing characteristics of life for the lower class. These patterns can be traced to the latter half of the nineteenth century, when communal landholdings were dissolved to facilitate the expansion of private holdings. This action created a dispossessed labor force whose movements came to be dictated by the cycles of coffee production.

Seasonal migrations from home communities to cash crop estates at times of harvest have been a way of life for many rural dwellers ever since coffee production came to dominate the

Moncagua displaced persons settlement, San Miguel Department
Courtesy United States Agency for International Development

Salvadoran economy (see The Oligarchy and the Liberal State, ch. 1). This type of migration was particularly important for land-poor peasants from the relatively infertile northern departments, hundreds of thousands of whom sought seasonal work in the central coffee regions. Similarly, as cotton farming developed in the coastal zone, both permanent laborers and thousands of seasonal harvest workers followed, particularly to land east of the Río Lempa and within the Sonsonate coastal plain in the southwest.

Between 1945 and 1969, population increase and land loss, particularly to cotton estates, led as many as 300,000 workers and dispossessed peasants—about 7 percent of the Salvadoran population—to migrate to neighboring Honduras. There, as farm laborers, squatters, tenants, or small farmers, they joined the land-poor rural population or moved to provincial towns where they were subsumed into the Honduran labor force. By the late 1960s, these Salvadorans constituted 12 percent or more of the Honduran population, and they had established contacts among that population, which was involved in its own agrarian reform efforts. The Honduran government targeted Salvadoran immigrants as the principal impediment to land redistribution efforts, encouraging anti-Salvadoran sentiments in an attempt to diffuse tensions among Honduran peasants and agricultural workers. In the wake of the ensuing Honduran agrarian reform, in which only native Hondurans were allowed to own land, as many as 130,000 Salvadorans were forced, or chose, to give up whatever jobs or land they had acquired and return to El Salvador. The exodus of Salvadorans from Honduras contributed to the so-called "Soccer War" of 1969 between the two countries, and the large number of returning Salvadorans worsened social and economic tensions within El Salvador itself.

In spite of ongoing tension with Honduras, Salvadorans continued to emigrate to that country, not only as landless laborers seeking work but, in the early 1980s, as refugees fleeing the civil conflict in El Salvador. Honduras seemed a logical refuge for many, given its proximity to the bordering Salvadoran departments of Morazán, Cabañas, and Chalatenango, all areas suffering under the civil conflict during the early 1980s. In 1981 some 60,000 refugees were in Honduras, many, particularly women and children, in refugee camps near the border, camps administered under the auspices of the office of the United Nations High Commissioner for Refugees.

Life was somewhat uncertain in the camps because of the unsettled circumstances stemming from the Salvadoran conflict. These pressures, as well as the monotony of life in the camps, induced thousands of Salvadorans to return home in spite of the dangers posed by ongoing warfare. In 1987 a reported 19,000 to 20,000 refugees still resided in camps in Honduras, the majority of whom were children and the rest mainly women and the elderly.

Some 20,000 Salvadoran refugees also sought sanctuary in Nicaragua, and an estimated 80,000 to 110,000 more relocated to Guatemala and thence to Mexico, many ultimately hoping to reach the United States. Indeed, between 1979 and 1988 as many as 500,000 Salvadorans were estimated to have reached the United States, the majority via Mexico. In overall terms, the extent of Salvadoran emigration to foreign countries was such that the United Nations (UN) in 1982 estimated that one-third of the work force had left the country. The number of refugees and displaced persons in general was estimated at 1 million, or 20 percent of the population, roughly half of whom had left the country.

Displaced persons remaining in El Salvador, internal refugees uprooted by the civil conflict, followed several migratory patterns. Some moved from one rural area to another; for example, some migrants from the war zones of the east moved to the far western provinces, where guerrilla groups were less active. Some fled from smaller cities and towns to the countryside, where the number of internally displaced persons was estimated at close to 250,000 in the early 1980s. The highest concentration of refugees, however,

Displaced family, Moncagua
Courtesy United States Agency for International Development

was found in the war-torn departments of Chalatenango, Morazán, and Cabañas.

In the early 1980s, many dislocated rural persons traveled to San Salvador seeking help largely through the auspices of the Roman Catholic Church. Conditions for these refugees were less than ideal, as many faced severe overcrowding, continued malnutrition and illness, and harassment from security forces in the camps where they sought shelter. Others faced extreme poverty in makeshift slum settlements, trying to earn a living as street vendors.

Urban Life

Well before the civil conflict of the 1980s, rural-urban migration was an economic fact of life in El Salvador. Most rural migrants were attracted to the capital, San Salvador. Yet prospects for a better life were limited in the cities too, and El Salvador did not experience a rush to urban migration on the same scale as most other Latin American countries.

Urbanization

In general, urbanization in El Salvador was stimulated by the success of coffee as an export crop and the growth and transformation of the wealthy coffee elite from a nineteenth-century rural gentry into a twentieth-century national elite. The political and economic dominance of the coffee oligarchy was particularly responsible for the growth of the San Salvador metropolitan area and, to a lesser extent, that of El Salvador's second city, Santa Ana.

77

During the nineteenth century, in fact, Santa Ana, situated in the heart of the coffee region, was the largest city in El Salvador. Both Santa Ana in the west and San Miguel in the east started as agricultural towns and regional centers; over time, both developed small industrial bases and commercial and service establishments.

Both these cities, however, were overshadowed by the growth of San Salvador. Over the years, especially during export agriculture "boom" periods, a portion of the earnings made by the elite was used to develop and support San Salvador as a modern urban center, using European and then North American models as a guide. Municipal services, communications, and transportation infrastructures were established to support the agricultural export trade. Small manufacturing and food-processing establishments developed, along with fledgling construction, commercial, and transport activities. A small middle class of civilian and military public employees, commercial middlemen, and small businessmen emerged. Educational, health, and welfare services were instituted, and urban workers, students, and artisans were allowed, within limits, to organize mutual aid associations, such as cooperatives, savings associations, and clubs, and to present grievances before the government.

Urban migration appealed to some members of the rural sector more than others. Persons leaving the northern departments were drawn to urban areas in large numbers. In addition, the capital, which attracted more than 90 percent of urban migrants, generally offered greater employment opportunities and better pay to women than to men, encouraging a relatively high percentage of women to trade rural for urban life. In the countryside, government regulations either restricted labor opportunities for women or compensated them at a lower rate. Similarly, income derivable from rural women's traditional handicraft production declined in the face of competition from urban manufactured goods; as a result, these traditional handicraft items were devalued both literally and figuratively. Partially as a result of such pressures, 44 percent of the urban labor force was female by 1975, compared with only 14 percent of the rural labor force. In fact, however, the participation of women in the rural work force probably was larger because many women effectively worked without pay during coffee or cotton harvests. Only men or heads of household officially contracted to provide labor, although women and children might work in men's crews. Thus, only men had a right to weekly payment, and only men had the legal right to a daily food allowance. When women were paid, their wages generally were one-third less than men's.

Stated differently, two-thirds of female workers in 1975 were employed in urban areas, predominantly in San Salvador; they worked at a wide variety of low-skill jobs characterized by low pay, long hours, and a lack of benefits or legal protections. The most common of these occupations was work as domestics in upper- and middle-class households and as street vendors, even though vending was against the law and vendors faced police harassment. Some women also found jobs in factories in the free-zone area of the capital, where North American-owned pharmaceutical and textile factories preferred to hire women because they were thought to be more reliable workers than men (see Foreign Economic Relations, ch. 3). Many women, especially the least educated, engaged in prostitution.

Quality of Life

Given the nature of available work, urban centers offered relatively little improvement in job opportunities for rural migrants. Although a small percentage of the work force was organized into labor unions, wages generally were kept low in the urban as well as in the rural sector. During the 1970s, an estimated 90 percent of urban workers received less than the legal minimum wage. In 1977 the average daily wage in urban manufacturing and service sectors was the equivalent of US$2.80. In 1983 observers estimated that a family needed 3.7 wage earners to buy a basic basket of goods. According to government figures, only 53,467 workers earned enough to buy the basic basket, while 1,283,058 did not. Of those who did not, approximately 800,000 could buy no more than 25 percent of the basic basket. In terms of purchasing power, poor urban workers earned about the same income as landless rural workers, so there was not a strong economic incentive for urban migration. In fact, like landless rural laborers, underemployed or unemployed city dwellers sometimes sought seasonal work as harvesters on agricultural estates.

The urban job market reflected the state of industrialization and manufacturing in El Salvador. During the decade of the 1960s, manufacturing growth was strong as the Central American Common Market enhanced export opportunities (see Manufacturing, ch. 3). During this period, the total number of persons employed in industry, including coffee, sugar, and cotton processing, increased markedly, mainly in San Salvador. The increase in manufacturing jobs, however, was not as great; this was attributable in part to the generally capital-intensive nature of manufacturing in El Salvador.

Street in Mercado Central District, San Salvador
Courtesy Inter-American Development Bank

Although the total number of industrial jobs grew, these jobs actually declined as a proportion of the total labor market during the 1960s, dropping from about 13 percent in 1961 to about 10 percent in 1971. Consequently, many urban workers displaced by manufacturing technology and newcomers from rural areas were forced into the informal job sector or into petty thievery and similar activities.

Because the cities, and especially San Salvador, were also the home, indeed the stronghold, of the elite, by the early twentieth century San Salvador displayed a sharp dichotomy between great wealth and extreme poverty, between those who owned expensive automobiles and those who walked barefoot beside ox carts. These differences became more pronounced during the course of the twentieth century. The families of the oligarchy and the high ranks of the military lived in material comfort and in a rather insulated fashion, avoiding contact with the poor, who were ridiculed, deprecated, and despised but also feared by the urban wealthy. The elite emulated West European and North American values and life-styles, emphasizing material goods, conspicuous consumption, and the "good life."

The city gave clear evidence of the social tensions and crises existing between the rich and the poor. Nowhere was this better illustrated than in the area of housing, which evidenced a severe shortage for the majority of poor and a kind of fortress mentality among the elite. Housing problems were dramatically increased in October 1986 by an earthquake centered on San Salvador, which left more than 200,000 homeless.

Of the 858,000 persons living in San Salvador in 1980, an estimated 643,000 lived in slum settlements either in the center of the city or on the periphery. Squatter communities included those newly arrived from the countryside as well as the long-term urban poor who, given the extensive unemployment and lack of opportunity in general, had not managed to improve their standard of living. In the approximately 100 *tugurios* (shantytowns), single-room dwellings were constructed of tin, cardboard, and cloth, sometimes with *bahareque* walls and tiled roofs. The majority had dirt floors, no electricity, and no access to any kind of water and sewage services. These hovels typically were crowded onto nationally or municipally owned land, such as riverbeds or rights-of-way.

Dozens of similar settlements also appeared on privately owned land held for speculation and rented at exorbitant rates. Often shanties were erected on such land before the owner was aware of the fact, and rent was a matter subsequently worked out between the squatters and the landowner. Just as municipal or national authorities did not guarantee permanent settlement on *tugurio* sites, so private landowners were not reconciled to permanent settlement by the tenants on their land and attempted to evict them if a more lucrative use for the land emerged.

Slums of a different sort, called *mesones,* were located in the central city. They were privately owned single-story compounds composed of a connected series of five, ten, or twenty or more rooms, each roughly four meters square, surrounding a common courtyard. *Mesones* typically lacked washing or cooking facilities; some included access to a common latrine. Each room was rented to a separate tenant, either an individual or a small family. Residents of *mesones* contrasted with those of *tugurios* in household size, as the latter tended to live in larger and more heterogeneous households, partly because of the general lack of landlord or government control over their living conditions.

Legally constructed private housing equipped with modern facilities and appliances was available only for middle- and upperclass Salvadorans. The homes of the elite, many of them located on the clean streets of San Benito, the wealthiest neighborhood in San Salvador, typically were surrounded by walls two to three meters high or more, topped with barbed wire and sometimes electrified. Watchtowers, gun ports, and closed-circuit television systems to monitor the grounds were not uncommon.

In urban slums, as in rural areas, poor housing, inadequate and unsafe water, poor sanitation, and overcrowding created medical problems, particularly infectious diseases, that compounded the ill effects of such poor living conditions. The urban infant mortality rate was, however, lower than the rural infant mortality rate (85 and 120 per 1,000 live births, respectively, in the mid-1970s).

Well-to-do Salvadorans had far better access than lower-class Salvadorans to medical facilities and social security benefits, especially in urban areas. Health service delivery, though planned on a nationwide scale, clearly favored urban dwellers (see Health and Welfare, this ch.).

Better education also was available in the city, and more people were able to take advantage of it. In 1976 about 61.7 percent of urban students reached the ninth grade, as compared with 5.7 percent of rural students. Some 90 percent of urban children attended primary school, and over 90 percent of all national enrollment in grades seven through twelve was urban. Nonetheless, the urban poor had the least likelihood of pursuing education beyond one or two years of primary classes, since school attendance required cash outlays for materials, special activities, or uniforms. Primary-school-age children, especially boys, also were able to earn a few centavos

(100 centavos equals 1 Salvadoran colón; for value of the colón—see Glossary) on the streets with odd jobs, such as selling newspapers, shining shoes, running errands, or watching cars, to supplement the family income.

University training was an important part of the urban education program in San Salvador, where university enrollment reached 35,000 in the 1970s. The main campus of the National University, or University of El Salvador, was located in the capital, but branch campuses were also found in the secondary cities, such as Santa Ana.

Traditionally, the National University enjoyed a high degree of institutional autonomy in its activities in spite of a long tradition of politically active students. As the political and economic problems of the nation deepened during the 1970s, however, the university came to function not only as a lively and protected forum for political dialogue but also as a haven for political activists, a center for communication and coordination of activities among politically active opposition groups, and a recruiting source for radical leftist guerrilla groups. All the mass organizations associated with the Farabundo Martí National Liberation Front (Frente Farabundo Martí de Liberación Nacional—FMLN) and the Revolutionary Democratic Front (Frente Democrático Revolucionario—FDR) came to have offices there, and the university was used as a press and a public forum by their representatives (see Political Parties, ch. 4; Left-Wing Extremism, ch. 5).

This situation changed abruptly in 1980 when the army closed the San Salvador campus based on evidence that it was being used as an armory and refuge by members of guerrilla groups. The university staff continued to operate on a greatly reduced, makeshift basis from rented space scattered throughout the city, enabling some 10,000 university students to continue their studies. In the violent atmosphere that prevailed at that time, some staff members were targeted for attack by right-wing groups, some were arrested, and the university rector was assassinated. With the closing of the university campus, some twenty-five private universities, with a combined enrollment of 25,000 persons, sprang up. These schools were both far more expensive to attend than the National University, which had charged only the equivalent of US$36 for annual tuition, and more conservative in attitude.

The Jesuit-operated Central American University José Simeón Cañas (Universidad Centroamericana José Simeón Cañas—UCA), originally established in 1966 by the elite to provide a conservative Catholic education for their children, continued to operate. The staff developed more liberal leanings than its oligarchical

Campus of the Jesuit-run Central American University
José Simeón Cañas, San Salvador
Courtesy Inter-American Development Bank

supporters originally intended, however. Members of the faculty and administration strongly supported political and economic reforms and published political, social, and economic studies on national and regional affairs. Although the university remained open during the 1980s, it was not immune from rightist attacks on its faculty and facilities.

Social Dynamics

The conditions of economic and social inequality that defined the basic cleavages within Salvadoran society also generated strong political and ideological dynamics within and among groups pressing either for change or for maintenance of the status quo. Further insights into the nature of Salvadoran life, especially during the 1970s and 1980s, may be obtained by considering the following within that broader societal context: the impact of governmental agrarian reform programs; the reaction of portions of the general populace, particularly popular organizations and guerrilla groups, to the political and economic climate; and the positions and actions taken by the Roman Catholic Church and by Protestant missionaries in these matters.

Agrarian Reform

During the 1970s, as Salvadoran emigrants returned from

Honduras, increased pressure for available land pushed the issue of agrarian reform to the forefront of national life. Various peasant and trade union organizations, with the tacit support of many others, including middle-sector business people, professionals, and public-sector employees, as well as certain church groups, increased their activities and demonstrations in support of reform. The response from the military-controlled government stressed the maintenance of public order, through repression if necessary, over political change. The polarizing effect of this attitude prompted concerned pro-reform military officers to take power in 1979. One of the priorities of the junta governments that followed was agrarian reform (see The Reformist Coup of 1979, ch. 1).

Peasant organizations were disorganized, mainly as a result of violent actions directed against their members by right-wing groups, and were unable to exert much influence on the junta government at the time of the original agrarian reform decree in 1980. For its part, the government also failed to consult with these groups regarding the best ways to proceed in such an undertaking. Having the most to lose in this process, the majority of the economic elite, particularly the agrarian and financial interests, bitterly opposed such measures on principle. These interests had opposed—and successfully defeated in the planning stage—several earlier agrarian reform measures suggested by previous governments (see The 1970s: The Road to Revolt, ch. 1).

The overall agrarian reform program was to be implemented in three phases, only the first of which achieved any effective results. Phase I called for the expropriation of all landholdings over 500 hectares, with owners allowed to keep as "reserve" 100 to 150 hectares, depending on land quality, in order to continue farming. The government, aided by the army, expropriated over 230 estates, comprising 15 percent of El Salvador's farmland (or 10 percent, if reserve lands are excluded). This included 14 percent of total coffee land, 31 percent of cotton land, and 24 percent of sugarcane land; over 60 percent of the expropriated holdings, however, were pasture or fallow land, including forests and mountains not well suited to cultivation.

The expropriated estates were not subdivided, but were turned into cooperatives run by a hierarchy of skilled managers and unskilled laborers. Under this arrangement, little changed in terms of day-to-day operations. In spite of the communal implications of the cooperative concept, the traditional social hierarchy of managers and unskilled labor remained. In many cases, the same administrators, who still had strong ties with previous landlords and their interests, gave the same orders to the same workers, who saw little evidence of change in their day-to-day situation. The former landowners initially continued to derive income from production on the cooperatives, as part of the cooperatives' profits went to an agrarian reform fund from which the former owners were to be compensated. In addition, because the former landowners could retain 100 hectares, they were often able to keep control of the best land or of processing facilities, which, if necessary, could be reclassified as urban properties. Some landowners also had sufficient time to begin to decapitalize their farms. Some had removed livestock and machinery; others had slaughtered cattle rather than transfer them to the newly created cooperatives. These actions significantly reduced the value of the cooperatives, especially considering that the majority of land affected by Phase I was pastureland.

Since the members of the cooperatives included only the few full-time workers on estates at the time of expropriation, which took place during an off-season period of low labor needs, Phase I did not affect the majority of the population in these regions. Similarly, because the expropriated estates were located in the coastal plain and central valleys, they did not benefit landless peasants in the north and east. Of an original 317 cooperatives, 22 had been abandoned by 1987 as a result of inadequate technical and credit assistance from the government, as well as the adverse economic effects of the civil conflict.

As of 1987, Phase II of the agrarian reform program had not been implemented. The official explanation for the prolonged inaction cited shortcomings in administrative expertise and financial resources; unofficially, political pressures appeared to be equally influential. Phase II originally called for expropriation of all estates between 100 and 500 hectares in size. Many larger landowners, sensing that land reform was imminent, had previously divided their larger estates among family members, and their holdings, including many coffee estates, now fell within this range.

The junta governments' failure to implement Phase II allowed the Constituent Assembly to redefine the provisions of land reform that eventually were incorporated into the Constitution of 1983 (see The Constitution of 1983, ch. 4). The assembly, dominated by representatives of conservative political parties, raised the ceiling on maximum allowable landholdings from 100 to 245 hectares. This had the effect of reducing the amount of land available for redistribution from about 72,400 hectares, or 5 percent of Salvadoran farmland, to about 54,300 hectares, or 3.7 percent of farmland. Owners of medium-sized farms had been prohibited by the original 1980 reform decree from selling their holdings; the assembly now granted these owners up to three years to sell their excess hold-ings to peasants or peasant associations. This provision shifted the onus of reallocation of land from the government to the landowners, thus ameliorating somewhat the problem of inadequate government resources for this purpose.

Phase III, also known as the Land to the Tiller program, man-dated that ownership of land that was leased, rented, or share-cropped would be transferred to the tiller. Implementation of this phase was slow and difficult. If fully realized, Phase III was pro-jected to involve some 13.6 percent of farmland and some 117,000 peasant families. Each beneficiary was allowed to seek title to no more than seven hectares; in practice, given the small size of exist-ing rental plots, many were granted title to plots well below that size; as of 1987, the average Phase III beneficiary had been granted title to a plot of less than two hectares.

By mid-1987 only 56,188 potential beneficiaries had applied for title to 79,142 parcels of land. The granting of definitive titles was hampered by bureaucratic inefficiency and chronic budget short-falls, so that the overwhelming majority of claimants were forced to continue working the land under provisional title. The failure to grant even provisional titles to the remaining 60,000 or so poten-tial beneficiaries was attributed in part to the inability of the govern-ment to contact all of these small farmers. Furthermore, the seven-hectare limit, also referred to as the retention rule, excluded some 12,000 beneficiaries who did not farm their land directly but were landlords of smallholdings. In its early stages, implementa-tion of Phase III was also complicated by the illegal eviction of peasants by landowners.

Moreover, the involvement of army personnel in the implemen-tation of agrarian reform led to an upsurge in combat between government and guerrilla forces in the countryside. This was the case particularly in the northern departments of Chalatenango, Morazán, and Cuscatlán, where there were few privately owned estates but where rural mass organizations were influential. The heightened army presence, combined with population dislocation, reportedly contributed to increased civil unrest in these areas.

Revolutionary Groups

During the 1960s and 1970s, some of the population sought expression and perhaps eventual redress for their problems by be-coming involved in a wide variety of ''mass organizations'' (also known as popular organizations), such as those included in the Revolutionary Coordinator of the Masses (Coordinadora Revolu-cionaria de las Masas—CRM) (see The Reformist Coup of 1979, ch. 1). These groups, once tens of thousands strong, were heavily urban oriented and included a range of trade unionists, teachers, clergy, professionals, students, and other middle-class and urban lower-class workers interested in social and economic reform. The tactics of the mass organizations included strikes, street demonstrations, mass rallies, and occupation of public buildings (churches, government buildings, and embassies), factories, and farms.

In the countryside, the mass organizations found some support among landless campesinos mainly in the hills around the central valleys and in the northern mountains (the departments of Chalatenango, San Salvador, Cuscatlán, Cabañas, and San Vicente). Laborers on the coastal plain, where estate owners and administrators exercised greater influence, showed less enthusiasm for the mass organizations.

Whereas some of the rural poor hoped to exert pressure for change through participation in the popular organizations, others joined the ranks of more conservative, officially sanctioned organizations. One of these, the Salvadoran Communal Union (Unión Comunal Salvadoreña—UCS), begun in 1966, sought to address the needs of small farmers through limited programs of technical assistance and credit facilities. By 1980 the UCS claimed 100,000 members.

Another peasant organization, the Nationalist Democratic Organization (Organización Democrática Nacionalista—Orden), claimed as many as 100,000 members in the late 1970s. Established in the 1960s under military rule, Orden had close ties to the GN (see The Security Forces, ch. 5). In return for cooperation with the GN in areas such as intelligence and civil defense, members of Orden were eligible for benefits such as favorable credit terms on government agricultural loans, priority consideration for permanent estate jobs, and employment on public works project. Orden was disbanded officially by a decree of the first 1979 junta government, but some observers believed that it continued to function unofficially after that date.

In the 1970s, activists from mass organizations joined the ranks of various guerrilla organizations (see The 1970s: The Road to Revolt, ch. 1; Left-Wing Extremism, ch. 5). Guerrilla membership was diverse and included trade unionists, students, teachers, other disaffected members of the middle class, urban workers, and peasants.

In early 1981, Salvadoran guerrilla groups who were united under the banner of the FMLN estimated that they controlled 10 percent of Salvadoran territory. By 1983 the FMLN's claims had risen to 30 percent. Although guerrilla forces exerted influence over certain areas, they had not achieved control in the sense of being able to secure territory against concerted efforts, usually "sweeps" by at least battalion-sized units, by government forces to reestablish access. Generally, the guerrilla movement was most active to the north and to the east of the Río Lempa, in the departments of Chalatenango, Cabañas, Morazán, Cuscatlán, San Vicente, and Usulután. Guerrilla activities were less frequent in the more affluent western half of the country, roughly to the west of the Río Lempa.

From the guerrilla perspective, El Salvador was seen as divided into three different "fields of struggle" depending on the nature of their activities there. The "liberated areas" or "zones of control," in the north and east, were areas where communications with the rest of the country had been cut off, where the government and the military had not established a permanent presence, and where strings of guerrilla camps exerted influence over the local population. The so-called "disputed" areas in the central part of the country were contested by guerrilla forces living among the rural population and by government forces stationed in towns. The third area, the cities, experienced comparatively little open antigovernment violence, although sporadic terrorist actions by both rightist and leftist groups persisted after the mid-1970s (see Threats to Internal Security, ch. 5).

In the isolated "zones of control," as in other rural areas, amenities were few: no electricity, water taken from streams and springs, and no sanitation facilities. Agricultural production on family plots and collective farms provided food for guerrilla combatants as well as for local residents. According to sympathetic foreign observers, the guerrillas provided some social services, including at least rudimentary medical care, using both modern and traditional herbal methods, and education programs. Although supplies were either limited or nonexistent, literacy programs for all ages, using sticks to scratch in the earth in lieu of pens and paper, and education in first aid and basic sanitation measures were conducted. These courses served to provide basic education to a largely illiterate population and to prepare them to provide medical and logistical support to FMLN combatants. Town meetings were held to discuss issues of local concern and to elect councils with representatives responsible for agriculture, health, education, and information. Religious activities compatible with the tenets of liberation theology (see Glossary) were encouraged. Security and early warning of armed forces operations in the area were provided by local militia drawn from the pool of younger residents.

Another aspect of the guerrillas' ideology stressed equality for women as comrades in the political-military struggle. This, in many cases, represented a considerable and sometimes difficult adjustment for people from a culture that placed an exceptionally strong value on machismo, where women traditionally were regarded as inferior. Discrimination against women was further reinforced in Salvadoran rural life, particularly in the area of labor. Government wage scales either excluded women from permanent labor positions; set a lower minimum wage for women, along with boys under sixteen and the handicapped; or did not pay women at all if they worked in a man's crew. Educational opportunities for girls were also more limited because of the need for their assistance at home at an early age. In territory influenced by the guerrillas, however, some observers reported that wife-beating was discouraged, an effort was made to assign tasks more equitably, and men were taught to view women as *compañeras* (comrades). Thus, men might cook and wash clothes, while women fought, or directed development projects, or did construction work. In fact, 40 percent of leadership and 30 percent of combatant roles were filled by women in guerrilla zones. Yet even in these communities, there were limits to change; tortilla-making, for example, remained a female task.

The Role of Religion

As a Hispanic country, El Salvador has always had a strong Roman Catholic identity. The majority of Salvadorans in the late 1980s were at least nominal Roman Catholics, and church rituals permeated the nation's culture and society. Church attendance, especially for women, remained important, church sacraments and ceremonies such as baptism and confirmation were observed, and fiestas were held to celebrate patron saints of villages, towns, and cities. Nevertheless, El Salvador tended to be somewhat more secular than its Central American neighbors. Birth control programs introduced in the late 1960s met with less opposition than elsewhere in Latin America. Marriage—in a religious or civil ceremony— was not as prevalent in El Salvador as in many other Latin American countries (this situation also reflected the strain exerted on social institutions by persistent poverty); many Salvadoran couples, especially in rural areas, lived together in common-law or free unions, many families were headed by women, and many children were born out of wedlock. Lastly, the ritual kinship practice of *compadrazgo* (selecting godparents for children) was becoming less widespread and less important in El Salvador.

Although the Roman Catholic Church, as typified by its hierarchy, was conservative in its approach to doctrine, a strain of reformist Catholicism called "social Christianity" emerged in El Salvador, as elsewhere in Latin America, in the 1930s in response to the hardships, uprisings, and repressions of that period. Social Christianity, which continued to have some appeal until the early 1960s, stressed the duty of lay persons to remedy social ills without waiting for the religious hierarchy, represented by its priests, to act. Although this movement did not advocate change in the basic social and political structure of the country, it called for improvements by working within the existing political order.

At least one influential individual at the top of the social and religious pyramid recognized and encouraged the need for improvements in the lives of those in the lower sector—the archbishop of San Salvador, Luis Chávez y González, who held this position from 1939 to 1977. Archbishop Chávez encouraged the priesthood as a vocation; built a seminary in San Salvador; established the Pius XII Institute, organized particularly to teach the Roman Catholic Church's social doctrine; and sent priests to study in Europe. It is also noteworthy that these Salvadoran priests came mainly from rural families, albeit fairly well-to-do ones, rather than from the urban middle class, and hence had closer ties to the peasantry. It is significant too that even in the early 1950s Chávez encouraged cooperatives as alternatives for peasants losing land to agribusiness expansion and that he sent priests to Canada to study cooperatives. In this sense, he presaged the communitarianism later advocated by the Salvadoran Christian Democratic Party (Partido Demócrata Cristiano—PDC).

In the late 1960s, the social attitudes of the Roman Catholic Church in El Salvador, as elsewhere, were deeply influenced by Vatican Council II (in 1965) and the social encyclicals of Pope John XXIII, as well as by the Second Latin American Bishops' Conference held in Medellín, Colombia, in 1968, which addressed the issues of Vatican II from a distinctly Latin American perspective. These gatherings, particularly the Medellín conference, emphasized the need for a more worldly involvement by the Roman Catholic clergy with the lives and problems of parishioners and advocated activist programs to improve the living conditions of the lower class. This "preferential option for the poor" was the germ of what later came to be known as "liberation theology." The church increased and encouraged involvement in programs for change after the Medellín conference, even if this involvement entailed secular political advocacy.

*Church of the Virgin
of Guadalupe,
San Salvador*

Toward this end, activist clergy and laity created grass-roots
Christian Base Communities (Comunidades Eclesiásticas de
Base—CEBs) to work toward their conception of social justice; these
groups encouraged church members to take the initiative in seeking social and political change and to act more independently of
the church hierarchy, if necessary, to achieve their goals. In short,
in contrast to the earlier social Christianity, where change was to
be effected within the existing social and political order, liberation
theology called for changes in social and political structures and
encouraged the laity to take an active role in bringing them about.
In El Salvador, the social concerns of Archbishop Chávez helped
pave the way for later advocates of liberation theology and, in a
way, linked this broad Latin American movement of the 1970s with
the social Christian movements of the prior decades.

A number of rural communities were receptive to the teachings
and methods of the base communities. Generally, the organization of the CEBs involved a priest or a trained religious worker
who met with twenty to thirty local parishioners for a few weeks.
As this group met to study and discuss selected passages from the
Bible and plan community activities, lay leaders were encouraged
to emerge, and the group was taught to appreciate and emphasize
the role of laypersons like themselves in social change. They discussed the earthly social, economic, and political reasons for their
plight as poor peasants and laborers and were taught by priests

93

and lay workers that the poor were equal before God with the rich landowners. During the 1970s, some 15,000 local lay leaders, catechists or delegates, underwent further training at seven centers set up throughout the country, studying the Bible, liturgy, agriculture, cooperativism, leadership, and health, all in preparation for their roles as religious, social, and political leaders in community development efforts. The role of local lay preachers and leaders also reflected the high ratio of laity to priests in El Salvador, which at that time was approximately 10,000 to 1.

The CEBs soon encountered harassment and hostility, apparently emanating from the economic and political elite. By the late 1970s, violence by right-wing groups was directed against members of the priesthood and other church workers known to be sympathetic to the CEBs on the grounds that assisting the poor constituted subversive activity. As civil unrest in general increased in the late 1970s, the church as a whole became increasingly polarized. The majority of the bishops supported the traditional role of the church, the traditional authority of the hierarchy, and the overriding authority of the government. Allied against this view was a faction of parish priests who favored the development of the CEBs and advocated expanded aid for the poor.

Once again, the position of the archbishop became crucial. In 1977 Archbishop Chávez resigned and was replaced by Monsignor Oscar Arnulfo Romero y Galdámez. Like his predecessor, Archbishop Romero spoke out publicly in favor of social justice for the general populace. He increasingly assumed the role of the leading advocate on behalf of the poor; his primary vehicles for expressing these views were his weekly Sunday morning homilies, broadcast throughout the nation and eagerly listened to on portable radios or the ubiquitous village loudspeakers in the plazas. As political tensions rose, the influential position and strong impact of the outspoken archbishop became intolerable to the Salvadoran right, and Romero was assassinated one Monday in March 1980 while saying mass.

Violence against grass-roots church activities continued during the early 1980s, with telling effect. The number of active priests declined, so that 40 percent of rural parishes lacked priests, and many CEBs were dismantled or forced underground. Of the 15,000 lay leaders active in CEBs, some joined the guerrillas, while others withdrew from church activities altogether. Monsignor Arturo Rivera y Damas, appointed archbishop after Romero's murder, found it appropriate to take a more distant or ambivalent position with respect to the question of the proper role of the church in Salvadoran national life, a position that also accorded more closely with the conservative attitude of the Vatican under Pope John Paul II. Meanwhile, although the church proper now lowered its public profile, a small, quasi-independent "people's church" emerged from the remnants of the CEB movement. Some priests, mainly Jesuits, continued to work in guerrilla-controlled areas, where the social and political importance of organized communities among the poor continued to be emphasized.

Protestant missionaries were quite active in El Salvador, the majority representing the evangelical branch of North American Protestantism. Evangelical activity was a multinational, multimillion-dollar enterprise developed and packaged in the United States, translated into Spanish, and exported not only to El Salvador but also to the other countries of Central America. Missionaries working for scores of organizations used crusades, door-to-door proselytizing, radio programs, food aid, and health care to advance their fundamentalist message of personal salvation through belief in Jesus, a salvation not to be gained in this world but in the afterlife. To these theologically conservative evangelicals, Roman Catholics were not Christians; only the "born-again" were God's chosen people, and efforts to achieve social gains by working for change in this life were inappropriate. Although "mainline" Protestant denominations encouraged expressions of concern over social problems, the brand of evangelical Protestantism that swept Central America in the 1970s and 1980s sought to remove its adherents from social action, to place the onus on God rather than on humans to act, and to inculcate passive, apathetic, and submissive resignation while waiting for the second coming of Christ. Put more bluntly, the thought of future salvation would cushion the impact of current suffering.

Protestantism was by no means new to Central America or to El Salvador. In the late nineteenth century, the majority of British and German immigrants, including coffee traders and financiers, were Protestants. In 1896 the aggressive Central American Mission (CAM), headquartered in North America and financed by North Americans, was established in El Salvador and Guatemala. The primary message of the CAM was that the sad state of the world was a necessary and predestined situation heralding the imminence of the second coming. In later years, the Seventh-Day Adventists, the Assemblies of God, and others joined the growing missionary movement in Central America.

Protestantism continued to grow steadily in El Salvador, particularly during the economic depression and political repression of the 1930s. The annual growth rate of the Protestant community in the country stood at 9 percent between 1930 and 1945 but dropped to 7 percent between 1945 and 1960. A dramatic resurgence appeared in the 1970s with an average annual rate of Protestant conversion of 11 percent. Some observers have attributed this impressive growth to a rejection of politicized social activism as exemplified by liberation theology. Others have interpreted the high rate of Protestant conversion as a withdrawal from the violence and instability of Salvadoran life in the late 1970s and 1980s.

Furthermore, the popularity of evangelical Protestantism seems to have correlated with the intensity and nature of population displacement. As the number of land-poor laborers grew and migrant labor increased, and as the bonds of community, extended family, and tradition were broken for many, traditional Catholicism was unable to fill the personal sense of emotional loss and lack of direction. This was particularly true because the number of priests and clerics was small. Protestantism, however, offered a personalistic message of Jesus' acceptance of the individual, emphasized each individual's direct relationship to God unmediated by a hierarchical clergy, and held out hope that sustained even desperately poor people with a sense of self-worth in the face of violence, displacement, and misery.

The elite found an ideological ally in this brand of Protestantism, not only for its apolitical approach but also for its laissez-faire, entrepreneurial, work-oriented values and its willingness to minimize the responsibility of the existing system for the nation's ills. Elites thus gladly supported evangelizing efforts on their landed estates, and significant numbers of upper-class Salvadorans converted to Protestantism.

* * *

The political events of the late 1970s and 1980s have given rise to a considerable number of readily available books, articles, and newspaper accounts detailing the conditions of life in El Salvador. An excellent introduction to both historical and current economic, political, and especially social conditions in El Salvador can be found in Philip L. Russell's *El Salvador in Crisis* and in Alastair White's *El Salvador. El Salvador: The Face of Revolution* by Robert Armstrong and Janet Shenk also provides an impassioned and readable account of the social and economic conditions underlying the civil war. *Margin of Life* by Cornell Capa and J. Mayone Stycos presents evocative photography and text illustrating the often harsh reality of everyday life for the impoverished majority living in both urban and rural settings in El Salvador and Honduras.

On more specific issues, Phillip Berryman's *The Religious Roots of Rebellion* discusses the background to liberation theology in Latin America and the specific role of the Roman Catholic Church in El Salvador. Articles in *NACLA Report on the Americas* by the North American Congress on Latin America present an overview of the activities and theology of Protestant missions in Central America. Also recommended for general reading is Part I of Enrique A. Baloyra's *El Salvador in Transition,* which contains a helpful overview of the nature of the military government and the oligarchical elite within a socioeconomic context. A. Douglas Kincaid's "Peasants into Rebels: Community and Class in Rural El Salvador" analyzes the significance of community solidarity as a factor in the history of social unrest in El Salvador. "Agrarian Reform in El Salvador" by David Browning provides an excellent overview of the social, political, and economic contexts of agrarian reform, and Robert G. Williams's *Export Agriculture and the Crisis in Central America* is highly recommended as a very readable account of the economic and social conditions underlying political instability in Central America in general. (For further information and complete citations, see Bibliography.)

Chapter 3. The Economy

Farm worker drying coffee

UNTIL THE GOVERNMENT IMPLEMENTED a major land reform in 1980, the most notable characteristic of El Salvador's economic structure was the unequal distribution of landownership. The economy was dominated by a few large plantations that produced cash crops, especially coffee, for export. The slow and difficult implementation of a sweeping three-phase land reform begun in 1980, however, considerably altered the pattern of unequal landownership.

El Salvador's economic development in the 1980s was hindered by a resource drain caused by the country's civil conflict, natural disasters, a lack of economic expertise, and adverse changes in the terms of trade (see Glossary). Consequently, by 1987 El Salvador's economic output barely equaled 80 percent of its 1978 level, and exports were only the third most important source of foreign exchange after foreign aid and remittances from Salvadorans living abroad. The most damaging of these factors was the civil conflict, particularly its impact on the country's infrastructure. By mid-1987 observers estimated that the total cost to the economy based on lost agricultural production, damaged infrastructure, and funds diverted from economic to military purposes was about US$1.5 billion.

El Salvador entered the 1970s as a relatively poor middle-income country with per capita income greater than that of Thailand and slightly less than that of the Republic of Korea (South Korea), Malaysia, and Costa Rica. Its overall level of development was roughly comparable to these countries as well, judging by such indicators as industrial contribution to the gross domestic product (GDP—see Glossary), life expectancy, the cost of labor, and per capita income. El Salvador had one other important characteristic in common with these other four countries—a hard-working, productive, and motivated labor force. El Salvador's annual rate of investment growth (3.5 percent), however, lagged substantially behind the other four during the 1960s. During this decade, gross investment grew annually by 24 percent in South Korea, 16 percent in Thailand, 7.5 percent in Malaysia, and 7.1 percent in Costa Rica. El Salvador's inferior rate of investment growth continued and in some cases widened during the 1970s.

By 1982 Salvadoran development had fallen far behind that of South Korea, Malaysia, Thailand, and even Costa Rica. Industrial production hovered around 20 percent of GDP, whereas in the other countries it accounted for between 27 percent (Costa Rica) and 40 percent (South Korea). Salvadoran per capita income fell to about a third of South Korea's and Malaysia's, half of Costa Rica's, and 15 percent below that of Thailand. Making matters worse, El Salvador's terms of trade had deteriorated much more rapidly than had those of the other countries.

Between 1982 and 1986, El Salvador fell even farther behind as it failed to diversify its exports away from agricultural commodities and into manufactured goods. In 1986 per capita GDP was almost half its level of 1977, and the country entered a period of disinvestment. As other middle-income countries appeared to be taking off, El Salvador was regressing.

Growth and Structure of the Economy

El Salvador's economy has always been highly dependent on a single agricultural export commodity. Following independence, indigo was the most important commodity to the Salvadoran economy and represented most of the country's exports. In the mid-nineteenth century, however, indigo was replaced in the European and North American markets by artificial dyes. Consequently, indigo producers were forced to seek alternative commodities that would permit them to maintain their level of earnings. Fortunately for El Salvador's wealthier landowners, the decline of indigo was concurrent with the rise in world demand for another crop that thrives in tropical climates—coffee. The coffee export sector dominated the Salvadoran economy by the 1870s.

During the 1950s and 1960s, coffee export earnings helped fuel the expansion of cotton and sugar cultivation (which subsequently became the country's second and third most important export crops, respectively) and financed the development of light manufacturing. In fact, in the years immediately following the Revolution of 1948, which reduced the direct political influence of the coffee interests, the taxes on coffee exports were increased tenfold in order to finance industrialization. These funds were used to develop the country's transportation infrastructure and electricity generation capabilities.

Light manufacturing developed rapidly in El Salvador during the 1960s, largely as a result of the establishment of the Central American Common Market (CACM—see Glossary). El Salvador's industrial development hitherto had been hindered by the absence of a domestic market for these goods. The small class of wealthy landowners generally preferred high-quality imports, while the large lower class lacked the disposable income to buy most manufactured goods. The CACM, however, improved this situation by expanding

Earthquake damage, San Salvador, October 1986
Courtesy Inter-American Development Bank

the market for Salvadoran goods through the elimination of intra-regional trade barriers. As a result, the manufactured goods produced in El Salvador became more competitive in Honduras than those from the United States or other non-Central American countries. The CACM-stimulated industrial growth never threatened the predominance of coffee production within the Salvadoran economy, however. Moreover, the stimulus proved to be short lived because the CACM broke down in the 1970s.

The civil conflict and the disincentives inherent in some government policies disrupted coffee, sugar, and cotton production during the 1980s, resulting in a general lack of dynamism in the Salvadoran economy (see table 4, Appendix). GDP increased at a 4.3 percent annual rate between 1965 and 1978 but, reflecting the effects of civil unrest, declined by 23 percent between 1979 and 1982. The economy modestly expanded between 1983 and 1986, with average annual growth rates of about 1.5 percent. The country's total GDP equaled approximately US$4.6 billion in 1986. Real per capita GDP was approximately US$938.

During the 1960s and 1970s, gross capital formation increased by an impressive 6.6 percent annual rate, reflecting investor confidence and the positive effects of the CACM. Between 1980 and 1986, however, as investors reacted to the instability caused by the civil conflict, depreciation outstripped investment at an annual rate of 0.8 percent. Private outflows of capital slowed in 1987, resulting in a less drastic capital account deficit of US$34 million, less than a quarter of the outflow registered in 1986.

El Salvador's economy expanded an estimated 2.5 percent in 1987, representing the largest single-year gain since 1978. This moderate improvement in the country's overall economic activity was primarily the result of a modest rebound in agricultural output and a substantial reactivation of construction activity led by the private sector. Gains in construction investment reflected efforts to replace structures damaged in the 1986 earthquake, which caused an estimated US$1 billion in damage to the country's buildings and infrastructure. Two additional sources of growth were transfer receipts (mostly from Salvadorans working in the United States) and official grants from the United States government. In 1987 net private transfers, or transfer receipts, accounted for over 4 percent of GDP, while grants or official transfers from the United States government represented 5 percent.

Although 1987 was the Salvadoran economy's most positive year since the beginning of the civil conflict, attempts to measure and judge the economy's health should compare the country's economic performance in 1987 with its most recent economic peak in 1978.

Using this method to evaluate El Salvador's economy casts a less favorable light than the alternative year-to-year measurement. Although El Salvador's economy grew rapidly in 1987 compared with other years in the 1980s, real income was still almost 20 percent below its 1978 level.

One important but ominous indicator of future economic health was the low level of gross fixed capital formation in 1987, which remained substantially below the levels necessary to expand production capacity and generate productivity gains. Gross fixed capital formation, 14 percent of GDP in 1987, was at a level significantly below those experienced in the 1960s and 1970s.

Consumption expenditures increased by less than 1 percent in 1987, primarily because of an 8.7 percent drop in general government expenditures. Because the International Monetary Fund (IMF—see Glossary) supervised the economic stabilization program, the government was obligated to reduce its budget deficit. Also, because revenue sources consistently failed to close the gap between expenditures and revenues, the government was forced to reduce consumption expenditures in 1987.

Income Distribution

Moderate economic growth in 1987 did not make up for the uneven income distribution in El Salvador. Poorer segments of the population did not share in the modest gains of the economy in 1987. In the agricultural sector, for example, the minimum wage remained unchanged at ¢8 (for value of the colón—see Glossary) per eight-hour day; at the same time, inflation, as measured by the consumer price index, rose by 27 percent during the first half of 1987. Real wages in both the private and the public sectors continued their precipitous descent to 13.3 percent in 1987. In 1987 private sector monthly wages averaged approximately ¢889. Although no current measure of income distribution was available in mid-1988, the combination of negative wage gains and positive aggregate growth implied a worsening of income distribution between employers and labor.

Sectors of the Economy

An examination of GDP by sector confirmed that, despite a modest recovery in 1987, El Salvador's economy was still vulnerable. Even though most sectors showed some growth in 1987, all registered below their 1978 or 1979 peaks.

Thanks to improved weather conditions, the agricultural sector recovered in 1987 from its 1986 decline, rising 3.1 percent, which merely erased the sector's 3.1 percent loss in 1986. The importance

105

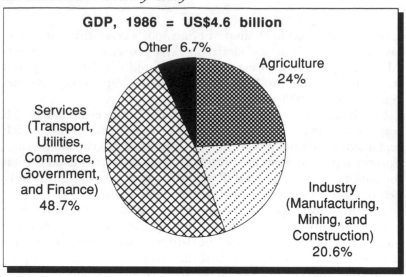

GDP, 1986 = US$4.6 billion

Other 6.7%

Agriculture 24%

Services (Transport, Utilities, Commerce, Government, and Finance) 48.7%

Industry (Manufacturing, Mining, and Construction) 20.6%

Source: Based on information from Economist Intelligence Unit, *Country Report: Guatemala, El Salvador, Honduras,* No. 3, London, 1988, 3.

Figure 5. Estimated Gross Domestic Product by Sector, 1986

of the agricultural sector, particularly coffee, in the economy cannot be overemphasized. In 1987, for example, despite a decrease in coffee production value attributable to lower international coffee prices, coffee still represented approximately 7 percent of GDP, 30 percent of agricultural output, and 60 percent of total exports. Coffee production recovered substantially, about 6 percent, in 1987 as a result of improved weather conditions and increased use of fertilizers. Fortunately, because most coffee was grown in the western part of the country, away from the civil conflict, production was unaffected (see fig. 5).

Analysts believed that in the future the fate of El Salvador's coffee earnings would depend on both producer prices and government-imposed price or exchange controls. According to some estimates, producer prices might eventually decline to levels at or below the average cost of production. Such a decline in prices could have catastrophic consequences for the country in both the short term and the long term. A decline in coffee prices would limit the country's ability to earn foreign exchange, resulting in foreign exchange allocation problems. Foreign currency shortages would then exert upward pressure on prices. Unprofitable production could impede further investment in coffee production and eventually reduce the coffee industry's capacity to generate export surpluses.

Government policies had a major impact on the profitability of coffee production. Price controls and exchange rate policies pursued by the government of José Napoleón Duarte Fuentes during the early 1980s led many coffee growers to claim that coffee growing was unprofitable. Even in years of strong world prices, coffee growers were adversely affected by the exchange rate manipulation and price controls effected by the National Coffee Institute (Instituto Nacional de Café—Incafe). It was unclear, however, whether Incafe would continue to operate under a more conservative government.

Sugar and cotton, once important agricultural crops, accounted for less than 10 percent of agricultural value added in 1987 and less than 5 percent of total Salvadoran export earnings. Low world prices adversely affected sugar production and inhibited investments. Cotton production declined because of the armed conflict and low international prices. For example, in 1986 average production costs of cotton exceeded international prices.

During 1987 manufacturing accounted for about 15 percent of total value added and continued its consistent recovery. Nevertheless, the sector's estimated 2.7 percent growth left value added in manufacturing almost 10 percent below the 1980 level. The gradual recovery in manufacturing could be attributed to increased demand for food products, beverages, and nonmetallic products. In 1987 food processing and beverages represented more than half of the value added in the manufacturing sector.

The construction industry proved to be the economy's only bright spot in 1987, registering growth for the third consecutive year with 14 percent growth above 1986. Compared with 1979, however, activity remained low. Moreover, rapid growth in 1987 reflected efforts to replace the structures and units damaged in the 1986 earthquake rather than a general revival of the construction industry.

Services represented almost half of GDP in 1986. Like construction and manufacturing, service activity continued on an upward trend in 1987 after falling by almost 25 percent between 1978 and 1982. As in other areas, however, 1986 value added by services remained approximately 17 percent below its 1978 peak. Between 1970 and 1978, service output grew by 54 percent. With the slowdown in economic activity after 1978, services declined by 17 percent between 1978 and 1987.

Service activity was tied closely to prevailing trends in the economy and therefore didn't have the dynamism of agriculture and industry. Service activity was also oriented exclusively toward domestic markets and thus did not affect the country's external economic position. Services included transportation, commerce,

107

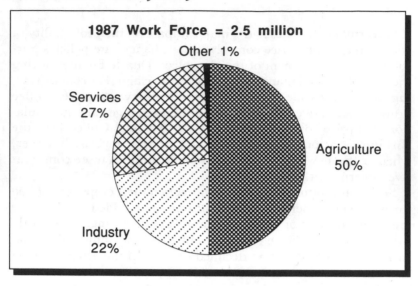

1987 Work Force = 2.5 million

Other 1%

Services 27%

Agriculture 50%

Industry 22%

Source: Based on information from United States, Department of State, Bureau of Public
Affairs, *Background Notes, El Salvador,* Washington, November 1987, 1.

Figure 6. Employment by Sector, 1987

insurance, health care, utilities, and other services provided by public enterprises.

The Labor Force

The Salvadoran labor force has been traditionally characterized as industrious, motivated, and reliable. Of new entrants to the labor force in 1986, it was estimated that 4 percent possessed executive, technical, or professional skills. Some 25 percent of all job seekers were classified as semi-skilled, while 71 percent were unskilled laborers. The labor force was young, reflecting the demographic profile of the population; in 1985 more than 52 percent of workers were less than thirty years of age (see table 5, Appendix). The labor force remained largely agrarian and rural in the late 1980s (see fig. 6).

Labor suffered because of a variety of economic and institutional circumstances: real wages declined, unemployment rose, and efforts to unify the fragmented labor movement were thwarted by the failure of President Duarte to implement promised labor reforms and by the polarization of union leadership (see Interest Groups, ch. 4). The negative trend for labor continued in 1987. The legal real minimum wage fell by 28 percent, and average real private sector and public sector wages dropped by 13.3 percent. Between 1983 and 1987, real wages declined by about one-third.

The Salvadoran Constitution details the right to organize unions and associations, but the establishment of "closed shops" (enterprises employing only union workers) was forbidden by law. The law also required the use of collective bargaining, conciliation, and arbitration before a strike could be called.

In 1986 there were approximately 150 recognized unions, employee associations, and peasant organizations, which represented 15 percent of the total work force. Although union membership stabilized in the 1980s, union activism fluctuated with prevailing economic and political conditions. For example, in 1982, while membership remained fairly constant in relation to past years, the number of workers involved in strikes fell from 13,904 in 1981 to just 373. In 1984 the number jumped to 26,111.

In 1987 the labor movement vocalized its frustrations as economic conditions stagnated and the civil conflict dragged on. Such frustrations were exacerbated by the perception that Duarte failed to implement the labor reforms he had promised during the 1984 presidential campaign. Labor leaders protested Duarte's failure to fulfill his end of the "social pact" after labor had put its weight behind him in exchange for pledges of increased inclusion of union members in the government and greater responsiveness to labor and peasant issues.

Between 1978 and 1984, private employment fell from 147,000 to 122,000, a 17 percent decline. Employment in the construction industry suffered the most during this period, declining almost 75 percent. Employment opportunities in 1987 continued the downward trend that began with the country's civil conflict. Although no official unemployment rates were available for 1986 or 1987, it is likely that counterbalancing forces stabilized the rate during these two years at the 1985 level, or 33 percent. First, the civil conflict continued to displace many workers and to limit employment growth. Second, the agricultural sector grew by 3.1 percent, recouping losses experienced in 1986. Finally, an estimated 2.5 percent economic growth rate in 1987 was insufficient to reduce the unemployment rate.

The impact of El Salvador's civil conflict was demonstrated in the evolution of the unemployment rate between 1978 and 1985. Over this period, the rate rose almost tenfold, from 3.1 percent to 33 percent. Labor's situation would have been even more grave without the emigration of an estimated 500,000 Salvadorans to the United States between 1978 and 1985. Remittances from workers abroad totaled US$350 million officially in 1987, although some estimates were as high as US$1 billion or more.

Role of Government

Traditionally, the government has played an important role in the country's economy. This role increased substantially after 1979, provoking considerable controversy and fueling domestic political polarization. Economic policy was coordinated among the central and municipal governments and seventeen decentralized agencies, which included the Salvadoran Social Security Institute (Instituto Salvadoreño del Seguro Social—ISSS) and the Salvadoran Institute for Agrarian Reform (Instituto Salvadoreño de Transformación Agraria—ISTA). Nine state-owned companies provided utility services to the Salvadoran public. In 1980 the government nationalized the marketing and export of coffee and sugar, two of El Salvador's most important export commodities. Since then, Incafe and the National Sugar Institute (Instituto Nacional de Azúcar—Inazucar) have acted as financial intermediaries between domestic producers and foreign markets. These bodies have been widely criticized by coffee and sugar producers because they imposed heavy export taxes and service charges that totaled some 50 percent of the sale price abroad.

Although considerable domestic criticism ⁿf the government's economic policy focused on the disincentives and inefficiency of land reform and the creation of Incafe and Inazucar, some critics maintained that another drawback of the government's economic policy was its failure to take into account the counterinsurgency effort. Many Salvadoran policymakers tended to accept the conflict as inevitable, calculating its effect only in terms of a shrinking growth rate. They apparently failed to assess a project's viability in the context of the civil conflict.

Monetary and Credit Policies

Between 1979 and 1982, El Salvador experienced a 23 percent fall in real per capita GDP, a 35 percent decline in export earnings, and a sharp rise in its unemployment rate to an estimated 27 percent. External and internal imbalance convinced the government to stabilize the situation under the guidance of the IMF. The government targeted monetary growth and other areas and, according to the IMF, accomplished most of its goals. In 1986, after a moderate reactivation of the economy in 1984 and 1985, the government adopted a short-term adjustment program to correct remaining internal and external imbalances. This program included the following changes: unification of the exchange rate, exchange and import restrictions, a more aggressive export promotion program, new fiscal revenue-generating mechanisms, agrarian reforms, a macroeconomic and external debt management committee, and strict monetary policies to curb the country's accelerating inflation rate, a major goal of government policy.

The rate of inflation in El Salvador was determined largely by the conduct of monetary policy and by variations in exchange rates and wages. Because of a net decline in capital formation and a major devaluation of the colón, inflation doubled during the 1980s relative to the 1965–80 period. El Salvador maintained an average annual inflation rate of 14.9 percent between 1980 and 1986, compared with 7 percent per year between 1965 and 1980.

Throughout the 1980s, the government employed monetary aggregate targets, price controls, wage controls, and exchange rate freezes as mechanisms to avoid accelerated price increases. On January 1, 1981, following a surge in wholesale and consumer price inflation, the government decreed a price freeze on basic goods and services. Efforts by the Regulatory Supply Institute (Instituto Regulador de Abastecimientos—IRA) to control prices through market intervention had failed to arrest the price rises for certain necessities, and prices seemed to be out of control. The government's price freeze in 1981 was accompanied by an intended six-month wage freeze, which actually lasted until the end of 1983. Over the 1981–83 period, real wages dropped by 29 percent in the private sector and 26 percent in the public sector.

In response to the increase in the number of transactions occurring in the parallel market as a result of the unofficial depreciation of the colón, 1985 price controls were relaxed. The result was a sudden increase in consumer price inflation from 12 percent to 22 percent, which by the end of 1985 had accelerated to a 32 percent annual rate.

When El Salvador unified its exchange rate in 1986, the price of some goods, such as oil derivatives, increased by 50 percent, while others, such as foodstuffs and clothing, held constant. Since 1986 some price controls have been lifted, allowing prices to reflect market forces. In 1986 inflation rose to 30 percent by year's end but declined to 27 percent in 1987. Continued wage controls through government intervention in employer-labor wage negotiations, an officially fixed exchange rate since 1986, and slow monetary growth ostensibly tamed the country's high inflation rate. Overall, the major results of the government's anti-inflation program were slower price inflation and real wage losses for workers.

The Central Reserve Bank of El Salvador (Banco Central de Reserva de El Salvador—BCR) set interest rates and rationed credit, generally targeting available capital for high-priority government projects. The Central Reserve Bank also regulated—and often executed directly—transactions involving foreign exchange, under a 1980 regulation to curb capital flight and control monetary supply. Small businesses, especially export businesses, were granted a majority portion of the credit, often at preferential low interest rates.

The Salvadoran government pursued restrictive monetary policies during 1987 to satisfy IMF recommendations for improving the Salvadoran balance of payments and for controlling inflation. By restricting credit to the private sector and to public enterprises, the government had hoped to curb demand, which in turn would have reduced imports and saved precious foreign exchange. In fact, despite the government's austerity program, imports increased by 9 percent in 1987. Furthermore, the government hoped to slow the monetary expansion that had tripled the money supply between 1979 and 1986 to 15 percent during 1987.

The government provided credit to the industrial sector through the National Industrial Development Bank (Banco Nacional de Fomento Industrial—Banafi), which was created in 1981 to replace the former Salvadoran Institute of Industrial Development (Instituto Salvadoreño de Fomento Industrial—Insafi). Banafi provided credit to promising new industries that were not able to obtain credit from other sources.

The Banking System

Since 1980 the entire Salvadoran banking system has been owned and operated by the government. Under nationalization, the Central Reserve Bank, through the Operative Fund (Fondo Operativo), rationed foreign exchange to the commercial banks. The Central Reserve Bank assigned each commercial bank a maximum allowable balance of foreign exchange and required a weekly balance report. The Central Reserve Bank also covered foreign exchange deficits of the commercial banks but required that they transfer large surpluses to the Central Reserve Bank. In turn, these commercial banks agreed to disburse foreign exchange for imports on priorities set by the Central Reserve Bank in exchange for the services rendered. The highest priorities for foreign exchange disbursements included food, medical supplies, raw materials, and petroleum products, followed by intermediate goods, money for medical expenses and activities abroad, and debt servicing.

Prior to the nationalization of the banking sector, El Salvador had numerous private financial institutions that were called banks but that actually functioned like investment companies. Members, who had contracts with the companies, contributed funds on a regular basis and then used this capital as collateral. Some of the more important "banks" included the Investment and Savings Bank, the Credit and Savings Bank, the Commercial Farm Bank, and the Popular Credit Bank. The Popular Credit Bank had broader powers than the others and could accept time deposits and savings accounts, deal in foreign exchange, and extend letters of credit. The Salvadoran Coffee Company and the Salvadoran Cotton Cooperative also provided seasonal credit to their members. Their activities were not financed by deposits, but rather by loans from foreign banks (mostly United States institutions).

As a result of the civil conflict and the 1980 government decree nationalizing the banking system, many Salvadorans transferred their savings out of the country. Consequently, private savings fell from a 34 percent share of GDP in 1979 to a 32 percent share in 1980. Capital outflows, however, were heavier than this statistic would indicate because GDP fell by 8 percent in the same year. By 1982, nonetheless, private sector confidence in the banking system had been tentatively restored, and private savings increased to 39 percent of GDP. The increase was primarily attributed to a 1982 rise in interest rates, which provided an incentive for saving.

The Tax System

Taxes, including sales, export, property, income, capital gains, profit, and stamp taxes (a 5 percent levy on goods and services), accounted for a 95 percent annual average of the Salvadoran government's revenue between 1976 and 1985. Tax revenue as a share of GDP increased from 11.6 percent in 1972 to 14.7 percent in 1986. Domestic sales taxes, representing 37 percent of total current revenue in 1986, were the most important source of revenue for the government. Taxes on international trade transactions provided an additional 27 percent of current revenue (two-thirds came from export duties), and taxes on income, profits, and capital gains provided 19 percent. Property taxes constituted only 5 percent of government revenue.

All residents, regardless of citizenship, were required to pay personal income tax, which was assessed according to a progressive scale, with a graduated minimum tax plus a percentage. In 1986 wage earners who garnered less than the equivalent of US$2,400 per year paid no income tax, while those whose income exceeded the equivalent of US$50,000 paid at a 60 percent rate. The maximum corporate tax was also set at 60 percent. In addition, businesses were subject to a net worth tax based on their net capital investment; the maximum rate of this levy was 2.5 percent.

The relative importance of export duties as a revenue source has been problematic for the government. Besides being unpopular among coffee producers, these taxes fluctuated with world coffee prices. In 1986, for example, government revenues rose by 57 percent, compared with 1985. Although higher income taxes, stamp taxes, and increased foreign aid also increased revenue in 1986, the size of the increase resulted largely from a jump in world coffee prices from US$1.43 per pound in 1985 to US$1.71 per pound in 1986. Conversely, when world coffee prices fell to only US$1.11 per pound in 1987, the Salvadoran government reported a fiscal deficit of US$160 million.

Fiscal Policy and the Budget Process

Salvadoran law stipulated that fiscal budgets of the central government, the decentralized agencies, and public enterprises such as Incafe and Inazucar had to be approved by the Legislative Assembly (see The Legislature, ch. 4). Budgets were generally approved for one fiscal year (FY—see Glossary) at a time. Special projects, such as those funded by the United States Agency for International Development (AID) and other foreign agencies, were considered extrabudgetary operations, however, and were not subject to legislative approval.

In nominal terms, government spending doubled between 1976 and 1982, from US$335 million to US$658 million. Government spending was stable relative to GDP, however; government expenditures represented 12.8 percent of GDP in 1972, compared with 12.9 percent in 1986. In 1986 the government maintained a surplus in its current account and an overall deficit equal to 5.4 percent of GDP.

The central government's fiscal deficit increased significantly as a share of GDP during the 1980s as compared with the 1970s. The deficit was 0.5 percent of GDP in 1976 but reached 3.4 percent in 1986. Most of the capital needed to cover the growing fiscal deficits between 1979 and 1987 was obtained from the Central Reserve Bank. The government could in fact cover about 85 percent of its annual fiscal deficit with financing from the Central Reserve Bank. In order to fund operations of public enterprises and additional development programs, however, the government had to rely heavily on foreign aid and international loans. The government owed only US$88 million to foreign creditors in 1970, but this indebtedness had increased to US$1.5 billion by 1986.

United States assistance greatly increased in importance to the Salvadoran economy during the 1980s. Between 1980 and 1986, the United States provided a total of US$2.5 billion in economic and military aid. This represented an increase of more than 3,000 percent over the US$7 million in economic, military, and development aid sent during the entire 1970–79 period. By 1987 United States assistance totaled US$608 million, larger than the fiscal budget of the Salvadoran government of US$582 million.

Allocation of Government Expenditures

The allocation of government spending changed markedly after 1978, mainly as a result of the civil conflict. While expenditures on education and health fell as a share of total government spending, military spending rose dramatically.

Military

The percentage of total government expenditures on the Salvadoran military increased from 6.6 percent in 1972 to 28.7 percent in 1986. Most of this increase was a result of the country's civil conflict and the need to establish and maintain the 59,000-member armed forces and security forces (see Defense Budget, ch. 5). If one also considers the military's operating expenditures (wages and purchases of goods and services related to national security), military spending increased from 22.2 percent of all government outlays in 1980 to 47.3 percent in 1986.

The huge amounts spent on counterinsurgency were further underscored when one considers foreign military aid; as much as 75 percent of the US$2.5 billion in United States assistance between 1980 and 1986 may have been applied directly or indirectly to the war effort. A study released in late 1987 by the bipartisan Arms Control and Foreign Policy Caucus of the United States Congress alleged that aid targeted for "stabilization, restoration, and humanitarian needs" was being used instead to repair damage, thus freeing more of the Salvadoran budget for military expenditures. The caucus advocated stricter measures to ensure that aid was used to improve health care, nutrition, and education.

Utilities and Communications

Most major utility companies in El Salvador were state owned and operated. These included the National Water and Sewerage Administration (Administración Nacional de Acueductos y Alcantarillados—ANDA), the National Telecommunications Administration (Administración Nacional de Telecomunicaciones—Antel), and the National Electric Company, known formally as the Río Lempa Executive Hydroelectric Commission (Comisión Ejecutiva Hidroeléctrica del Río Lempa—CEL). These companies, responsible for providing public services, operated fairly autonomously, even though their budgets were controlled by the Legislative Assembly. Government expenditures on economic services

115

(including road construction and maintenance, communications facilities, and power plants and lines) declined from 29 percent of total expenditures in 1976 to only 12 percent in 1985. Spending on these services increased by 37 percent in nominal terms from US$98 million in 1976 to US$135 million in 1985; during the same period, government spending increased by 31 percent, from US$334 million to US$1.1 billion. In 1978 about 70 percent of these service-oriented expenditures went for the building and maintenance of roads, communications facilities, and power plants and lines. This share declined to 53 percent in 1986, largely because of increased spending on services to the agriculture sector and the fishing industry.

Health, Education, and Entitlements

Historically, El Salvador's health care system has fallen short of the country's needs (see Health and Welfare, ch. 2). The government's ability to provide adequate health care eroded during the 1980s because of the civil conflict's costliness and guerrilla attacks that destroyed many previously existing facilities. Spending on health care, as well as other social services, was supplanted by increases in military spending. Consequently, government spending on health services declined as a share of total expenditures from 10 percent in 1978 to 7.5 percent in 1986.

Nevertheless, compared with its performance earlier in the decade, health care improved in the mid-1980s, largely because of AID efforts. With AID assistance, the Salvadoran government circumvented drastic reductions in social services—despite cuts to these services in the fiscal budget—and progressed in a number of areas. Between 1984 and 1986, malaria cases declined from 62,000 to 23,500; officials from the Ministry of Public Health and Social Services were able to make 914 prenatal visits per 1,000 births in 1986, compared with 876 in 1984; health officials also increased distribution of oral rehydration packets (vital to reducing infant mortality) by 130 percent, from 650,000 in 1984 to 1.5 million in 1986.

Education's share of government expenditures declined, a side effect of the civil conflict, from 21.4 percent in 1976 to 14.5 percent in 1986. As a result, by 1986 over 1,000 schools had been abandoned.

Government spending on social security and welfare increased from US$11 million in 1976 to US$31 million in 1985, an increase in line with that for total government spending. Spending on housing and amenities, however, declined in nominal terms, from US$11 million in 1976 to US$6 million in 1985. This category

Municipal buses, San Salvador
Courtesy Inter-American Development Bank

included spending on sanitary services, which declined from US$800,000 in 1976 to US$200,000 in 1985, after dropping to a low of US$100,000 between 1979 and 1981.

Public Enterprises

In El Salvador in the late 1980s, there were nine state-owned companies, the most important of which were public utility companies, such as CEL, Antel, ANDA, IRA, and the Autonomous Executive Port Commission (Comisión Ejecutiva Portuaria Autónoma—CEPA). IRA, which operated under the Ministry of Agriculture and Livestock, was responsible for marketing imported or domestic foodstuffs, such as corn, rice, beans, and powdered milk. Some of these foods were sold in government stores at subsidized prices. The state also owned shares of the cement and textile industries. The establishment of the two state-owned marketing companies, Incafe and Inazucar, expanded the public sector significantly and increased public revenue at the expense of coffee and sugar producers.

Most state-owned companies turned a profit in the 1980s. Between 1980 and 1983, for example, state-sector profits increased from 0.8 percent to 1.7 percent of GDP. Some state-owned companies, however, tended not to adjust prices during inflationary periods. IRA regularly incurred large deficits by trying to provide affordable foodstuffs. IRA's deficits were generally covered by the central government. Most other state-owned companies financed

117

their deficits abroad, or through loans from the Central Reserve Bank.

Agriculture

Industry and agriculture were the most dynamic sectors of the economy during the 1965–80 period, growing each year by 5.3 percent and 3.6 percent in real terms, respectively. Between 1980 and 1986, the value of agricultural output dropped by an average 2.3 percent per year. This decline was influenced by a number of factors, among them guerrilla sabotage, the comparative inefficiency of farms created by the land reform program, and the ineffectiveness of many government policies. Despite the general decline of agricultural output, coffee, which generated half the country's export earnings in 1987, continued as the most important commodity produced in El Salvador.

The agricultural sector accounted for nearly 25 percent of GDP in 1987 and was responsible for about 80 percent of the country's export revenue. Although the number of people employed in agriculture increased from 3.5 million in 1970 to 5.7 million in 1986, the share of the economically active population employed in agriculture declined from 56 percent in 1970 to only 40 percent in 1986. After coffee, sugar and cotton were the most important agricultural commodities. Basic grains (wheat, rice, and corn) were also grown extensively, but for domestic consumption.

Despite the relative importance of agriculture to El Salvador's economy, absolute levels of production declined dramatically after 1979. Several factors, especially the civil conflict, were blamed for the decline. Guerrilla attacks on farms, processing plants, and infrastructure undermined efficiency, precluded investment, and intimidated laborers. The impact of the conflict varied, however, depending on the crop. For example, the geographical location of the most important coffee-growing area—the western sector of the country—insulated most coffee producers from the violence. In contrast, cotton production, centered in the eastern part of the country, was devastated by guerrilla activities.

The Land Tenure System

Historically, landownership in El Salvador has been highly concentrated in an elite group of wealthy landowners. Most of the good arable land in El Salvador was located on large coffee plantations, while lower quality land was rented to peasants, who grew staple crops (see Standard of Living, ch. 2). Because these plots often failed to provide even a subsistence-level existence for them, the tenant farmers often worked as laborers for the coffee plantations as well.

During the colonial period, a certain tension existed between the hacendados—the owners of private plantations—and Indian communities that laid claim to, but did not always make productive use of, communal lands known as *ejidos* or *tierras comunales*. Although some encroachment by hacendados on Indian lands undoubtedly took place, this practice was not apparently widespread, mainly because the Spanish crown had supported the integrity of the Indian lands. After independence, however, the process of private seizure of communal lands accelerated, aided by the confusing and incomplete nature of the inherited colonial statutes dealing with the ownership and transfer of land. The rapid growth of coffee production in the late nineteenth and early twentieth centuries led the government to formalize the favored status of private, export-oriented agriculture over subsistence farming through the passage of the legislative decree of March 1, 1879. This decree allowed private individuals to acquire title to *ejido* land as long as they planted at least 25 percent of that land with certain specified crops, most notably coffee and cocoa. *Tierras comunales* were formally abolished in February 1881; the abolishment of *ejidos* in March 1882 left private property as the only legally recognized form of land tenure.

During the twentieth century, the conflict over land tenure pitted commercial export-crop producers against campesinos who sought to raise subsistence crops—mainly corn—on land to which they rarely held legal title. Some campesinos worked under various rental and sharecropping arrangements; however, an increasing number functioned as squatters, with no claim to their land beyond their mere presence on it. This occupation of private and public lands was intensified by rapid population growth, the expansion of cotton production that removed further acreage from the total available for subsistence agriculture, and the expulsion of thousands of Salvadorans from Honduras following the 1969 war between the two countries (see The 1969 War with Honduras, ch. 1).

As of 1988, the most recent agricultural census had been conducted in 1971, but data on the 1980 land reform program corroborates that extremely unequal land distribution patterns persisted throughout the 1970s. According to the 1971 agricultural census, 92 percent of the farms in El Salvador (some 250,500 in all) together comprised only 27 percent of all farm area. The other 73 percent of farmland was combined in only 1,951 farms, or 8 percent of all farms; these parcels were all over 100 hectares. Farms between 100 and 500 hectares represented 15 percent of El Salvador's cultivated area.

119

The land distributed under Phase I of the land reform program included the largest plantations—all those larger than 500 hectares. Phase I divided up 469 individual properties, with a combined area of 219,400 hectares, almost 18 percent of all Salvadoran farmland. Nearly 31,400 Salvadoran heads of household benefited directly from Phase I of the land reform; if family members are included, the beneficiaries totaled almost 188,200. Most of these lands were expropriated by the government and divided among 317 cooperatives. The government hoped that the economies of scale possible under a cooperative framework would keep the farms efficient.

The government guaranteed the former landholders that they would be compensated and had planned to pay them out of the cooperatives' earnings. However, because the cooperatives experienced major difficulties during their initial years, much of the compensation had to be paid by the government. According to a report released by the inspector general of AID in February 1984, the cooperatives established under Phase I of the land reform ''had massive capital debt, no working capital, large tracts of nonproductive land, substantially larger labor forces than needed to operate the units, and weak management.'' By the end of 1985, only 5 percent of the 317 cooperatives formed under the land reform were able to pay their debts, in spite of US$150 million in assistance from AID. Many lacked capital to buy fertilizer, so yields steadily declined. Nevertheless, by the end of 1987 almost all Phase I compensation had been paid. The restrictions placed on Phase II by the Constituent Assembly greatly limited its effect on land tenure because of the small size of the plots (see Agrarian Reform, ch. 2). As of 1987, however, Phase II of the agrarian reform program had not been implemented.

Major Crops and Commodities

Coffee

Coffee has fueled the Salvadoran economy and shaped its history for more than a century. It was first cultivated for domestic use early in the nineteenth century. By mid-century its commercial promise was evident, and the government began to favor its production through legislation such as tax breaks for producers, exemption from military service for coffee workers, and elimination of export duties for new producers. By 1880 coffee had become virtually the sole export crop. Compared with indigo, previously the dominant export commodity, coffee was a more demanding crop. Since coffee bushes required several years to produce a usable harvest, its production required a greater commitment of capital,

Salvadoran coffee cooperative
Courtesy
United States Agency for
International Development

labor, and land than did indigo. Coffee also grew best at a certain altitude, whereas indigo flourished almost anywhere.

Unlike those of Guatemala and Costa Rica, the Salvadoran coffee industry developed largely without the benefit of external technical and financial help. El Salvador nonetheless became one of the most efficient coffee producers in the world. This was especially true on the large coffee *fincas,* where the yield per hectare increased in proportion to the size of the *finca,* a rare occurrence in plantation agriculture. The effect of coffee production on Salvadoran society has been immeasurable, not only in terms of land tenure but also because the coffee industry has served as a catalyst for the development of infrastructure (roads and railroads) and as a mechanism for the integration of indigenous communities into the national economy.

In the decades prior to the civil conflict of the 1980s, export earnings from coffee allowed growers to expand production, finance the development of a cotton industry, and establish a light manufacturing sector. After 1979, however, government policies, guerrilla attacks, and natural disasters reduced investment, impeding the coffee industry's growth. To make matters worse, after a price jump in 1986 world coffee prices fell by 35 percent in 1987, causing coffee exports to decline in value from US$539 million to US$347 million.

Government control of coffee marketing and export was regarded as one of the strongest deterrents to investment in the industry.

121

In the first year of Incafe's existence, coffee yields dropped by over 20 percent. During each of the ensuing four years, yields were about 30 percent lower than those registered during the 1978–80 period. Although the area in production remained fairly constant at approximately 180,000 hectares, production of green coffee declined in absolute terms from 175,000 tons in 1979 to 141,000 tons in 1986; this 19 percent drop was a direct result of lower yields, which in turn were attributed to decreased levels of investment. According to the Salvadoran Coffee Growers Association (Asociación Cafetalera de El Salvador—ACES), besides controlling the sale of coffee, Incafe also charged growers export taxes and service charges equal to about 50 percent of the sale price and was often late in paying growers for their coffee.

Coffee growers also suffered from guerrilla attacks, extortion, and the imposition of so-called "war taxes" during the 1980s (see Left-Wing Extremism, ch. 5). These difficulties, in addition to their direct impact on production, also decreased investment. Under normal conditions, coffee growers replaced at least 5 percent of their coffee plants each year because the most productive coffee plants are between five and fifteen years old. Many coffee growers in El Salvador, in an effort to avoid further losses, neglected to replant.

Although most coffee production took place in the western section of El Salvador, coffee growers who operated in the eastern region were sometimes compelled to strike a modus vivendi with the guerrillas. During the 1984–85 harvest, for example, the guerrillas added to their "war tax" demand a threat to attack any plantation they thought underpaid workers. They demanded that workers receive the equivalent of US$4.00 per 100 pounds picked, a US$1.00 increase over what was then the going rate. The fact that growers negotiated with the guerrillas—while the government looked the other way—demonstrated the continuing importance of coffee export revenue to both the growers and the government.

Sugar

Sugar was the most dynamic of all agricultural commodities during the 1980s, showing increases in production and amount of area cultivated. Salvadoran farmers devoted 42,000 hectares to sugar production in 1986, compared with 33,000 hectares in 1979. Production rose from 2.7 million tons in 1979 to 3.2 million tons in 1986, after peaking at a record 3.4 million tons in 1984. Despite rising production, however, sugar producers still experienced problems. World sugar prices crashed from US$0.085 per pound in 1983 to US$0.04 per pound in 1984 and did not begin to recover until late 1987.

Cotton

Salvadoran farmers did not produce much cotton until after World War II, when several technological developments combined to facilitate farming on the coastal lowlands. One of these was the increased availability of drugs to combat malaria and yellow fever; another was the production of cheap chemical insecticides (insect infestation being the major obstacle to high cotton yields in El Salvador); and yet another was the development during World War II, when imports of cloth and clothing dried up, of a domestic textile industry. During the 1950s, cotton production increased fifteenfold. Production was boosted still further in the 1960s by the completion of the Carretera Litoral, the coastal highway running almost the length of the country.

Although it was one of the country's top sources of export revenue in the 1960s and 1970s, cotton was the major economic casualty of the civil conflict, virtually disappearing as an export commodity during the 1980s. The value of exports fell precipitously, from US$87 million in 1979, to US$56 million in 1983, and to only US$2.3 million in 1987. Many plantations in the eastern part of the country were abandoned as a result of the violence, while other plantations affected by the land reform shifted production to other crops. Those farms that continued to operate reported declining yields and a virtual cessation of investment and replanting. The cultivated area devoted to cotton declined from 82,000 hectares in 1979 to only 27,000 hectares in 1986, a drop of almost 70 percent. Production of seed cotton declined from 169,000 tons in 1979 to 55,000 tons in 1986.

Basic Grains

During the late 1970s, the Salvadoran government shifted the emphasis of agricultural policy away from traditional export commodities toward increased production of staple crops for domestic consumption. Food security, defined as the ability to produce enough food domestically, was a goal of the government in the 1980s, but one that proved increasingly elusive. The area under cereals cultivation declined from 422,000 hectares in 1979 to 390,000 hectares in 1986 because farms located in conflict zones were abandoned. The shortfall was made up by an increase in imports. Salvadoran food imports totaled only 75,000 tons in 1974; by 1986, however, this figure had risen to 212,000 tons. In response to the insurgency, food aid was increased. In 1974–75, for example, El Salvador received only 4,000 tons of food aid; by 1985–86 this figure had risen to 278,000 tons.

Corn production declined steadily from 517,000 tons in 1979 to 391,000 tons in 1986. The area for corn cultivation also declined from 281,000 hectares to 243,000 hectares, while yields shrank from 1.8 tons per hectare to 1.5 tons per hectare. Rice production, however, remained fairly steady. Salvadoran farmers maintained approximately 15,000 hectares in rice from 1979 to 1986 (rising to 17,000 hectares in 1985); harvests rose from 56,000 tons in 1979 to 69,000 tons in 1985, only to drop to 53,000 tons in 1986. Sorghum production and cultivation also declined slightly. In 1979 farmers devoted 126,000 hectares to the cultivation of sorghum, compared with 119,000 hectares in 1986. Sorghum harvests declined from 145,000 tons in 1979 to 135,000 tons in 1986.

Livestock

Cattle raising accounted for some 10 percent of the value added in agriculture for 1986. The cattle population dropped from 1,317,000 head in 1979 to only 1,010,000 head in 1986. Salvadoran farmers raised only 400,000 pigs in 1986, an 11 percent decline from 1979. The declines in production were attributable to widespread overslaughtering—a result of the land reform, which caused some large landowners to slaughter their livestock and sell them rather than lose them to the cooperatives—smuggling, to avoid export taxes, and the effects of the civil conflict.

Fisheries

El Salvador's fishing industry, although responsible for only 0.1 percent of GDP, produced the fourth largest source of export revenue for the country in 1986. In 1987 the fishing industry consisted of two main sectors, a modern, capital-intensive shrimp fishery, and a small artisanal fishery. Of the two, the shrimp industry was the big money-maker, with shrimp exports totaling 3,700 tons in 1986, valued at US$18.4 million. Shrimp fishermen caught an annual average of about 5,400 tons from 1980 through 1987, up from the 3,000 to 4,000 tons caught each year during the 1960s and 1970s. The abundant shrimp resource supported both a modern shrimp fleet and an artisanal shrimp fishery.

In 1981 the government established the Center for Fisheries Development (Centro de Desarrollo Pesquero—Cendepesca) to develop the fishing industry. Cendepesca regulated the industry and promoted its expansion through such devices as tax credits on the importation of machinery, fishing boats, and inputs for processing and exemptions of five or ten years on municipal and income taxes for companies devoted to fishing. Cendepesca also tried to manage the shrimp fishery (to prevent overfishing) through required

Shrimp fishermen
Courtesy United Nations Food and Agriculture Organization

registration and licensing of shrimp boats. Cendepesca repeatedly sought to impose a closed season during shrimp reproduction periods, but these efforts were thwarted by powerful lobbyists in the face of opposition from major shrimp companies. Consequently, there was a fear that overfishing would deplete stocks, a development that could reduce the shrimp catch and have a major impact on the country's export earnings.

El Salvador also had an embryonic shrimp culture industry. According to an AID feasibility study, El Salvador has 5,000 hectares of land particularly well suited for shrimp farming. By the end of 1987, however, only four small shrimp farms were operating in El Salvador.

The government also tried with a US$50 million loan from France to establish a major tuna fishery. The funds were used to build a large tuna port, complete with processing facilities, at La Unión, already a major shrimp fishing port. The project was completed in 1981 but was never initiated because of the government's poor management of the vessels and the project. The Salvadoran government, which purchased two large tuna seiners for operation in 1981 and 1982, reported meager catches because of technical difficulties. By 1985 the facilities at La Unión had languished, and the government was unable to sell the vessels. The weakness of the Salvadoran tuna industry became clear in September 1986 (and

125

again in August 1988) when the Salvadoran government ignored the United States Marine Mammal Protection Act, an act that requires tuna exporters to the United States to report their efforts to reduce concomitant porpoise mortalities. Consequently, the United States embargoed Salvadoran tuna in September 1986 and again in 1988.

Forestry

El Salvador's forestry industry developed rapidly after 1969, when the "Soccer War" cut off shipments of lumber from Honduras, a primary supplier (see The 1969 War with Honduras, ch. 1). The lumber industry was encouraged by the developing paper and wood pulp production industries and the ongoing traditional furniture industry. By the mid-1980s, however, El Salvador was once again highly dependent on wood imports. Lumber imports in 1985 totaled US$36.7 million, compared with US$13 million in 1974, while lumber exports reached US$6.6 million in 1985, compared with only US$400,000 in 1974.

Industry

The creation of the CACM fostered development of industry in El Salvador during the 1960s by reducing intraregional trade barriers, which increased aggregate demand for manufactured goods. The Salvadoran and Guatemalan manufacturing sectors benefited the most and conversely suffered the most when the CACM lost momentum after the 1969 Salvadoran-Honduran war. During the 1980s, however, industrial output, affected by guerrilla attacks on power plants and by reduced investor confidence, also suffered declines by an average of 0.7 percent each year between 1980 and 1986.

Manufacturing of consumer goods predominated in the industrial sector. About 50 percent of manufactured goods produced were either food products or beverages. Intermediate goods, such as chemicals and pharmaceuticals, increased in importance during the 1970s but still constituted only about 15 percent of manufacturing output in 1986. El Salvador also had small industries that produced tobacco products, petroleum products, clothing, textiles, wood products, and paper products. Construction was the second leading contributor to the industrial sector, but its contribution to GDP was considerably less than that of manufacturing.

Manufacturing

The manufacturing industry developed slowly. In 1950, when manufacturing accounted for about 7 percent of GDP, it comprised mostly cottage industries. Of the fourteen larger manufacturing firms (with more than 100 employees), thirteen were located in San Salvador and produced mainly textiles, tobacco, and beverages; most of the smaller firms manufactured clothing, shoes, furniture, and wood or straw products.

The development of manufacturing industries was slowed by a shortage of reliable year-round labor—most Salvadorans worked seasonally as agricultural laborers—and an even more acute lack of skilled workers. In 1952, however, when the government offered tax breaks to small businesses, industry grew almost 5 percent a year from 1955 to 1958. During this period, cement, chemical, and transportation equipment industries began. The intermediate goods sector was much more dynamic than the capital goods sector; with the development of modern chemical, pharmaceutical, and petroleum product industries, it grew rapidly in the 1960s and 1970s. The production of machinery and transport equipment remained fairly stable in terms of its share of the value added for total Salvadoran manufactured goods, rising from 3 percent of total value added in 1970 to 4 percent in 1985.

By 1960 the manufacturing sector represented 14.6 percent of El Salvador's GDP, the highest percentage of any Central American country at the time. The creation of the CACM boosted the rapid development of manufacturing firms in El Salvador through out the 1960s. By 1965, following three years of 12 percent average annual growth, manufacturing represented 17.4 percent of GDP. Between 1961 and 1970, value added in manufacturing increased (in nominal terms) from US$89.2 million to US$194.1 million.

The manufacturing sector received a temporary setback because of the 1969 war with Honduras, which disrupted CACM trade. Even the CACM's share of Salvadoran exports fell from 40 percent in 1968 to 32 percent in 1970. Nevertheless, manufacturing output increased by a modest 3.9 percent in 1969. Following the war, however, foreign investment replaced CACM trade as the engine of growth for the Salvadoran manufacturing industry.

During the 1970s, manufacturing was the most dynamic segment of the Salvadoran economy, growing by an impressive 16.8 percent yearly between 1971 and 1978. Consumer goods (especially foodstuffs, textiles, clothing, and shoes) continued to be the most important products. Because of the CACM's decline, El Salvador was forced to seek new export markets like the United States, which in the 1970s imported over 20 percent of the country's food exports and almost 35 percent of its exports of beverages and tobacco products. El Salvador also sought export markets for textiles and other light manufactures in the United States and the Federal Republic of Germany (West Germany). The project was not competitive, however, because of poor product quality and outmoded manufacturing techniques and expensive foreign materials. Eventually Japan and West Germany became important export markets for the bulk of El Salvador's nonedible raw materials, fats, and oils.

Because foreign investors funneled their capital to industries producing intermediate goods, these industries increased in importance relative to consumer goods during the 1970s. As a result, El Salvador increased the percentage of its exports of manufactured goods exported to industrialized countries. In 1965 over 90 percent of Salvadoran manufactured exports went to other developing countries (primarily CACM states), but by 1986 about 87 percent were being shipped to industrialized countries. Overall exports of manufactured goods increased (in real terms) from US$32 million in 1965 to US$170 million in 1986.

During the 1980s, the manufacturing sector, buffeted by the chaos of the civil conflict, labor unrest, declining investor confidence, and world recession, experienced a major decline. Aside from the generalized capital flight spurred by political instability, the second most damaging effect of the conflict, after guerrilla sabotage of the electrical grid, was attacks on factories.

The industries hit hardest by guerrilla attacks were those producing nontraditional capital goods such as transportation equipment, intermediate goods such as metal products and machinery, and capital-intensive consumer goods such as electric appliances. Traditional industries (foodstuffs, beverages, tobacco, wood products, and furniture) were least affected because their factories tended to be smaller and thus less subject to guerrilla attacks. These industries also had well-developed domestic markets and consequently were less affected by the 1980–82 world recession. Exports of manufactured goods declined by 48 percent in value and almost 80 percent in volume between 1979 and 1982, mainly as a result of lower shipments of chemicals, textiles, clothing, and petroleum products.

Labor unrest became a major contributing factor in declining manufacturing output. But it is unclear whether or not there is a direct relationship between guerrilla activity and that unrest. There were, however, eighty-six strikes in 1979, involving almost 23,000 workers, compared with only one strike, involving 700 workers, in 1975.

Other Leading Industries

The construction industry was one of the most dynamic in El Salvador during the 1970s. Value added increased from US$50 million in 1977 to US$80 million in 1978 but then declined precipitously, reaching a low of US$17 million in 1980. The industry reported only moderate growth in the early 1980s. Also, the number of workers employed in construction declined by over 75 percent between 1980 and 1986, from 13,100 workers to only 3,100.

Paradoxically, despite the industry's general decline, the number of building permits issued tripled between 1979 and 1984. The increase, however, went for housing; the number of permits issued for the construction of factories or other commercial buildings dropped from 320 in 1979 to only 35 in 1984. It is unclear whether or not all the approved buildings were actually built. When the October 1986 earthquake prompted massive capital inflows for reconstruction, however, the construction industry grew by 14 percent in 1987 and stimulated the economy's 2 percent increase in GDP that year.

El Salvador's mining industry was first established in the late nineteenth century when Charles Butters, who had pioneered the cyanide process for mineral separation, opened several gold mines. Two of his gold mines (San Sebastian and Divisadero) were highly productive; the San Sebastian mine by itself yielded US$16 million worth of gold between 1908 and 1928. Mining declined significantly by the early 1930s because world gold and silver prices dropped and costs rose. Mining, which generated only a fraction of GDP in 1987, has not played an important role in the Salvadoran economy since. El Salvador also has deposits of silver, copper, iron ore, sulfur, mercury, lead, zinc, and limestone; of these, only gold, silver, and limestone were mined in 1987, and only in limited amounts.

Infrastructure

El Salvador's infrastructure was the primary target of guerrilla sabotage in the mid- to late 1980s. Insurgent forces of the Farabundo Martí National Liberation Front (Frente Farabundo Martí de Liberación Nacional—FMLN) regularly damaged or disrupted the country's transportation, communications, and energy systems to erode the government's popularity. The front hoped to emphasize the government's inability to move the nation's economy, to increase the economic strain on the country, and to create the "objective conditions" necessary for a successful antigovernment insurrection. Guerrillas attacked a wide variety of economic targets, from trucks and buses to bridges, roads, and power plants, but they were not responsible for all the damage to the infrastructure in the 1980s. A 1982 flood washed out numerous roads and bridges, and in October 1986 an earthquake severely damaged many water and power plants and communications facilities, causing an estimated US$1 billion in damage.

Transportation

El Salvador's transportation sector, which included railroads, major highways, and air transport, connected the country's major regions (see fig. 7). Even though these systems were extensive, the disruptions of the civil conflict made travel dangerous and undependable.

El Salvador has had a fairly complete railroad system since the early twentieth century. In 1987 there were 602 kilometers of railroads in El Salvador. Over one-half of the tracks (380 kilometers) were owned by Salvador Railroads, which was built with British capital in the late 1890s to transport coffee from Sonsonate and Santa Ana to the port of Acajutla. By 1985 Salvador Railways, which was nationalized in the mid-1960s, was forced to curtail operations because of guerrilla attacks.

By 1980 the country had over 10,000 kilometers of roads, of which some 1,500 were paved. The major arteries were the Pan American Highway and the Carretera Litoral. The Pan American Highway ran through Santa Ana, San Salvador, and San Miguel. The Carretera Litoral ran mainly along the coast but also went through Zacatecoluca and Usulután. Road transportation was periodically blocked by the guerrillas, who intermittently controlled extensive eastern portions of both highways. For example, during the October 1982 guerrilla offensive alone, more than 100 vehicles were burned on the Pan American Highway. Truckloads of soldiers were needed to convoy fuel trucks on the highway between San Salvador and San Miguel. The transportation stoppage reportedly caused a major gasoline shortage in San Miguel, where motorists sometimes had to visit several service stations in order to fill up their tanks. The guerrillas also sabotaged the Litoral and Cuscatlán bridges, the two primary routes across the Río Lempa, one of El Salvador's most significant geographic obstacles (see fig. 3).

The two major ports in El Salvador were Acajutla and La Unión, both large shipping ports with significant infrastructure for fisheries. Ilopango International Airport, located near San Salvador, was one of Central America's most modern airports, and it was the only airport in the country suitable for jet aircraft. El Salvador's only commercial airline, Central American Air Transport (Transportes Aéreos Centroamericanos—Taca), owned seven commercial aircraft that provided service to Central America, Mexico City, Miami, and Los Angeles. Nevertheless, considering its size in the late 1980s, El Salvador had a large number of airfields. Of the country's 138 airfields, 95 were usable, but of these, only 5 were paved. Although noncombatant crop dusters used most of the airfields, some were caught in the crossfire of the civil conflict. One cotton cooperative reported that one of its pilots had been killed and that two others had been wounded by guerrilla snipers.

Communications

Telecommunications in El Salvador, although still not highly developed, showed significant growth from the mid-1960s to the mid-1980s. The country had a nationwide trunk radio-relay system and was connected to a Central American microwave network. There were about 116,000 telephones in the country in 1986, or about 2.3 phones for every 100 people. This represented a 900 percent increase over the 13,000 phones in the country in 1964.

The National Telecommunications Administration (Administración Nacional de Telecomunicaciones—Antel) has owned and operated the telephone and telegraph services since 1963. The postal service, operating under the Ministry of Interior, carried both domestic and international mail.

Throughout the civil conflict, the telecommunications network was devastated by the guerrilla attacks on repeater stations and on an earth station parabolic antenna for international satellite communications (see Left-Wing Extremism, ch. 5). Telephone function boxes reportedly were also destroyed daily. AID provided generators to maintain telephone service during the frequent power outages and also replaced damaged equipment.

Energy

Because El Salvador has no known oil deposits, it has long depended on imported oil (which frequently has constituted a large share of total imports). The oil shocks of 1973 and 1979 prompted the government to develop alternative forms of energy, such as hydroelectric and geothermal power. Although dependence on foreign oil lessened during the 1980s, about one-third of El Salvador's energy in 1986 still came from imports. The government owned a monopoly on imported petroleum products and sold them at a high profit to domestic refineries. In turn, to keep bus fares low the government used these oil sales revenues to subsidize diesel bus fuel. This policy, ironically, greatly increased commercial and industrial gasoline prices.

The growth of energy production was impressive through the 1960s and 1970s (largely as a result of the construction of geothermal and hydroelectric power plants) but slowed significantly in the 1980s. Energy production rose by 9 percent a year between 1965

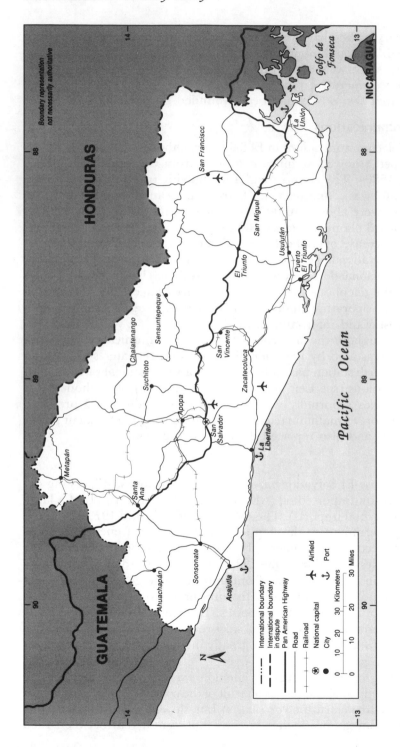

Figure 7. Transportation System, 1988

and 1980 but decreased to only 3.6 percent a year in 1980–86. The growth in energy consumption also slowed, from 7 percent a year in the 1965–80 period to only 1.5 percent annually from 1980 to 1986. Per capita energy consumption, however, increased from 140 to 216 kilogram equivalents of oil per capita between 1965 and 1986.

From 1981 to 1985, four hydroelectric power plants (Guajoyo, Cerrón Grande, 5 de Noviembre, and 15 de Septiembre) provided about 50 percent of the country's electricity, geothermal plants provided about 40 percent, and thermal plants generated about 10 percent. Guerrilla sabotage continually targeted electric power plants and power lines. In fact, the steady growth in energy production and consumption was quite remarkable, given the frequency of these attacks. By 1985 guerrillas had destroyed over 1,000 high-tension electrical towers and had damaged almost every power plant in the country. During a three-week period in January 1986, guerrilla forces blew up over 120 electrical posts and 9 electrical towers, intermittently leaving about 85 percent of the country's population without electricity.

To diminish the impact of guerrilla attacks on power plants, the Salvadoran government signed an agreement with Honduras in early 1987 for the annual purchase of about US$15 million in energy from the El Cajón hydroelectric power plant, scheduled to open in 1989. In 1987 the government also announced that a Belgian company was planning to build a US$8 million geothermal power plant; the company agreed to accept Salvadoran shrimp as barter payment.

Foreign Economic Relations

Balance of Payments and the External Sector

In 1987 El Salvador was one of the few countries in the world to maintain a large current account deficit and experience a net outflow of private capital while achieving a large increase in international reserves. This increase was equivalent to almost 1 percent of GDP. These seemingly inconsistent results were reconciled by a flow of US$275 million in official aid to El Salvador, 90 percent of which came from AID.

El Salvador's total exports equaled approximately US$573 million in 1987, a decline of almost 20 percent compared with 1986. The country's weak export performance reflected a deterioration in its terms of trade, growing protectionism in Organisation for Economic Co-operation and Development (OECD) countries, and continuing stagnation of the CACM. Coffee prices fell 35 percent from their 1986 high levels, and other agricultural products, such as cotton, sugar, and nontraditional exports, did not compensate. In 1987 foreign assistance and emigrant remittances surpassed coffee as the most important sources of foreign exchange. Both continued to finance the country's balance of payments deficit by an amount equal to 10 percent of GDP. In 1987 remittances from Salvadorans living in the United States easily exceeded the country's debt-service payments.

The total value of imports in 1987 was approximately US$911 million. Import volume and value rose in 1987 by about 3 percent and 18 percent, respectively, stimulated by the recovery in the construction sector, the overvalued colón, and a moderate recovery in consumer spending (see table 6, Appendix). Raw materials continued to account for over 50 percent of total imports, followed by consumer goods (24 percent) and capital goods (23 percent).

Factor services in 1987 (income from factors of production employed outside the owner's locale, such as interest paid on or received from external debt), remained in deficit in 1987 at US$127 million. With exports falling, the country's debt-service ratio rose to 37 percent of exports in 1987. A large surplus in nonfactor payments, consisting primarily of insurance disbursements from the 1986 earthquake, negated a significant amount of the factor-service deficit, leaving a small US$14 million services account deficit.

Trade with other Central American countries continued to diminish in 1987. In 1977 El Salvador exported US$216 million, or about 25 percent of its total exports, to other CACM countries. In 1987, because of the stagnation of the CACM, exports to this market fell below US$100 million, or less than 15 percent of total exports. In turn, the fall of exports to CACM countries forced El Salvador to solicit other trading partners, such as the United States and Canada, which increased Salvadoran imports by their combined total of more than 100 percent between 1981 and 1987. Exports to these two countries accounted for almost 50 percent of Salvadoran exports in 1987. Even with rising demand, total exports dropped by almost 50 percent in dollar terms between 1977 and 1987.

Trade and Trade Policy

El Salvador's degree of dependence on imports of intermediate and capital goods changed little between 1978 and 1985. Moreover, its dependence on a few agricultural export commodities, such as coffee and sugar, and its failure to explore nontraditional exports continued to limit growth potential. Despite government promotion of nontraditional export products, exports actually became less diversified throughout the seven-year period, with manufactured

Cerrón Grande hydroelectric project, northwestern El Salvador
Courtesy Inter-American Development Bank

goods falling as a share of total exports from a 40 percent share to only 20 percent, and coffee rising to a 40 percent share from 24 percent.

The country's import trade dependence also continued unchanged. Intermediate and capital goods represented about 60 percent of imports in 1985. That imports of these goods continued to constitute such a significant share of total imports reflected the failure of import substitution industrialization (see Glossary) programs to replace imports with locally produced goods.

The value of imported and exported goods and services was equivalent to over 50 percent of GDP in 1985. Lacking a diversified export sector and given its high degree of dependence on imports of capital and intermediate goods, the Salvadoran economy was vulnerable to variations in the terms of trade. Since the world market prices of El Salvador's primary exports, especially coffee, were highly volatile, fluctuations in the terms of trade were common. For example, if 1980 equals 100 percent, the country's terms of trade went from 72 percent in 1984 to 90 percent in 1986 and to 54 percent in 1987. These fluctuations underscored the economy's instability and stunted the country's potential growth.

Trade policy in El Salvador changed significantly between 1960 and 1987, reflecting the emergence—and subsequent decline—of the CACM, price fluctuations for coffee and other commodities, and the evolution of the Salvadoran economy. Past failures and mismanagement prompted the IMF to effect commercial policy changes in 1982 and 1986.

The 1960s have been characterized as the Golden Age for El Salvador and the rest of Central America. The establishment of the CACM in 1960 reduced intraregional trade barriers and drastically cut import duties—normally an important source of government revenue. The CACM made it possible for the Salvadoran government to pursue import substitution industrialization policies then in vogue in Latin America because the reduction in intraregional trade barriers effectively increased aggregate demand for nontraditional export products. For El Salvador—more than for any other CACM member—these policies favored the development of a significant manufacturing sector. The protective tariffs established by the CACM on manufactured goods encouraged its countries to develop competitive domestic industries. Trade barriers restricted imports of finished goods from non-CACM members and reduced tariffs on foreign raw materials.

Even with these and other changes, however, El Salvador's trade policy continued to center on the promotion of agricultural exports, a promotion essential to the government's industrialization plans. The earnings from agricultural exports were diverted (through export taxes and other charges) to the purchase of raw materials, machinery, and other unavailable domestic capital goods. Despite the rapid growth of manufacturing industries in El Salvador during the 1960s, most manufactured exports by 1970 (especially food products, beverages, and textiles) were shipped to the CACM. Three export products—coffee, cotton, and sugar—accounted for 90 percent of extraregional exports.

When the CACM began to decline in the 1970s, policymakers established an industrial free zone, which provided some incentives to export manufactured goods outside the CACM. The industries that were in the free-trade zone, however, tended toward the production of intermediate goods that required costly imported inputs. Consequently, these industries neither created value added for the Salvadoran economy nor improved El Salvador's balance of payments position. These new industries, however, increasingly tailored Salvadoran manufactured exports to North American and West European markets by the end of the 1970s. Nevertheless, a fixed exchange rate program continued to discriminate against exports because the dollar exchange rate remained overvalued. As a result of this policy and the country's increasing political instability, by the end of 1980 only four foreign companies continued to operate joint ventures in the free-trade zone.

Port expansion at Acajutla
Courtesy Inter-American Development Bank

The establishment in 1982 of a dual exchange rate pegged the United States dollar at ¢2.50 on the official market, while the rate on the parallel market fluctuated with market forces. Until 1985, as the country responded to balance of payments pressures, an increasing percentage of external transactions was shifted to the parallel market. Even with the gradual shift of transactions toward the parallel rate, a 20 percent real appreciation of the colón undercut the competitiveness of Salvadoran tradables. Following the rates' unification in 1986, the colón remained fixed, and currency was overvalued.

Two other important changes affected Salvadoran trade policy in the 1980s. First, producers of goods exported outside of the CACM were allowed to establish United States dollar-denominated accounts in Salvadoran banks. Second, exporters of nontraditional goods, e.g., beverages and processed food, were permitted to hold dollar accounts and sell them to the Central Reserve Bank at their discretion; the exporters were not required to report the exchange rate of these transactions. In a sense, these changes signaled the return to a nonunified exchange system.

Direct Foreign Investment and External Debt

Foreign capital, especially from the United States, played a crucial historical role in El Salvador's economic development. In the early decades of the twentieth century, foreign capital (primarily British,

American, and Canadian) contributed to the development of a mining sector that produced gold and silver for external markets. Investment from these countries also spurred the development of the Salvadoran railroad and electrical systems. Between 1930 and 1950, direct investment increased for the processing of agricultural commodities and for the service sector.

The amount of foreign capital flowing into the Salvadoran economy during the 1960s and 1970s paralleled the rise and decline of the CACM. During the 1960s, foreign capital supported the development of import substitution industries, such as Alcoa's 1963 joint venture to produce semi-finished products from imported industrial extrusion ingot and Lenox's 1964 investment to produce plastic products. The strong performance of the CACM during the 1960s attracted direct foreign investment. Between 1963 and 1968, the stock of direct foreign investment increased from US$43 million to US$110 million. Between 1968 and 1978, however— the period of the CACM's decline—direct foreign investment increased to only US$124 million. In the 1970s, a larger share of direct foreign investment went to industries with low value added, like those in the industrial free zone, rather than toward import substitution industries. Until 1979 foreign capital played an important role in El Salvador's most dynamic industries, with the exception of brewing and cement. During the 1980s, capital inflows slowed in response to the country's political and economic instability. Between 1980 and 1984, foreign direct capital flowed in at a rate of about US$7 million per year.

Increased foreign investment, particularly in export-oriented industries, was an economic goal of the Duarte administration. Although the instability engendered by the civil conflict militated against it, the export promotion law of 1986 sought to attract more foreign capital by granting a ten-year (renewable for an additional ten-year period) exemption from most import duties on inputs for industries that exported at least 25 percent of their production. These industries were also exempted from all revenue and net worth taxes. In an effort to simplify the often frustrating procedure of registering foreign firms with the government, a central documentation center was established to address the needs of export-oriented firms.

Salvadoran external debt was mostly a result of extensive government borrowing after 1979, which increased the government's indebtedness from US$88 million in 1970 to US$1.5 billion in 1987. The private sector owed US$120 million to foreign creditors in 1987. El Salvador's total external debt of approximately US$1.7 billion represented less than half of the country's estimated 1987 GDP.

As a share of exports, debt service rose to 37 percent from 33 percent in 1986, slightly below the debt service of other large debtor countries such as Brazil, Mexico, and Argentina. On a per capita basis, El Salvador's debt was well below that of Costa Rica, Mexico, Argentina, and Brazil.

Of the country's total 1987 debt service of US$182 million, about US$113 million went toward principal, while only US$64 million went toward interest payments. Low interest payments reflected the favorable terms associated with El Salvador's external debt. The average interest rate on the debt in 1987 was 3.1 percent, and the average maturity was thirty-nine years, with an average 8.6-year interest-free grace period. Thus, relative to other heavily indebted countries, El Salvador's external debt represented less of an obstacle to economic development. Over 90 percent of the Salvadoran debt was held by nonprivate lenders and was publicly guaranteed Almost half of the public debt was bilateral, most of it held by the United States government. Other factors, such as the civil conflict, deteriorating terms of trade, and an antagonistic relationship between the private sector and the Duarte administration, have more adversely affected the country's economy than has the government's indebtedness.

In addition to multilateral aid from the World Bank (see Glossary) and bilateral aid, El Salvador made use of US$43 million of its IMF credit in 1987. To qualify for this credit, the government initiated a short-term structural adjustment program with limitations on credit and public sector spending and the adoption of monetary targets, unification of the exchange rate regime, the creation of new export promotion incentives, and the formation of an external debt management committee to ensure that autonomous and semiautonomous institutions did not accumulate external debt too rapidly.

Future economic development in El Salvador seemed in the late 1980s to be highly dependent on political factors. The lingering instability caused by the civil conflict inhibited investment, damaged the infrastructure, denied secure access to certain parts of the country, and forced the government to allocate an abnormally high percentage of its budget to the military. Even a complete cessation of hostilities, however, would be unlikely to lead to complete recovery in the short term, given the structural shortcomings of the economy.

*   *   *

The lack of broad, accurate, and up-to-date government statistics from El Salvador is compensated for to some extent by the working relationships established in the late 1980s between the Salvadoran government and the IMF and the United States Department of State, particularly AID. Several Department of State reports compiled by the embassy staff in San Salvador provide an overview of the economy. Because Salvadoran statistical reporting to the IMF was required by the stabilization packages implemented in the mid-1980s, the IMF has reliable statistics for the country. A good source for both economic and political reporting is the quarterly *Country Profile: Guatemala, El Salvador, Honduras* produced in London by the Economist Intelligence Unit. A more historical perspective on the economy is provided by Marc W. Herold's article "Finanzekapital in El Salvador, 1900–80," as well as by David Browning's *El Salvador: Landscape and Society.* (For further information and complete citations, see Bibliography.)

Chapter 4. Government and Politics

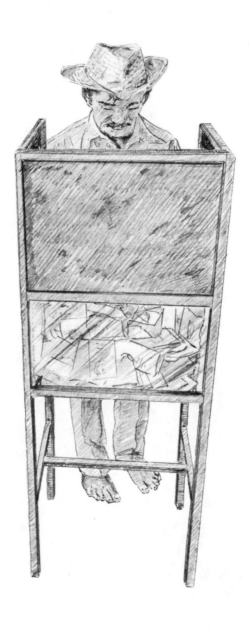

Voter casting his ballot

SINCE THE REFORMIST COUP of 1979, El Salvador has experienced wrenching political turmoil as numerous actors, movements, and forces contended for the right to shape the country's future. By the late 1980s, the most extreme of these forces—the oligarchic elite and the Marxist-Leninist guerrilla forces—appeared to have lost some of their previous influence, as a still-tentative democratic process continued to evolve amid trying circumstances. The United States loomed large in this process as the country's major source of economic and military aid and assistance and the most enthusiastic foreign supporter of its democratic efforts. Despite consistent support from Washington and a certain amount of progress in human rights and economic reform, many problems remained intractable, and the overall political situation was still volatile and, to some extent, unpredictable. The conservative Nationalist Republican Alliance underscored this fact by capturing a surprising legislative majority in the March 1988 elections.

Although the system established by the Constitution of 1983 was functional, some observers questioned its legitimacy because it excluded the Salvadoran left from the political process. As the 1989 presidential elections approached, however, these claims lost some of their validity in the face of the return to El Salvador of such opposition figures as Guillermo Manuel Ungo Revelo and Rubén Zamora Rivas, the establishment of the Social Democratic Party and the possibility, however dubious, of a settlement between the government and the Farabundo Martí National Liberation Front-Revolutionary Democratic Front within the framework of the Central American Peace Agreement signed in Esquipulas, Guatemala, on August 7, 1987 (the so-called Arias Plan).

Observers were reluctant to predict the odds of successful implemention of a genuine democratic system in El Salvador, a country with no real democratic tradition to draw on, where economic conditions were tenuous at best and where a destructive and divisive insurgent conflict wore on with no resolution in sight. It was clear, however, that the El Salvador of the late 1980s was different from the El Salvador of the 1970s and that further change was inevitable, even if the exact nature of that change remained uncertain.

Constitutional Background

The Constitutions of El Salvador, 1824–1962

El Salvador has functioned under fifteen constitutions since it achieved independence from Spain in the early nineteenth century. The vast majority of these documents were drafted and promulgated without the benefit of broad popular input or electoral mandate. The nature of the country's elite-dominated political system and the personalistic rule of presidents drawn from either the oligarchy or the military accounted for the relatively short life span of most of these documents. Some of them were drafted solely to provide a quasi-legal basis for the extension of a president's term, whereas others were created to legitimize seizures of power on an ex post facto basis.

The first Salvadoran constitution was produced in 1824. It declared El Salvador independent as a member of the United Provinces of Central America (see El Salvador and the United Provinces of Central America, ch. 1). The dissolution of the United Provinces necessitated the promulgation of a new constitution in 1841 as El Salvador emerged as an independent republic in its own right. The 1841 constitution was a liberal document that established a bicameral legislature and set a two-year term for the nation's president with no possibility of reelection. The latter feature contributed directly to the demise of the document in 1864, when President Gerardo Barrios dispensed with it and extended his term by legislative decree.

That same year, Barrios replaced the 1841 constitution with one that, not surprisingly, increased the presidential term to four years and allowed for one reelection. This issue of presidential tenure proved to be a major point of contention for the next two decades. The 1871 constitution, drafted by resurgent liberal forces, restored the two-year term, prohibited immediate reelection, and strengthened the power of the legislative branch. This document too, however, fell victim to individual ambition when President Santiago González replaced it with the constitution of 1872, which restored the four-year term. Similarly, the constitution of 1880 was used to extend the term of President Rafael Zaldívar. The four-year term was retained in the constitution of 1883, but presidential tenure was reduced to three years in the constitution of 1885. The latter document, although it never formally came into force, owing to the overthrow of Zaldívar by Francisco Menéndez, was nonetheless an influential piece of work, primarily because it formed the basis for the constitution of 1886, the most durable in Salvadoran history.

The constitution of 1886 provided for a four-year presidential term with no immediate reelection and established a unicameral legislature. Some limits on presidential power were incorporated, most notably the stricture that all executive decrees or orders had to comply with the stated provisions of the constitution. This constitutional litmus test of executive action was, at least in theory, a significant step toward an institutionalized governmental system and away from the arbitrary imposition of power by self-serving caudillos. The constitution of 1886 showed remarkable staying power by Salvadoran standards, remaining in force in its original form until January 1939. It was reinstated in amended form after World War II. The 1939 constitution that filled the wartime gap was designed by President Maximiliano Hernández Martínez to ensure his uninterrupted rule; it increased the presidential term from four to six years. Martínez's effort to extend his rule still further by inserting a provision for the one-time legislative election of the president was one of several grievances fueling the public unrest that drove him from office in 1944.

The wartime constitution was revised in that same year. Although technically titled the Reforms of 1944, this document is also sometimes referred to as the Constitution of 1944. It was supplanted in 1945 by yet another charter, the constitution of 1945, which endured for only one year. The 1886 constitution, in amended form, was reinstated in 1946. These changes reflected the political uncertainty that prevailed in El Salvador between the termination of Martínez's long tenure as president and the advent of the military-led Revolution of 1948.

The constitution that grew out of the Revolution of 1948, under which Oscar Osorio was elected president, was the constitution of 1950. It retained a unicameral legislature and changed the name from National Assembly to Legislative Assembly. The 1950 charter also restored a six-year presidential term with no immediate reelection and, for the first time, granted Salvadoran women the right to vote.

A Constituent Assembly appointed by the military-civilian junta and headed by Colonel Julio Adalberto Rivera drafted a document that was promulgated as the constitution of 1962 but that was basically quite similar to the 1950 constitution. Relatively long lived by Salvadoran standards, it was not superseded until 1983, by which time the personal and political guarantees of the constitution had been suspended by a state of emergency.

The Constitution of 1983

The Political Setting

The sixty-member Constituent Assembly elected in March 1982 was charged with producing a new constitution. This new document was expected to institutionalize, although perhaps in modified form, the reform measures taken by the various junta governments after 1979; it was also to serve as the master plan for a system of representative democratic government. In addition to crafting the structure of that government, the Constituent Assembly was responsible for issuing a schedule for presidential elections.

A majority of the members, known as deputies, of the Constituent Assembly represented conservative political parties. All told, conservative parties had drawn approximately 52 percent of the total popular vote. The moderate Christian Democratic Party (Partido Demócrata Cristiano—PDC) had garnered 35.5 percent. These results equated to twenty-four seats for the PDC and thirty-six seats for a loose right-wing coalition made up of the Nationalist Republican Alliance (Alianza Republicana Nacionalista—Arena), the National Conciliation Party (Partido de Conciliación Nacional—PCN), Democratic Action (Acción Democrática—AD), the Salvadoran Popular Party (Partido Popular Salvadoreño—PPS), and the Popular Orientation Party (Partido de Orientación Popular—POP). Representatives of these five parties issued a manifesto in March 1982 decrying both communism and Christian democratic communitarianism and declaring that both ideologies had been rejected by the people by way of the ballot box. The coalition leaders suggested that they were preparing to limit Christian democratic influence on the drafting of the constitution and to exclude the PDC from participation in the interim government that was to be named by the Constituent Assembly.

The original exclusionary aims of the rightist coalition, however, were never completely fulfilled. During its existence, from April 1982 through December 1983, the Constituent Assembly came under pressure from a number of sources, most significantly from the United States government and the Salvadoran military. United States envoys from both the White House and Congress pressed Salvadoran political leaders to incorporate the PDC into the interim government and to preserve the reform measures, particularly agrarian reform. At stake was the continuation of United States aid, both economic and military, without which El Salvador would have been hard pressed to sustain its democratic transition in the face of growing military and political pressure from the Farabundo Martí National Liberation Front-Revolutionary Democratic Front (Frente Farabundo Martí de Liberación Nacional-Frente Democrático Revolucionario—FMLN-FDR), the leftist guerrilla (the FMLN) and political (FDR) opposition groups that unified in 1981 in an effort to seize power by revolutionary means (see The Civil Conflict Begins, ch. 1). El Salvador's military High

Command (Alto Mando) recognized this reality and lent its considerable influence to the cause of continued PDC participation in government. The Christian Democrats had been brought into the junta governments at the urging of reformist officers; by 1982 the PDC and the military had come to a practical understanding based on their shared interest in maintaining good relations with the United States, expanding political participation, improving economic conditions for the average Salvadoran, and fending off the challenge from the Marxist left. Realistically, the last objective was preeminent and encompassed the other three. Lesser influence was exerted on the deputies by popular opinion and demonstrations of support for specific reforms. For example, campesino groups staged rallies outside the Constituent Assembly's chambers to press their demand for continuation of the agrarian reform decrees.

The actual drafting of the constitution was delegated by the Constituent Assembly to a special commission composed of representatives of all the major political parties. The assembly agreed to reinstate the 1962 constitution with only a few exclusions until a constitution was produced and approved. At the same time, the deputies voted to affirm the validity of the decrees issued by the junta governments, including those that enacted agrarian, banking, and foreign commerce reforms. Having reestablished a working legal framework, the assembly voted itself the power to act as a legislature through the passage of constituent decrees.

Since it could not serve as both the legislative and the executive branch, the Constituent Assembly was required to approve the appointment of a provisional president. Many observers believed that Arena leader Roberto D'Aubuisson Arrieta, who was elected president of the assembly on April 22, 1982, was the most likely candidate. D'Aubuisson's reputed ties with the violent right wing, however, militated against him. It was reported that the United States and the Salvadoran High Command lobbied persuasively against D'Aubuisson's appointment, mainly on the grounds that his negative image outside El Salvador would complicate, if not preclude, the provision of substantial aid from Washington. Apparently swayed by this argument, the members of the Constituent Assembly appointed Alvaro Magaña Borja, a political moderate with ties to the military, to the post on April 26. In an effort to maintain a political equilibrium, Magaña's cabinet included members of all three major parties—Arena, the PDC, and the PCN.

Despite its defeat on the issue of the provisional presidency, Arena continued to hold the balance of power in El Salvador through its leadership of the conservative majority in the Constituent Assembly. The *areneros* (members or adherents of Arena) vented their

147

frustration with the political process primarily in the area of agrarian reform. In May 1982, Magaña proposed a partial suspension of Phase III of the reform, the Land to the Tiller program, for the 1982–83 harvest season in order to avoid agricultural losses occasioned by the transfer of land titles (see Agrarian Reform, ch. 2). The Arena-led coalition in the assembly seized on this proposal and expanded it to include some 95 percent of Phase III landholdings. This action was interpreted by interested parties both in El Salvador and abroad as a bid by the right to eliminate agrarian reform and to encourage the eviction of land recipients, a process that was ongoing at the time, although its extent was difficult to quantify; it led directly to a limitation by the Senate Foreign Relations Committee of the United States Congress on military and Economic Support Funds (ESF) aid to El Salvador. Although Arena's most important domestic constituency—the economic elite—continued to advocate the limitation if not the elimination of agrarian reform, it was clear that such efforts in the Constituent Assembly would have negative repercussions. The failure of Arena's leadership to take this fact into account and its seeming inability—or unwillingness—to seek compromise and accommodation on this and other issues contributed to its eventual loss of influence among center-right assembly delegates and the military leadership.

In August 1982, in an effort to bring the *areneros* under control and to prevent them from sabotaging not only the reforms but perhaps the entire fledgling democratic system, Magaña, apparently at the strong urging of the military chiefs and the United States, brought together representatives of Arena, the PDC, and the PCN to negotiate a "basic platform of government." In what became known as the Pact of Apaneca, the parties agreed on certain broad principles in the areas of democratization, the protection of human rights, the promotion of economic development, the preservation of economic and social reforms, and the protection of the country's security in the face of the violent conflict with leftist insurgent forces. Organizationally, the pact established three commissions: the Political Commission to work out a timetable and guidelines for future elections, the Human Rights Commission to oversee and promote improvements in that area, and the Peace Commission to explore possible resolutions of the civil conflict. The guidelines established by the pact eased the chaotic governmental situation to some degree; they were also significant in that they brought Arena into a formal governmental association with more moderate actors, such as the PDC, and committed the *areneros,* at least in principle, to the preservation of some degree of reform.

The pact did not put an end to infighting among the political parties, however. Magaña, lacking a political power base or constituency beyond the good will of the military, found it frustrating to try to exert authority over his cabinet ministers, particularly those drawn from the ranks of Arena. This conflict came to a head in December 1982, when Magaña dismissed his health minister, an *arenero,* for refusing to comply with the president's directives. Arena party leadership advised the minister to reject the president's action and to retain his post. This proved to be a miscalculation on the part of Arena, as Magaña went on to have the dismissal approved by a majority of the Constituent Assembly. Again in this instance, the behind-the-scenes support of the military worked in favor of the provisional president and against Arena.

The damage done to Arena's prestige by the dismissal of the health minister was compounded by the party's efforts to influence the appointment of his successor. Magaña proposed a member of the small, moderate AD for the post. The *areneros,* particularly Constituent Assembly president D'Aubuisson, saw this (not without justification) as an effort to diminish their influence in the government and sought to defeat the appointment through parliamentary maneuvering. They succeeded only in delaying approval, however. Furthermore, after the vote the assembly amended its procedures to limit the power of the assembly president.

Arena was not the only party to see its standing diminish after the signing of the Pact of Apaneca. The PCN delegation in the Constituent Assembly suffered a rupture immediately after the signing of the pact, as nine conservative deputies split from the party to establish a bloc they dubbed the Salvadoran Authentic Institutional Party (Partido Auténtico Institucional Salvadoreño—PAISA). This move left the assembly more or less evenly split between conservative and centrist deputies.

The special commission charged with drafting the constitution finished its work in June 1983. At that time, it reported that it had reached agreement in almost all respects. Two major exceptions, however, were agrarian reform and the schedule and procedure for presidential elections. These issues were left to the Constituent Assembly to resolve.

Of all the constitutional provisions debated in the Constituent Assembly, those dealing with agrarian reform were the most contentious. In light of the decline in the Arena coalition's standing and influence and the corresponding gains of the PDC and its moderate allies, eliminating the reforms altogether was ruled out. The conservatives retained enough clout, however, to limit the provisions of the original decrees. Their major victory in this regard was the raising of the maximum allowable landholding under Phase II of the reform from 100 to 245 hectares, an action that addressed the concerns of some well-to-do landowners but that put a crimp in redistribution efforts by reducing the amount of land subject to expropriation. After the 1982–83 suspension, the Constituent Assembly twice extended Phase III of the reform; the government accepted applications for title under this phase until July 1984.

Aside from the sections dealing with agrarian reform, the draft constitution was approved by the Constituent Assembly without an excess of debate. One exception was the article dealing with the death penalty. The version finally approved by the assembly endorsed capital punishment only in cases covered by military law when the country was in a state of declared war. These restrictions effectively eliminated the death penalty from the Salvadoran criminal justice system. Consideration of the draft document by the full Constituent Assembly began in August 1983; the final version was approved by that body in December. The effective date of the Constitution was December 20, 1983. The Constituent Assembly, having completed its mandate, was dismissed at that point, only to be reconvened on December 22 as the Legislative Assembly. The membership of the body remained the same.

The Document

The Constitution of 1983 is in many ways quite similar to the constitution of 1962, often incorporating verbatim passages from the earlier document. Some of the provisions shared by the two charters include the establishment of a five-year presidential term with no reelection, the right of the people to resort to "insurrection" to redress a transgression of the constitutional order, the affirmation (however neglected in practice) of the apolitical nature of the Salvadoran armed forces, the support of the state for the protection and promotion of private enterprise, the recognition of the right to private property, the right of laborers to a minimum wage and a six-day work week, the right of workers to strike and of owners to a lockout, and the traditional commitment to the reestablishment of the Republic of Central America (see El Salvador and the United Provinces of Central America, ch. 1).

The Constitution consists of 11 titles, subdivided into 274 articles. Title One enumerates the rights of the individual, among them the right to free expression that "does not subvert the public order," the right of free association and peaceful assembly for any legal purpose, the legal presumption of innocence, the legal inadmissibility of forced confession, and the right to the free exercise of religion—

again, with the stipulation that such exercise remain within the bounds of "morality and public order."

Title One, however, also specifies the conditions under which constitutional guarantees may be suspended and the procedures for such suspension. The grounds for such action include war, invasion, rebellion, sedition, catastrophe (natural disasters), epidemic, or "grave disturbances of the public order." The declaration of the requisite circumstances may be issued by either the legislative or the executive branch of government. The suspension of constitutional guarantees lasts for a maximum of thirty days, at which point it may be extended for an additional thirty days by legislative decree. The declaration of suspension of guarantees grants jurisdiction over cases involving "crimes against the existence and organization of the state" to special military courts. The military courts that functioned from February 1984 until early 1987 under a suspension of guarantees (or state of siege) were commonly known as Decree 50 courts, after the legislative decree that established them.

According to the Constitution, all Salvadorans over eighteen years of age are considered citizens. As such, they have both political rights and political obligations. The rights of the citizen include the exercise of suffrage and the formation of political parties "in accordance with the law" or the right to join an existing party. The exercise of suffrage is listed as an obligation as well as a right, making voting mandatory. Failure to vote has technically been subject to a small fine, a penalty rarely invoked in practice.

Voters are required to have their names entered in the Electoral Register. Political campaigns are limited to four months preceding presidential balloting, two months before balloting for legislative representatives (deputies), and one month before municipal elections (see Political Dynamics, this ch.). Members of the clergy and active-duty military personnel are prohibited from membership in political parties and cannot run for public office. Moreover, the clergy and the military are enjoined from "carry[ing] out political propaganda in any form." Although military personnel are not denied suffrage by the Constitution, the armed forces' leadership routinely instructed its personnel to refrain from voting in order to concentrate on providing security for polling places.

Title Five defines the outlines of the country's "Economic Order." As noted, private enterprise and private property are guaranteed. The latter is recognized as a "social function," a phrase that may function as a loophole for the potential expropriation of unproductive land or other holdings. Individual landowners are limited to holdings of no more than 245 hectares but may dispose of their holdings as they see fit. The expropriation of land may be undertaken for the public benefit in the "social interest" through legal channels and with fair compensation.

Amendment of the Constitution is not a simple procedure. Initial approval of an amendment (or "reform") requires only a majority vote in the Legislative Assembly. Before the amendment can be incorporated, however, it must be ratified by a two-thirds vote in the next elected assembly. Since legislative deputies serve three-year terms, an amendment could take that long or longer to win passage into law.

Governmental Institutions

The Constitution of 1983 affirms the Salvadoran government as republican, democratic, and representative, as had the constitution of 1962. The government is divided into executive, legislative, and judicial branches. The military, although not a constitutional branch of government per se, exerts considerable influence over the country's governance and serves as the most immediate representative of the government for many Salvadorans, particularly those in rural areas and in the zones most affected by the insurgency.

The Executive

The executive branch is made up of the president of the republic, the vice president, ministers and vice ministers of state, and their subordinate officials (see fig. 8). The president must be Salvadoran by birth, over thirty years of age, of good character, and a member of a legally recognized political party. The president is elected by direct popular vote, serves a five-year term, and may not run for reelection. Several categories of individuals are proscribed from seeking the office of president: anyone who has held the office of president for more than six months prior to the beginning of a presidential term; the spouse or relatives to the fourth degree of consanguinity of said officeholder; anyone who had held the office of president of the Legislative Assembly or president of the Supreme Court of Justice for one year prior to the beginning of a presidential term; anyone who has held the post of minister, vice minister, or head of an official autonomous institution for the same one-year period; or any professional member of the military who is or has been on active duty during a three-year period prior to the beginning of a term. The same restrictions apply to those holding the offices of vice president or *designado* (the two individuals designated by the legislature as next in line after the vice president for presidential succession).

The powers of the president are circumscribed to some extent by the Constitution. The president requires the approval of the Legislative Assembly in order to leave the country. He is required to report to the assembly upon request on any subject except secret military strategy. In addition, the president can be declared physically or mentally incapacitated by a two-thirds vote of the assembly.

The president is charged with the ''direction of foreign relations'' and is designated the commander in chief of the armed forces. He is required to report to the Legislative Assembly within the first two months of each year on developments within the country and the government during the course of the previous calendar year (the Salvadoran ''state of the union'' address).

Ministers and vice ministers are named and removed by the president. They are required to be Salvadoran by birth and over twenty-five years of age. Together with the president and vice president, the Council of Ministers (or cabinet) produces the government plan—the projected requirements of the government for the coming year—and proposes a budget to the assembly at least three months before the beginning of the fiscal year.

The Legislature

The legislature is a unicameral body known as the Legislative Assembly. Its members are referred to as deputies (*diputados*). They are elected every three years according to a system of proportional representation. The assembly elected in March 1988 was composed of sixty deputies and sixty alternates (*suplentes*).

There is no restriction on the reelection of deputies. To serve in this capacity, however, one must be a Salvadoran by birth and over twenty-one years of age. Those prohibited from seeking election to the assembly include the president and vice president of the republic, government ministers and vice ministers, active-duty military personnel, and relatives of the president within the fourth level of consanguinity or the second level of affinity. Elected deputies, however, may serve as ministers or vice ministers, heads of official autonomous institutions, or chiefs of diplomatic missions. Such individuals do not participate in the business of the assembly but may be reintegrated into that body at the conclusion of their service in such a post.

The powers of the Legislative Assembly are considerable. It is the body that determines the statutory laws of El Salvador. It has the power to levy taxes, to ratify or reject treaties negotiated by the executive branch with foreign governments or international organizations, and to regulate the civil service. The assembly also wields the power of the purse as the body that approves the national

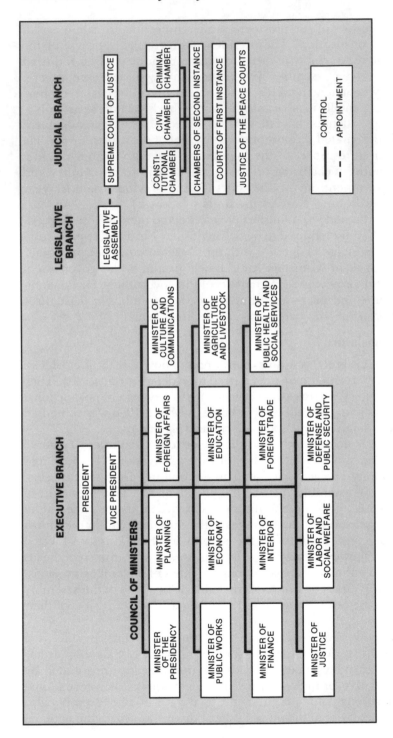

Figure 8. Organization of the Government, 1988

budget in its final form. Perhaps just as important in a political sense is the assembly's power to place individuals, through a majority vote, in the following posts: president (chief justice) and magistrates of the Supreme Court, president of the Central Electoral Council, president and magistrates of an independent government auditing body known as the Court of Accounts (Corte de Cuentas), the attorney general, and the procurator general. By naming to these positions members of parties or factions opposed to the president, the Legislative Assembly can (and has, in some instances) impede the workings of government to a significant degree. The assembly also has the power to declare war, ratify peace treaties, and grant amnesty for political offenses or common crimes.

Legislation may be introduced not only by deputies but also by the president, by way of his ministers; the Supreme Court, in the case of laws pertaining to the judiciary; and local municipal councils, with regard to municipal taxation. A presidential veto of a law passed by the Legislative Assembly may be overridden by a two-thirds vote of that body. The executive may raise objections to a law on constitutional grounds; in such a case, the Supreme Court serves as the arbiter. If a law submitted to the Supreme Court by the president is ruled to be constitutional, the president is compelled to sign it into law.

The Judiciary

The judicial branch of government is headed by the Supreme Court of Justice. The number of magistrates on the Supreme Court is not stipulated in the Constitution but is determined by other statutes. Magistrates are required to be Salvadoran by birth, more than forty years of age, and lawyers who have practiced for at least ten years or who have served as judges in a chamber of second instance for six years or on a court of first instance for nine years. Clergymen are prohibited from serving as magistrates. The president of the Supreme Court directs the business of the Supreme Court and functions as the head of the judicial branch. Magistrates are appointed by the Legislative Assembly to five-year terms.

The Supreme Court is divided into three chambers, or *salas*. The Constitutional Chamber (Sala de lo Constitucional), composed of the Supreme Court president and four other magistrates, rules on the constitutionality of laws and hears cases involving the invocation of *amparo* (restraint against the infringement of an individual's rights) or of habeas corpus. The remaining chambers of the Supreme Court, the Civil Chamber and the Criminal Chamber, serve as the last level of appeal in these legal categories.

155

Below the Supreme Court are the chambers of second instance, or courts of appeal. Each chamber is composed of two magistrates, who hear appeals of decisions handed down in the courts of first instance. There were fourteen chambers of second instance in 1986. The courts of first instance hear both civil and criminal cases; there were some eighty-seven such courts in 1986. The broadest level of the legal system is the justice of the peace courts. Numbering approximately 193 in 1986 and located throughout the country, the justice of the peace courts decide only cases involving misdemeanors and minor civil suits.

The Military

The constitutional role of the Salvadoran armed forces is spelled out in Title Six, Chapter Eight of the Constitution. The military is charged with maintaining a representative democratic form of government, enforcing the no-reelection provision for the country's president, guaranteeing freedom of suffrage, and respecting human rights. The armed forces as an institution is defined as "essentially apolitical" and obedient to established civilian authority.

It should be borne in mind that such documents tend to reflect ideals and goals for conduct, not the prevailing state of affairs at the time of their drafting. In the late 1980s, the Salvadoran armed forces was an evolving institution attempting to deal simultaneously with a left-wing insurgency and the institutionalization of a democratic form of government while also seeking to deflect what it perceived as threats to its internal cohesion. One such threat was the potential investigation and possible prosecution of officers on human rights charges, many of them connected with the prosecution of the war against the guerrillas, although such action was rendered less likely by the amnesty approved by the Legislative Assembly in 1987 as well as by the political ascendancy of Arena (see The Criminal Justice System, ch. 5). Given its history, the heightened importance of its role in dealing with the insurgents, and its interest in preserving its institutional integrity, the Salvadoran military certainly exerted political influence, particularly in areas of policy directly related to national security. Indeed, the armed forces was expected by all political actors in the country to play a role in the country's affairs, and its power and influence were accepted by all those participating in the democratic system.

Since the political influence of the armed forces, usually exerted through the High Command, was exercised largely behind the scenes, it was in many ways difficult to measure. There were indications, however, that the military was attempting to cooperate

Government office buildings at Government Center, San Salvador

with civilian democratic leaders. The minister of defense and public
security, General Carlos Eugenio Vides Casanova, accompanied
President José Napoleón Duarte Fuentes to the October 1984 meeting with representatives of the FMLN–FDR in La Palma (see Left-
Wing Extremism, ch. 5). General Vides also appeared before the
Legislative Assembly a number of times at the request of that body
to testify on military issues. Both the air force, by restricting aerial
bombing, and the security forces, by showing restraint in dealing
with radical demonstrators in San Salvador, followed directives laid
down by the president (see The Military under Democratic Rule,
1984–88, ch. 5). Perhaps the best evidence of military restraint
under the emerging democratic system was the fact that, as of late
1988, the High Command had made no move to overthrow the
existing government by force, despite several reported appeals from
Salvadoran political factions to do so.

Another important development with regard to the military's
political role concerned its relationship with other actors, particularly the elite and the political parties. By supporting a government headed by a Christian democratic president and assisting in
the implementation of agrarian reform measures, the armed forces
demonstrated in the 1980s that their previous ties with the elite,
particularly the agrarian elite, no longer compelled them to resist
almost every form of social and political change. The dissociation
by the military from direct institutional support of any political

157

party—in contrast to its virtual control of the PCN during the 1960s and 1970s—also enhanced the armed forces' political independence.

Local Government

El Salvador is divided into fourteen administrative divisions called departments, the equivalent of states in the United States (see fig. 1). Each department is administered by a governor appointed by the president. An alternate for each governor is also designated. Governors must be Salvadoran by birth, over twenty-five years of age, and residents of their department for at least two years prior to their appointment.

Below the departmental level, El Salvador is divided into 261 municipalities (or *municipios,* the equivalent of counties in the United States). Each *municipio* is governed by a municipal council composed of a mayor (*alcalde*), a legal representative (*síndico*), and two or more council members (*regidores*). The number of *regidores* is determined by the population of the *municipio.* Members of the municipal councils must be more than twenty-one years of age and residents of the *municipio* in which they serve. Directly elected, municipal officials serve three-year terms and may be reelected. *Municipios* are not all of equal size but are required to have a population of at least 10,000; municipal boundaries are determined by the Legislative Assembly.

The powers of local government are circumscribed by those of the central government. Because department governers are appointed by the president, their independence is questionable. Despite their status as elected representatives, the powers of municipal officeholders are also limited in certain key areas. The most glaring example is taxation. Although the municipal councils are allowed to suggest local taxes and tax rates, only the Legislative Assembly has the power to actually levy taxes. Therefore, all funds utilized by the councils are appropriated and disbursed by the assembly, although such funds are earmarked in the budget and are not incorporated into the central government's general fund. Among the duties relegated to the municipal councils under the Salvadoran Municipal Code are the holding of town meetings (*cabildos abiertos*) at least once every three months. The council is enjoined from acting against the majority opinion expressed at the *cabildos abiertos.* The municipal councils also grant legal recognition (*personalidad jurídica*) to communal associations in their *municipios.* The councils are required to meet periodically with representatives of the communal associations and to consult with them on the appointment of representatives to advisory and other local commissions. The councils also issue local ordinances and regulations.

Political Dynamics

Electoral Procedures

Electoral procedures in El Salvador are governed by the Electoral Code, which was updated by the Legislative Assembly in January 1988. The system it established is in some ways cumbersome and open to abuse but adheres closely to electoral procedures followed in most Latin American countries.

The organization in charge of administering electoral procedures is the Central Electoral Council (Consejo Central de Elecciones), which consists of three members and three alternates elected for five-year terms by the Legislative Assembly. Nominees for the council are drawn from the ranks of the leading political parties or coalitions, as determined by the vote totals in the most recent presidential elections. The president of the Central Electoral Council serves as the chief administrator and the ultimate authority on questions of electoral procedures.

In order to cast their votes, all citizens are required to obtain from the Central Electoral Council an electoral identification card (*carnet electoral*) certifying their inscription in the national Electoral Register. The *carnet electoral* is presented at the individual's polling place and is the only form of identification accepted for this purpose. The card must bear the voter's photograph, signature (if literate), and right thumbprint. The *carnet electoral* is valid for five years from the date of issue.

The issuing of *carnets electorales* and the related maintenance of the Electoral Register are the most cumbersome aspects of the electoral system, particularly in rural areas where voters' access to their municipal electoral boards frequently is impeded by poor transportation and the effects of the insurgent war. Rural voter registration has also been hampered by direct and indirect coercion by the guerrilla forces, who have described national elections as a sham and a component of a United States-designed counterinsurgency strategy. These and other factors, including a general disenchantment with the electoral process based in large part on the failure of the government to end the insurgency and improve economic conditions, contributed to a gradual decline in voter turnout during the 1982–88 period. Whereas some 80 percent of the electorate turned out for the Constituent Assembly balloting in 1982, only an estimated 65 percent voted in the first round of presidential balloting in March 1984. This was followed by turnouts of

159

approximately 66 and 60 percent in the 1985 and 1988 legislative and municipal elections, respectively.

The Central Electoral Council, in coordination with its departmental and municipal electoral boards, determines the number and location of polling places. This process is to be completed at least fifteen days prior to balloting. Although the Electoral Register and final vote tallies are processed at least partially by computer, paper ballots are utilized at the polling places. Ballots are deposited in clear plastic receptacles to reduce the possibility of fraud. All political parties are entitled to station a poll watcher at each balloting site to reduce further the opportunity for vote manipulation.

Polling places are open from 7:00 A.M. until 5:00 P.M., at which time the officials at each site begin the preparation of an official record of the results. This record includes a preliminary vote count by party, an inventory of ballots issued to the polling place (the discrepancy between ballots issued and ballots used is not to exceed 300), and accounts of challenges received and any unusual incidents or occurrences during the course of the voting. Poll watchers scrutinize the record's preparation and are entitled to a copy of the final product. As a result, political parties frequently are able to issue preliminary electoral results well in advance of the official tally.

These records from the polling places are forwarded to the local municipal electoral board, where a record for the entire *municipio* is prepared. The municipal voting records are conveyed to the Central Electoral Council by way of the departmental electoral boards. The council conducts the final scrutiny of the records; this process must be undertaken no later than forty-eight hours after the closing of the polls. Copies of voting records are also provided to the office of the attorney general as a further safeguard against tampering.

In the case of presidential elections, the Central Electoral Council can declare a winner only if one ticket receives an absolute majority of all votes cast. If no one party or coalition receives such a majority, as happened in the March 1984 elections, the council is required to schedule within thirty days a runoff election between the two leading vote-getters. The declaration of winners in legislative balloting is less direct; here, voters cast their ballots for parties more than for individuals, since seats in the Legislative Assembly are allotted to registered candidates roughly on a proportional basis according to the departmental vote totals of their party or coalition. Municipal elections are more straightforward, with the winners decided according to their showing in the municipal vote tallies.

Voters in line at a polling place
Courtesy United States Department of Defense

The protracted insurgent war exerted pressure on the government to adjust its electoral procedures. In areas where guerrilla control prevented the establishment of polling places, voters were urged to cast their ballots at the nearest secure location. Some polling places in departmental capitals were required to have on hand electoral records for rural voters who had relocated from war zones. In some towns, so-called national polling stations were set up to accommodate displaced voters from other departments. These stations were required to have on hand electoral registration data for the entire country. Guerrilla-engineered transportation stoppages, attacks on public buildings, and sabotage of the electrical system impeded voting as well, especially in rural areas. Indeed, many of these actions were undertaken with the specific intention of deterring voters from participation.

In addition to overseeing elections, the Central Electoral Council is also charged with the official recognition of political parties. Initial petitions to the council for the formation of a party require the support of at least 100 citizens. This group then is granted sixty days to secure the signatures of at least 3,000 citizens and submit them to the council. If all the signatures are verified, the party is then granted legal recognition, referred to as inscription (*inscripción*). The party's inscription can be revoked if it fails to receive at least 0.5 percent of the total national vote cast in a presidential

161

or legislative election, or if the party fails to participate in two consecutive elections. Parties are allowed to form coalitions at the national, departmental, or municipal levels without forfeiting their separate inscriptions.

Political campaigns are underwritten to some extent by the state through the provision for "political debt." The Electoral Code stipulates that each party can expect to receive reimbursement according to the following formula: ¢10 (for value of colón—see Glossary) for each valid vote cast for the party in the first round of a presidential election, ¢6 for each vote in legislative elections, and ¢4 for each vote in municipal elections. All parties are eligible for payment, regardless of their showing at the polls.

The Electoral Process

From March 1982 to March 1988, Salvadorans went to the polls five times to cast their ballots for members of the Constituent Assembly (later converted to the Legislative Assembly), the president, deputies of the Legislative Assembly, and municipal officials. This flurry of electoral activity was occasioned by the transition to a functional representative system of government, a decidedly new experience for Salvadorans.

The first round of the 1984 presidential election was held on March 25. Some 1.4 million Salvadorans went to the polls. Although eight candidates competed, most voters cast their ballots for the representative of one of the three leading parties, the PDC's Duarte, Arena's D'Aubuisson, or the PCN's Francisco José Guerrero Cienfuegos. The results were not immediately decisive. Duarte received 43 percent of the vote, D'Aubuisson 30 percent, and Guerrero 19. This necessitated a runoff election on May 6 between Duarte and D'Aubuisson. Despite entreaties from Arena, Guerrero declined to endorse either candidate. It is doubtful that his endorsement would have made much difference in the balloting, given Duarte's relative popularity and D'Aubuisson's reputed connections with right-wing violence and the disapproval of his candidacy by the United States government. It was reported in the United States press after the election that the United States Central Intelligence Agency had funneled some US$2 million in covert campaign aid to the PDC. Nevertheless, the results of the runoff were surprisingly close, with Duarte garnering 54 percent to D'Aubuisson's 46 percent. Some observers criticized the presidential election on the grounds that it excluded parties of the left, such as those represented by the FDR. Political conditions at that time, however, were not favorable to participation by such groups. If nothing else, the inability of the government to provide for the physical security of leftist candidates militated against their inclusion in the electoral process.

The 1985 legislative and municipal elections were carried overwhelmingly by the PDC. The party achieved an outright majority in the Legislative Assembly, increasing its representation from twenty-four to thirty-three seats, and carried over 200 of the country's municipal councils. Arena and the PCN joined as a two-party coalition for these elections in an effort to secure a conservative majority in the assembly. The terms of the coalition, whereby Arena agreed to split evenly the total number of seats won, resulted in a political embarrassment for D'Aubuisson's party, which took 29 percent of the total vote but was awarded only one more seat (thirteen to twelve) than the PCN, which had drawn only 8 percent of the vote. PAISA and AD also won one seat apiece.

The style of Salvadoran political campaigning bore little resemblance to that of the United States and other institutionalized democracies. Personal verbal attacks between competing candidates and parties predominated in the media, in campaign literature, and at public rallies. Debate on specific issues was largely eschewed in favor of emotional appeals to the electorate. It was therefore not uncommon to hear candidates and leaders of the PDC refer to Arena as a "Nazi-fascist party," whereas *areneros* openly denounced Christian Democrats as "communists." One of Arena leader D'Aubuisson's favorite campaign embellishments was to slash open a watermelon with a machete; the watermelon, he told the crowds, was like the PDC—green (the party color) on the outside but red on the inside. This dramatic, personalistic type of appeal highlighted the lack of institutionalization of the Salvadoran democratic system, the intensity of emotion elicited by the political process, and the polarizing effect of the ongoing struggle between the government and leftist insurgent forces. Observers reported, however, that Arena spokesmen toned down their appeals during the 1988 legislative and municipal elections in an effort to project a moderate, responsible image.

Political Parties

By 1988 El Salvador had a number of registered political parties participating in the democratic process. Only three, however, had significant followings: the PDC, Arena, and the PCN.

Christian Democratic Party

The ideological position of the Christian Democratic Party (Partido Demócrata Cristiano—PDC) was more liberal than that of most Christian democratic parties elsewhere in Latin America or in Western Europe. In the Salvadoran context, taking into account the existence of radical leftist groups such as those constituting the FMLN–FDR, the PDC could be characterized as a party of the center-left. The party was born out of the frustration of urban middle-class professionals who felt themselves excluded from the political process in El Salvador (see The Christian Democrats: A Centrist Alternative? ch. 1). From its founding in 1960 until the early 1980s, the party and its leaders showed considerable tenacity and staying power in the face of right-wing repression, the adamant refusal of the economic and political elite (with the backing of the military) to allow broad-based popular participation in government, and the eventual defection of some of its members to the radical left, in the form of the FDR. The year 1979 was a turning point for the Christian Democrats, as it was for the country as a whole. Party leaders' participation in the junta governments established after the reformist coup gave them an opportunity to organize and prepare to participate in the democratic process initiated in 1982. Their involvement also attracted the support of the United States. Despite its failure to win a majority of the seats in the 1982 balloting for the Constituent Assembly, the PDC nonetheless emerged from that election as the leading political party in the country, a position it went on to demonstrate in the 1984 and 1985 elections.

The PDC reached the peak of its power after the 1985 elections. At that point, Duarte was still a popular figure. The party's absolute majority in the legislature was seen by him and his fellow Christian Democrats as a mandate for the continuation and extension of reforms. The opposition was weakened and divided. Resentment among the *areneros* over their unsuccessful coalition with the PCN provoked a rupture between the two conservative parties. Subsequently, the PCN became more supportive of the PDC and its political program.

Duarte and his party used their control of the executive and legislative branches to further the agrarian reform program first established by decree in 1980, to draft a new Electoral Code, to approve an amnesty for political prisoners, and to pass additional economic reform measures. The momentum that had seemed so compelling in the wake of the March elections, however, was eroded by events and was eventually lost in the tumult of politics and insurgency. Perhaps the first of the blows to the PDC's position was the kidnapping of the president's daughter, Inés Guadalupe Duarte Durán, in September 1985. This incident preoccupied Duarte personally, so that his support within the armed forces weakened, and a leadership vacuum developed in both the government and the PDC (see Left-Wing Extremism, ch. 5).

Another major dilemma for the PDC government was the direction of a war-ravaged economy. Although it could be justified on an economic basis, Duarte's 1986 package of austerity measures drew political fire from most major interest groups (see Interest Groups, this ch.; Role of Government, ch. 3). The associated currency devaluation, always a controversial step, was especially unpopular. The impression that the president implemented the austerity measures largely in response to pressure from the United States also did little to enhance his prestige or that of the party.

For most Salvadorans, the civil conflict and its attendant violence were the problems of uppermost concern, especially insofar as pocketbook issues such as inflation, standard of living, and employment were seen as closely related to the war against the leftist guerrillas. Duarte's personal popularity was boosted after the October 1984 meeting in La Palma with representatives of the FMLN–FDR; a war-weary population began to believe that a resolution to the conflict might be in sight. These optimistic expectations, however, were dampened considerably as the negotiating process bogged down and stalled. The kidnapping of Duarte's daughter further hardened the president's attitude and rendered the prospect of a negotiated settlement during his administration highly unlikely. Although the majority of Salvadorans had little sympathy for the FMLN, Duarte's failure to achieve peace nonetheless undermined his popularity and diminished the public perception of the PDC as a viable mediator between the extremes of left and right.

Another issue that tarnished the reputation of the PDC was corruption. Rumors and allegations that had become common in El Salvador came to a head in March 1988 with the publication of an article in the *New York Times* indicating that as much as US$2 million in United States economic aid might have been embezzled. One of the individuals named in the article was an associate of Alejandro Duarte, the president's son. Although the president himself was never linked with corrupt practices of any kind, the apparent failure of other members of the PDC to resist the temptations of office was a blow to the image of a party that had throughout its history protested and decried the abuses of power perpetrated under previous governments.

The post-1985 decline in the fortunes of the PDC government closely paralleled a general popular disillusionment with the democratic process. By 1987 polls conducted by the Central American University José Simeón Cañas showed that slightly over three-quarters of the electorate felt that no existing political party represented their interests. Of those respondents who did express a party preference, only 6 percent identified with the PDC and 10 percent with Arena.

Given the lack of clearly demonstrable progress in the economic, political, and security spheres, most observers correctly predicted that the PDC would lose its legislative majority in the March 1988 elections. The scale of that loss, however, was greater than most had anticipated. The final official vote count yielded thirty Legislative Assembly seats for Arena, twenty-three for the PDC, and seven for the PCN. Arena's leaders initially protested the results, claiming that they had captured at least thirty-one seats and thus a majority in the legislature. The protest was rendered academic in May 1988, when a PCN deputy switched his party allegiance to Arena. A September 1988 ruling by the Supreme Court awarded the contested seat to Arena, raising its majority to thirty-two. In a stunning turnaround, the Christian Democrats had dropped eleven seats in the assembly and lost more than 200 municipal races to Arena. A particularly sharp blow to PDC pride was the loss of the mayoralty of San Salvador, a post the party had held continuously since Duarte's election as mayor in 1964. Ironically, Duarte's son Alejandro was the PDC candidate who was forced to concede defeat to the Arena candidate, Armando Calderón Sol.

The internal cohesion of the party had begun to erode well before the 1988 elections. While Duarte was struggling to deal with affairs of state, his own party was polarizing into two personalistic, competitive factions. One of these factions was led by Julio Adolfo Rey Prendes, a longtime party member and associate of Duarte's. The other faction supported Fidel Chávez Mena, a younger technocrat who had disrupted a seemingly harmonious and supportive relationship with Duarte by opposing him for the 1984 presidential nomination. Rey Prendes's faction was commonly known as "the Ring" (La Argolla) or "the Mafia." The latter designation, used by members of the faction themselves, perhaps reflected Rey Prendes's reputation as a backroom political wheeler-dealer. Chávez's followers were referred to as *institucionalistas* or simply as *chavistas*.

Through his accumulated power within the party, Rey Prendes was able to influence the nomination of PDC legislative candidates in the 1988 elections. These deputies served as his political power base. The *chavistas*, although frozen out of the nominations to the Legislative Assembly, rallied to have their man nominated for president at a party convention in June 1988, but only after an earlier convention dominated by members of the Rey Prendes faction was ruled invalid by the Central Electoral Council. Not surprisingly, the earlier convention had nominated Rey Prendes as the party's standard bearer.

Judging by his public inaction in the matter, Duarte awoke fairly late to the trouble in his own party. In an effort to settle the conflict between the two contentious factions, the president proposed in April 1988 that both Rey Prendes and Chávez renounce their campaigns for the presidency in favor of a unity candidate, Abraham Rodríguez. Rodríguez was a founding member of the PDC who had run unsuccessfully for president in 1967. The fact that Duarte's attempt at reconciliation was rejected immediately by both factional leaders demonstrated the president's diminished status and authority among the party's ranks.

The decline in the fortunes of the PDC was tragically and almost symbolically accentuated by the announcement in June 1988 that President Duarte was suffering from terminal liver cancer. The illness might have explained to some extent Duarte's faltering leadership of both the government and his party. In any case, the announcement seemed to punctuate the end of an era in Salvadoran politics.

Nationalist Republican Alliance

The nature of the Nationalist Republican Alliance (Alianza Republicana Nacionalista—Arena) as a political force in El Salvador was the object of some debate as it moved toward becoming a ruling party with its 1988 electoral victory. Some observers characterized Arena as the institutional representative of the "disloyal right," meaning those conservative forces that played the game of democracy while privately harboring preferences for authoritarian or even dictatorial rule and a restoration of the absolute political preeminence of the elite. Others felt that after a rocky beginning, Arena had moderated and extended its ideology beyond simplistic, reflexive anticommunism and was ready to assume the role of a conservative party that would support private enterprise and be willing to accept some economic reforms in response to popular demands.

The fortunes of Arena, like those of the PDC, were cyclical in nature. Although the 1982 Constituent Assembly elections yielded the party a leading role in that body, subsequent elections appeared to reflect a growing public rejection of the extremist image of Arena and its leader, D'Aubuisson. The nadir of the party's influence was reached after the 1985 elections and the unsuccessful coalition with the PCN. Much of the blame for the party's electoral defeats fell on the shoulders of D'Aubuisson. In an effort to moderate the party's image, D'Aubuisson was persuaded to step down as party president in October 1985. He was replaced by Alfredo Cristiani Burkard, a member of a prominent coffee-growing family. Although Cristiani, who in May 1988 was designated the party's 1989 presidential nominee, subsequently went on to project a less hyperbolic public image for the party, D'Aubuisson was nevertheless retained as an "honorary president for life," and he continued to serve as a charismatic drawing card at public rallies and as a party spokesman in the media. San Salvador mayor Calderón Sol also emerged from the 1988 elections as a leading figure in the party.

Arena's journey from obstructionist opposition to apparent majority status was attributable to a number of factors. With its support from private enterprise and large agricultural interests, Arena enjoyed a distinct advantage in funding over its rivals. Along with superior liquidity came superior organizational and propaganda capabilities. Although its elitist supporters were the most influential, Arena's base of support also incorporated significant numbers of rural peasants and, particularly in the March 1988 elections, the urban poor. The party consistently drew some 40 percent of the peasant vote, reflecting the basic conservatism of this voting bloc as well as the ingrained appeal of strong caudillo leadership and a visceral response to the party's promises to prosecute more forcefully the war against the guerrillas. Arena also benefited from the intractable nature of the country's problems and the PDC's apparent inability to cope successfully with the challenge of governing a country torn by violence and instability.

Arena also reportedly counted a significant percentage of the military officer corps as sympathizers with its views, particularly the party's call for a more vigorous prosecution of the counterinsurgent war. D'Aubuisson, a 1963 graduate of the Captain General Gerardo Barrios Military Academy, apparently maintained contacts not only with members of his graduating class (*tanda*) but also with conservative junior officers. It was reported by some observers that D'Aubuisson's behind-the-scenes appeals from 1984 to 1988 were intended to foment a rightist coup d'état against the PDC government. After the party's March 1988 electoral victory, such a drastic method of taking power appeared to be ruled out by Arena's seemingly bright prospects in the 1989 presidential race.

Although Arena's surprisingly strong showing in the 1988 elections was to a great extent a rejection of the PDC, it also seemed to reflect a hardening of public attitudes, particularly with regard to the conflict between the government and the leftist guerrillas. Whereas Duarte and his party had drawn support among the electorate at least in part by promising to end the fighting through negotiations, Arena suggested that the more effective approach was to step up military efforts in the field. This approach seemed to have the greatest appeal among the residents of conflict zones in the north and east of the country, where resentment of the protracted fighting ran high. Some urban middle-class voters, once strong supporters of the PDC, also reportedly responded favorably to this hard-line position.

Another aspect of Arena's appeal revolved around nationalism and rejection of foreign interference in Salvadoran affairs. Some *areneros* bitterly resented the perceived favoritism shown the PDC by the United States and blamed much of their party's misfortune from 1984 through 1988 on manipulation by the *norteamericanos*. Some party spokesmen such as Sigifredo Ochoa Pérez, a flamboyant retired army colonel elected to the Legislative Assembly in 1988, extended their criticism beyond the political sphere into the arena of military tactics, publicly criticizing the role of United States military advisers in formulating counterinsurgent strategy. Cristiani also spoke out against such United States-backed innovations as the switch to small-unit tactics and suggested that an Arena government would move to abandon them (see Left-Wing Extremism, ch. 5). The seeming inability of the armed forces to resolve the insurgency by military means appeared to sharpen the public's receptiveness to these criticisms.

The most immediate advantage gained by Arena through its control of the Legislative Assembly was its ability to dictate the appointment of candidates to important government posts, such as magistrates of the Supreme Court and the attorney general of the republic. The party's legislative agenda was uncertain in mid-1988, but it seemed to entail some tinkering with land reform provisions, such as changing the titling procedure for cooperatives; easing the tax and regulatory burden on the private sector, especially the coffee industry; restoring private banking; and, perhaps, reprivatizing the foreign trade procedures.

National Conciliation Party

The National Conciliation Party (Partido de Conciliación Nacional—PCN) was the dominant political party in El Salvador during the 1960s and 1970s, when it was closely associated with the military. Although its level of popular support was all but impossible to quantify because of institutionalized electoral fraud, the PCN had supporters among both the elite and the rural population, especially in areas where the armed forces served as the primary governmental presence. The party's showings in the 1982 Constituent Assembly elections and the first round of the 1984 presidential elections were respectable; it was Guerrero's almost

20 percent total that forced the voting to a runoff between Duarte and D'Aubuisson. From that point on, however, the PCN's support at the polls declined steadily. This appeared to be a by-product of the democratic transition in El Salvador. Under a system allowing open electoral competition, the military shifted its support to the party best positioned to ensure continued aid from the United States and to provide some measure of stability to the government. Until 1988 this party was the PDC. Deprived of its military connection, the PCN was left to fend for itself in a new and unfamiliar scheme of things. Given the polarizing tendencies of Salvadoran politics, parties without a mass base or superior organization tended to be marginalized. This clearly seemed to be the case with the PCN in the wake of the 1988 elections.

During its years in power, the PCN was a rightist party that implemented limited and controlled reform in an effort to placate nonelite sectors, such as the peasantry and the urban middle class. The image of the party, however, was tarnished severely by the harsh repression undertaken by the military and the so-called "death squads" in response to growing popular unrest in the 1970s (see The 1970s: The Road to Revolt, ch. 1). When the armed forces turned to the PDC in 1980 in an effort to lend legitimacy to the post-1979 junta governments, the separation of the PCN from the military was begun. Unfortunately for the PCN, however, the association between the two was strong in the public mind. Although this lingering perception may have helped the party among some rural voters, overall it was judged a liability by most observers. In response to this perceived image problem, the PCN in the mid-1980s was attempting to moderate its policy positions, adopt a social democratic platform, and reach out to labor and peasant groups. Any support that the PCN might pick up from these sources was expected to come at the expense of the PDC.

Left-Wing Parties

The major representative of the political left in El Salvador was the Revolutionary Democratic Front (Frente Democrático Revolucionario—FDR), a grouping of social democratic parties and the remnants of some of the "popular organizations" that led antigovernment protests in the late 1970s. Up to and including the elections of 1988, the left had been excluded from the electoral process. The most frequently cited impediment to leftist participation was right-wing violence. This was certainly a very valid consideration in the early 1980s, when the level of human rights violations was extremely high (see Right-Wing Extremism, ch. 5).

Anti-FMLN demonstration,
San Miguel
Courtesy Donald C. Keffer

By the mid-1980s, however, political violence had declined considerably, rendering the possibility of leftist participation more plausible. Such an eventuality was complicated considerably by the direct association of the FDR with the violent, rejectionist left as represented by the Farabundo Martí National Liberation Front (Frente Farabundo Martí de Liberación Nacional—FMLN). The leadership of the FMLN clung to the position that the only legitimate elections would be those undertaken after the conclusion and implementation of a power-sharing arrangement between the government and the FMLN–FDR. Participation in elections held in the absence of such an agreement only served to legitimate what the insurgent commanders described as a puppet government of the United States. This extremism and intransigence by its allies made problematic the FDR's full inclusion in the electoral process. Yet another consideration for the leftist parties was the potential for a weak showing at the polls and the loss of prestige and bargaining power that would entail.

Nevertheless, despite the numerous factors weighing against them, members of the two leading parties in the FDR coalition began to return from foreign exile to organize and possibly to compete in the 1989 presidential elections. Rubén Zamora Rivas, the leader of the Popular Social Christian Movement (Movimiento Popular Social Cristiano—MPSC), and Guillermo Manuel Ungo Revelo, head of the National Revolutionary Movement (Movimiento

Nacional Revolucionario—MNR), returned to El Salvador in November 1987. Wearing body armor beneath their suits, the two made several public appearances and were interviewed on Salvadoran radio and television stations. The groundwork for their dramatic reappearances had been established by other, less prominent members of their parties who had returned to assess the political climate prevailing under the Duarte government.

In December 1987, the MPSC and MNR announced that they were forming a political coalition that would also include the Social Democratic Party (Partido Social Demócrata—PSD), a small left-of-center party established in 1986. The new grouping was dubbed the Democratic Convergence (Convergencia Democrática—CD). Many observers felt that the CD was set up in order to contest the legislative and municipal elections of March 1988. The CD's announcement in January of that year that it would not field candidates put an end to such speculation and bought the coalition additional time to contemplate its strategy for the 1989 elections. Public statements by Ungo and Zamora shed little light on their intentions in this regard. In one such statement, Ungo denied that the CD was intended to function as an electoral coalition. Zamora adhered closely to the FMLN line in a December 1987 statement in which he advocated the creation of a "transitional government" prior to the holding of general elections. Nevertheless, in March 1988 the MPSC began the process of legal registration as a political party under the procedures established by the Electoral Code; subsequent press reports also indicated that electoral participation had been approved by the leadership of the FMLN.

Although Ungo and Zamora denied any possibility of a split between the FDR and the FMLN, there were definite signs of uneasiness between the two groups. Most of the open disagreements involved the FMLN's continued advocacy and employment of terrorism as a political instrument. The FDR leaders particularly disagreed with the kidnapping of Duarte's daughter and the June 1985 murder of thirteen people, including six United States citizens, in San Salvador. The return of MPSC and MNR members and their possible participation in the established electoral process was seen by some as another manifestation of the growing strains within the FMLN–FDR alliance.

Other Parties

The 1985 crisis within the ranks of Arena produced a splinter party that initially referred to itself as Free Fatherland (Patria Libre). It was led by D'Aubuisson's 1984 running mate, Hugo Barrera Guerrero, a prominent businessman. The early prospects for the party, which subsequently changed its name to the Liberation Party (Partido Liberación—PL), seemed promising. A number of observers felt that a center-right, probusiness party could pick up much of the support that Arena seemed to have lost in the 1984 and 1985 elections. The PL, however, was unable to compete with Arena on an organizational basis and fared poorly in the 1988 elections, coming away without a single seat in the Legislative Assembly.

There were several other small political parties that ran candidates in the 1988 elections but failed to garner any seats in the Legislative Assembly. One of these was the Salvadoran Authentic Institutional Party (Partido Auténtico Institucional Salvadoreño—PAISA), the conservative PCN splinter party. Another small conservative party was the Authentic Revolutionary Party (Partido Auténtico Revolucionario—PAR). Democratic Action (Acción Democrática—AD) was a moderate party that supported Duarte and the PDC in the 1984 elections but subsequently differed with the government's economic policies and assumed a more independent stance. Rounding out the field was the extreme right-wing Popular Orientation Party (Partido de Orientación Popular—POP).

Interest Groups

Private Enterprise

Members of the private business sector relied on a number of organizations to articulate their positions on economic and political issues. These organizations served as pressure groups, injecting themselves regularly into the political arena through criticism of government policies, the actual or threatened shutdown of business and industry, and behind-the-scenes lobbying with politicians. The leading private enterprise organizations were the National Association of Private Enterprise (Asociación Nacional de la Empresa Privada—ANEP), the Association of Salvadoran Industrialists (Asociación Salvadoreña de Industriales—ASI), the Salvadoran Chamber of Commerce and Industry (Cámara de Comercio e Industria de El Salvador), the Salvadoran Coffee Growers Association (Asociación Cafetalera de El Salvador—ACES), and the Association of Coffee Processors and Exporters (Asociación de Beneficiadores y Exportadores de Café—Abecafé). Their membership was drawn from the economic elite, and their leadership consistently advocated a reduction in government involvement in industry, the reprivatization of coffee exports and foreign trade in general, no increase in taxes on business (usually referred to as "the productive sector"), no extension of the agrarian reform, and reductions in government spending (see Role of Government, ch. 3).

173

Most economic issues usually found the private enterprise organizations aligned on one side and labor and peasant organizations on the other, with the Duarte government somewhere in between, attempting to mediate between the two blocs. This was especially true with regard to agrarian reform. The private enterprise organizations, particularly the coffee growers' associations, opposed agrarian reform from its inception in 1980. They were unable to prevent implementation, however, because of a shift in the political climate that brought too many other actors, including the PDC, the reformist military, and the United States, down on the side of some measure of reform. Denied their first preference in the matter, the private sector groups went on to advocate limitations on the terms of the reforms. These were enacted by the Constituent Assembly and incorporated into the 1983 Constitution. By the late 1980s, the line taken by the private sector reflected that espoused by Arena, namely, that the reforms should not be rescinded but should be made more efficient.

Private-enterprise organizations provided the most significant opposition to the Duarte government's 1986 economic austerity package. From the businessmen's point of view, the most offensive aspect of the package was the so-called "war tax" on all income above US$20,000 with revenues derived from the tax to be applied directly to the war effort against the leftist guerrillas. In this as in other matters, the private sector groups worked in concert with Arena. While *arenero* legislators boycotted sessions of the Legislative Assembly in an effort to deny the PDC a quorum, the private-enterprise organizations called for a shutdown of business and industry on January 22, 1987. The business strike was quite effective, closing a reported 80 percent of Salvadoran stores, factories, and professional and nonprofessional services. Although impressive, this demonstration of economic power by the private sector had no immediate effect on government policy. The issue eventually was rendered moot, however, in February 1987 when the war tax was declared unconstitutional by the Supreme Court.

The January 1987 strike was but another chapter in a long history of confrontation between the private sector and the PDC. Bitterly opposed to Duarte's election in 1984, the ASI publicly denounced Duarte and his party as adherents to the same ideology as that of the FMLN. The PDC, according to the industrialists, differed only in its "method and strategies" for achieving socialism. Although he responded to the attacks in kind during the campaign, Duarte attempted after his election to reassure business leaders that he was not antagonistic to private enterprise. The agendas of the PDC and the private sector were too divergent, however, and attitudes generally were hardened between the two as economic conditions failed to improve and the insurgency ground on interminably.

Labor and Campesino Groups

Although labor confederations have existed for decades in El Salvador, their political input has been limited by their small membership—officially, only nonagricultural workers have been allowed to organize—and by the exclusionary nature of the political system. Under military rule, the only unions with influence were those with ties to the armed forces or its associated ruling party. The political ferment that began to make itself felt in the late 1970s, however, was reflected in the labor movement. The real and pressing grievances of workers and peasants, who began to organize into unsanctioned interest groups of their own, led them to enlist in the growing number of unions affiliated with the so-called mass organizations or popular organizations. These organizations took a much more militant, antigovernment line than did the old, established labor unions. Ultimately, the leaders of the mass organizations, supportive of the revolutionary goals of the FMLN, were more concerned with the promotion of their political agenda than with the attainment of better wages and working conditions for the rank and file. By the early 1980s, strikes, demonstrations, and protests by these groups had contributed to an atmosphere of uncertainty, instability, and political polarization in El Salvador. In the violent right wing backlash that followed, members of moderate, prodemocratic, nonconfrontational unions were murdered along with the militant supporters of the mass organizations. This repression—both official and unofficial—temporarily removed labor groups as participants in the political arena. The situation began to change as democratic institutions evolved in the wake of the 1982 Constituent Assembly elections.

Duarte won the presidency with the support of a number of groups in Salvadoran society who felt that their interests could best be served by the extension of economic reform. Most of these groups—middle-class professionals, small business people, labor unions, and peasants—also believed that a just resolution to the civil conflict was a necessary prerequisite to economic reactivation. In terms of numbers, the most important of these sectors were the labor and peasant organizations. In February 1984, Duarte signed a "social pact" with the major centrist grouping, the Popular Democratic Unity (Unidad Popular Democrática—UPD). This agreement called for the full implementation of agrarian reform, government support for union rights, incorporation of union and

175

peasant leaders into the government, and continued efforts to curtail human rights violations and to end the civil conflict.

From the point of view of labor and peasant groups, the Duarte government failed to follow through on the pledges made under the social pact, and, as a result, the UPD began to unravel. In early 1984, the UPD had been the leading labor and peasant grouping in both numbers and influence. It was an umbrella group made up of the country's leading labor federation—the Federation of Unions of the Construction Industry and Kindred Activities, Transportation, and Other Activities (Federación de Sindicatos de la Industria de la Construcción, Similares, Transporte y de Otras Actividades—Fesinconstrans); its largest peasant group, the Salvadoran Communal Union (Unión Comunal Salvadoreña—UCS); and three smaller groups. In August 1984, some three months after Duarte's election, the leadership of the three smallest UPD affiliates called a press conference to denounce Duarte for his lack of compliance with the social pact. Leaders of Fesinconstrans and the UCS, who were not consulted before or included in the press conference, publicly dissociated themselves from the statements made there. This incident precipitated a political and ideological split within the labor movement that showed little sign of abating by the late 1980s.

Documents seized by government forces after a shootout with a rebel group in April 1985 shed some light on the leadership crisis within the UPD. According to the documents, three union leaders (although not named, they were presumed by most analysts to be the leaders who called the 1984 press conference) were collaborating clandestinely with the FMLN and were receiving bribes to assume a confrontational stance with the government. The coordination of actions among the FMLN, leftist unions, and certain militant human rights and refugee groups seemed to be confirmed by another cache of rebel documents seized in April 1987. Whatever the motivation, the split in the UPD leadership prompted the more moderate leadership of Fesinconstrans and the UCS to explore the possibility of establishing a new labor confederation. This organization, christened the Democratic Workers' Confederation (Confederación de Trabajadores Democráticos—CTD), was founded in December 1984. In March 1986, the CTD and the UCS joined with a number of other labor and peasant groups to form the National Union of Workers and Peasants (Unión Nacional de Obreros y Campesinos—UNOC). UNOC characterized itself as a labor organization supportive of the moderate political left; it advocated the continuation of the democratic process in El Salvador as well as the political incorporation of workers and the making of improvements in their quality of life.

The leaders of the more militant and radical labor and peasant groups almost simultaneously established a parallel umbrella group to UNOC, dubbing it the National Union of Salvadoran Workers (Unión Nacional de Trabajadores Salvadoreños—UNTS). It included the remaining members of the UPD, several established leftist labor groups, some of which maintained ties to the World Federation of Trade Unions, a front group of the Communist Party of the Soviet Union; a peasant organization known as the National Association of Peasants (Asociación Nacional de Campesinos—ANC); and a leftist student group, the General Association of Salvadoran University Students (Asociación General de Estudiantes Universitarios Salvadoreños—AGEUS). Although it claimed that its membership rivaled that of the 350,000-strong UNOC, most observers agreed that the UNTS represented only 40,000 to 50,000 members at most.

President Duarte, the armed forces, and representatives of the United States maintained that the UNTS was penetrated and controlled by the FMLN. This allegation was not universally accepted, however. Whether coordinated with FMLN strategy or not, the actions of the UNTS appeared calculated to undermine the legitimacy of the Duarte government and to promote unrest and instability in urban areas, particularly San Salvador. UNTS affiliates staged numerous strikes, mainly in the capital, most of which were declared illegal by the government because the demands of the union leadership were judged to be more political than economic in nature. Some unions demanded the president's resignation as a condition of settlement. Many of the strikes were endorsed by the FMLN over the clandestine radio station Radio Venceremos operated by the guerrilla group known as the People's Revolutionary Army (Ejército Revolucionario del Pueblo—ERP). The largest mass antigovernment demonstration organized by the UNTS took place in February 1986; estimates of the number of participants ranged from 7,000 to 12,000. A generally progovernment rally organized by UNOC the following month drew a considerably larger turnout, estimated at up to 65,000.

Although it opposed the militant strategy of the UNTS and supported the reforms decreed by the junta governments and maintained under the PDC, UNOC also displayed disillusionment with Duarte and his seeming inability to improve workers' standard of living or to wind down the insurgency. UNOC's influence, however, began to wane by 1985. This development was attributable mainly to internal leadership struggles within Fesinconstrans

177

and the UCS. Ironically, the catalyst for these conflicts was found not in the failure of the social pact with the PDC but in its partial fulfillment. Labor and peasant leaders who had been appointed to government posts, mainly in the institutions administering agrarian reform and credit facilities, were exploiting the patronage potential of their positions to expand their personal following among the rank and file. Resentment over this tactic prompted challenges from union leaders and members who either felt excluded from the patronage process or who objected to the practice on ethical grounds. UNOC's lack of concerted involvement in the PDC legislative victory of 1985 lessened its influence with the government and perhaps made it easier for Duarte to follow the course of economic austerity that eventually drew fire from both the private sector and labor groups from across the political spectrum.

Just as the UNTS represented the militant leftist position among Salvadoran labor and peasant groups and UNOC affected a more moderate, center-left stance, there were also conservative labor groups still functioning in the late 1980s. The two leading organizations in this category were the General Confederation of Unions (Confederación General de Sindicatos—CGS) and the National Confederation of Workers (Confederación Nacional de Trabajadores—CNT). Their numbers were small—CGS membership was estimated at 7,000 in 1986—and their political influence correspondingly low. By 1988, however, as Arena took control of the legislative branch and seemed poised to win the presidency, the position of these conservative labor groups may well have been enhanced, if only because moderate organizations such as UNOC were all but certain to see their leverage with the government diminish considerably. The radical UNTS, which was condemned as a rebel front group even by the Duarte administration (although it seemed clear that the majority of rank-and-file UNTS members were not FMLN sympathizers), could look forward to little or no sympathy from an Arena government.

The Roman Catholic Church

The Salvadoran Roman Catholic Church has been affected by the country's political and social turmoil. During the tenure of Monsignor Oscar Arnulfo Romero y Galdámez as archbishop of San Salvador (1977-80), the positions of the church, as expressed by Romero, drifted in favor of those activist Roman Catholics who advocated liberation theology (see Glossary). By the time of his assassination in March 1980, Romero had become the leading critic of official and unofficial repression in El Salvador. Judging by the content of his weekly homilies, some observers felt that his moral

Cathedral of Santa Ana,
Santa Ana

outrage over abuses committed by armed forces personnel and death squad forces was drawing him closer to a public recognition of the legitimacy of armed struggle against the government (see The Role of Religion, ch. 2).

Romero, however, never spoke for a majority of the Salvadoran bishops. The only other member of the hierarchy at the time who was known to harbor some sympathy for Romero's proliberationist views was Arturo Rivera y Damas. Rivera, who had been a leading candidate for the archbishop's position in 1977 but was passed over in favor of the reputedly more conservative Romero, was a critic of government and military human rights abuses, especially when they involved the persecution or murder of Roman Catholic clergy or lay workers. Under Romero, he occupied a swing position between the activist stance of the archbishop and the more conservative attitudes of the country's three remaining bishops. Although they readily endorsed condemnations of military repression, the three bishops differed sharply with the thrust of liberation theology, which they saw as excessively politicized. Their concerns for the role of the church under a leftist government were strengthened by the example of postrevolutionary Nicaragua, where the traditional church was viewed by the ruling party as a rival and was harassed by the state security and propaganda apparatus.

Rivera succeeded Romero as archbishop in April 1980. He began to take the sort of moderate political stance that most observers

179

had expected of Romero. Rivera spoke out against abuses by all parties and refused to take sides in the civil conflict. He initially advocated the cessation of foreign military aid to both sides. By the late 1980s, however, the church's position on this point had softened somewhat, owing to the ideological intransigence of the FMLN and the seemingly indiscriminate deployment of antipersonnel mines by its forces. In line with the position of the Vatican, Rivera sought to eschew political advocacy in favor of moral suasion so as to render the church a viable mediator in the conflict.

Rivera and other representatives of the church, particularly San Salvador auxiliary bishop Gregorio Rosa Chávez, have served as mediators in situations ranging from labor disputes to negotiations between the government and the FMLN–FDR. At President Duarte's request and with the acquiescence of the rebel leadership, Archbishop Rivera served as an intermediary throughout the fitful process of dialogue that began with the October 1984 meeting in La Palma (see Left-Wing Extremism, ch. 5). When that process broke down, the archbishop maintained contacts with both sides in an effort to keep tenuous lines of communication open.

By the late 1980s, the attitude of the Salvadoran hierarchy toward the guerrillas had hardened considerably. Public statements by Rivera and others condemned the insurgents' tactics in the field, their ideology, their political intransigence, and their efforts to disrupt the electoral process. The FMLN, in turn, denounced the bishops as tools of the "Duarte dictatorship" and questioned their fitness as objective mediators. Although they hinted that they might reject the church's participation in future negotiations, the leadership of the FMLN suggested in May 1988 that contacts between it and the Legislative Assembly be channeled through Rivera.

The church publicly supported the electoral process begun in 1982 and urged citizens to participate in it. At the same time, church spokesmen were quick to criticize the mudslinging nature of Salvadoran campaigning and urged politicians to stress substantive issues over personal attacks. Although they did not interject themselves as advocates or lobbyists, the bishops generally supported the reform programs initiated and maintained by the PDC government and opposed on moral grounds any effort by the elite to restrict or eliminate those reforms. In the tradition established by Romero, Rivera continued to condemn in his weekly homilies reported excesses by the military or security forces.

Mass Communications

By Central American standards, the Salvadoran media enjoyed a moderate freedom of expression and ability to present competing political points of view. They were not as restricted as the media in Nicaragua, but neither were they as diverse, pluralistic, and unrestricted as those of Costa Rica. Although the government did not exercise direct prior censorship, the owners of most publications and some broadcast media outlets exercised a form of self-censorship based either on their personal political conservatism, fear of violent retaliation by right- or left-wing groups, or possible adverse action by the government, such as refusal to renew a broadcast license.

Article 6 of the Constitution guarantees freedom of expression that does not "subvert the public order, nor injure the morals, honor, or private life of others." This language, taken directly from the 1962 constitution, was rendered meaningless by official and unofficial repression and left-wing terrorist action against the media and its practitioners in the early 1980s. With the post-1982 advent of a freely elected democratic system of government, however, and the accompanying decline in politically motivated violence, the climate under which the press and broadcast media operated began to improve.

This expansion in freedom of expression was not as evident in the print medium as it was in the broadcast media. Most newspapers were owned by conservative business people, and their editorial policies tended to reflect the views of their publishers rather than to adhere to the standards of objectivity normally expected in the North American or West European press. This did not mean, however, that the Salvadoran press was monolithically conservative. The weekly publication of the archdiocese of San Salvador, *Orientación,* presented critical analysis of the political scene. Readily available publications emanating from the Central American University presented a generally leftist, antigovernment perspective on events. Small private presses also produced pamphlets, bulletins, and flyers expressing opinions across the political spectrum. The leading daily newspapers in the late 1980s were *El Diario de Hoy,* with a circulation of approximately 75,000; *El Mundo,* with approximately 60,000; and *La Prensa Gráfica,* with approximately 100,000, all published in San Salvador.

Freedom of expression in print was best exemplified by the common practice of taking out paid political advertisements, or *campos pagados.* Most newspapers accepted such advertisements from all sources. *Campos pagados* were one of the few means of access to the print medium available to leftist groups such as the FMLN–FDR and other like-minded organizations. *Campos pagados* also were frequently employed by political parties, private sector groups, unions, government agencies, and other groups to express their opinions.

181

The content of the advertisements was unregulated and uncensored. Their cost effectively limited their use to groups and organizations rather than to individuals.

The influence of the press was limited by illiteracy and the concentration of publishing in the capital. Radio did not suffer from these handicaps and consequently was the most widely utilized medium in the country. In 1985 Salvadorans owned an estimated 2 million radio receivers. Although the majority of the seventy-six stations on the air broadcast from San Salvador, the country's small size and the use of repeater stations meant that virtually all of the national territory was within broadcast range. There was only one government-owned radio station. Although the commercial stations tended to emphasize music over news programming, the representation of competing political viewpoints in news segments was becoming a common practice by the mid-1980s. In addition to the ERP's Radio Venceremos, the Farabundo Martí Popular Liberation Forces (Fuerzas Populares de Liberación Farabundo Martí— FPL) operated a second clandestine station, Radio Farabundo Martí. Both stations served as propaganda organs of the FMLN.

According to many observers, television was the medium where increased political latitude was most evident. Television news crews covered press conferences held by diverse political groups, interviewed opposition politicians such as the FDR's Ungo and Zamora, and investigated allegations of human rights abuses by the military and security forces. Like radio stations, television stations enjoyed virtually complete coverage of the country. Television did not have the market penetration exhibited by radio, however, because of the higher cost of television receivers. A 1985 estimate placed the number of receivers at 350,000. There were six television channels operating in the late 1980s. Of these, two were government-owned educational channels with limited air time. The remaining four were commercial channels.

Foreign Relations

Relations with the United States

As the civil conflict intensified after 1981 and its effects rippled through the economic and political life of the nation, El Salvador turned toward the United States in an effort to stave off a potential guerrilla victory. The administrations of presidents Jimmy Carter and Ronald Reagan responded to the Salvadorans' appeals, and by the mid-1980s government forces appeared to have the upper hand in the field (see The United States Takes a Hand, ch. 1).

Total United States aid to El Salvador rose from US$264.2 million in fiscal year (FY—see Glossary) 1982 to an estimated US$557.8

million in FY 1987. On average over this period, economic aid exceeded military aid by more than a two-to-one ratio. Economic aid was provided in the form of Economic Support Funds (ESF), food aid under Public Law 480 (P.L. 480), and development aid administered by the United States Agency for International Development (AID). ESF was intended to provide balance of payments support to finance essential non-food imports. Assistance with food imports as well as the direct donation of foodstuffs was accomplished through the P.L. 480 program. Development aid covered a broad spectrum of projects in such fields as agriculture, population planning, health, education, and training. For FY 1987, regular non-supplemental ESF appropriations totaled US$181.7 million, and combined food and development aid amounted to US$122.7 million. The regular FY 1987 appropriation for military aid was US$116.5 million.

This aid was crucial to the survival of the Salvadoran government and the ability of the armed forces to contain the insurgency. The situation amplified the personal importance of Duarte after his 1984 election to the presidency. Well known and respected in Washington, Duarte was able to foster a consensus within the United States Congress for high levels of aid as a show of support for the incipient democratic process in his country. These large aid allocations, in turn, promoted stability by deterring possible coup attempts by conservative factions of the military and other opponents of PDC rule. At the same time, the lifeline of aid also rendered El Salvador dependent to a large degree on the United States. A certain amount of popular resentment over this dependence was reflected in adverse reaction from some Salvadoran politicians, journalists, and other opinion makers to Duarte's October 1987 gesture of kissing the United States flag while on a visit to Washington. Some analysts also identified an element of anti-United States sentiment in Arena's March 1988 electoral victory.

El Salvador's dependence on United States support sometimes led to policy moves or public pronouncements that were perceived as responses to pressure from Washington. The 1986 economic austerity measures were one example. Another was Duarte's repeated call for the Nicaraguan government to negotiate with its armed opposition—the so-called *contras*—in spite of the president's public refusal to endorse the United States policy of aid to the *contras*. El Salvador also was quick to condemn Panamanian strongman General Manuel Antonio Noriega Moreno for his February 1988 ouster of President Eric Arturo Delvalle; most Latin American countries were somewhat circumspect with regard to the Panamanian situation, not wishing to be seen as favoring United

States intervention in that country. Some actions by the Salvadoran government were clearly and unequivocally influenced by direct United States pressure, such as Duarte's April 1987 decision to deny political amnesty to the convicted killers of six United States citizens and others in a June 1985 terrorist attack in San Salvador. By taking this action, Duarte averted the loss of US$18.5 million in economic aid.

Although the United States exerted significant influence over government policy in El Salvador, it did not enjoy the absolute control ascribed to it by leftist propaganda. In some areas, Washington's policy goals were frustrated by the intransigence of certain political actors. The obstruction of full implementation of agrarian reform by conservative legislators was one example; another was resistance among the officer corps to the introduction of counterinsurgency tactics. Perhaps the most vexing issue for United States policymakers was human rights. Despite an impressive statistical decline in the mid-1980s, political killings continued. These acts, perpetrated by both right-wing and left-wing groups, helped to feed the climate of violence that inhibited the institutionalization of the democratic process.

United States influence in El Salvador was also diminished temporarily by the 1986–87 revelations surrounding the so-called Iran-Contra Affair. The Reagan administration's preoccupation with these revelations, its loss of international prestige in connection with them, and the embarrassing disclosure of covert Salvadoran military involvement in the *contra* supply network all combined to lessen United States involvement in and influence over Salvadoran affairs. Many observers have seen evidence of waning United States influence in Central America in the Duarte administration's decision to sign the Central American Peace Agreement in August 1987 at Esquipulas, Guatemala, despite the last-minute announcement of an alternative peace plan by Reagan and United States speaker of the House of Representatives, James Wright.

Another point of contention between the two governments was United States immigration reform. By most estimates, there were some 500,000 Salvadorans residing illegally in the United States in the late 1980s. Modifications of the United States immigration law enacted in 1987 technically mandated the expulsion of illegals who had entered the country after 1982. Since the bulk of Salvadoran illegal immigration took place after that date, the new law threatened the majority of this population with repatriation. This prospect was worrisome to the Duarte government for two major reasons: such a large influx was certain to place added strain on employment and public services, already areas of serious concern

*President José Napoleón Duarte
Fuentes confers with President Ronald Reagan, October 1987
Courtesy The White House*

for the government; and the return of Salvadorans resident in the United States meant the loss of dollar-denominated remittances regularly transmitted to family members who had remained behind in El Salvador. Estimates of the total amount of remittance income—a valuable source of foreign exchange for the economy—ranged as high as US$1.4 billion a year. Duarte's pleas for a Salvadoran exemption from the immigration reform were denied by the White House. Action to deport Salvadoran illegals, however, was held up pending consideration in the United States Congress of bills granting exemptions to Salvadoran and Nicaraguan immigrants.

Relations between the United States and El Salvador appeared to be entering a period of transition after the March 1988 elections. Under both the Carter and the Reagan administrations, United States policy had supported the centrist PDC as the surest path to the development of a functional democratic system. The decline of the PDC and the ascendancy of Arena called for some adjustment in that policy. Despite some marked anti-United States sentiment among the *areneros,* there were no early indications of potential friction between the United States and an Arena government. The nomination of Cristiani as the party's 1989 presidential candidate instead of the more controversial D'Aubuisson was seen by some observers as a conciliatory gesture toward Washington.

The Crisis in Central America

During the Duarte administration, most Salvadoran foreign policy efforts were focused on Central America and the potential resolution of political conflict that manifested itself in the form of antigovernment insurgencies in El Salvador, Nicaragua, and Guatemala. Although Costa Rica and Honduras had not experienced insurgencies, their governments were concerned with potential political spillover from neighboring states. By the early 1980s, most observers agreed that, given the historical, familial, geographic, and economic interrelationship of the Central American states, a regional solution to this crisis was the most logical and efficacious approach. Early efforts toward this end in the United Nations (UN) and the Organization of American States (OAS), as well as tentative mediating efforts by the governments of Mexico and Venezuela, failed to make any substantive progress toward the institution of a regional negotiating process. It was not until 1983 and the establishment of the Contadora Group that serious negotiating efforts began among the five Central American states.

The Contadora Process

The Contadora negotiating process was initiated in January 1983 at a meeting of the foreign ministers of Mexico, Venezuela, Colombia, and Panama on Contadora Island in the Gulf of Panama. The idea of a purely Latin American diplomatic effort to stabilize the Central American situation and prevent either military confrontation between neighboring states or direct military intervention by the United States was attributed to then-president of Colombia Belisario Betancur Cuartas. These "Core Four" countries served as mediators in subsequent negotiating sessions among the five Central American states.

By September 1983, the negotiations had arrived at a consensus on twenty-one points or objectives. These included democratization and internal reconciliation, an end to external support for paramilitary forces, reductions in weaponry and foreign military advisers, prohibition of foreign military bases, and reactivation of regional economic mechanisms such as the Central American Common Market. The twenty-one points were incorporated into a draft treaty, or *acta,* one year later.

In September 1984, the Nicaraguan government took the other four government delegations by surprise with its call for the immediate signing of the *acta* as a final treaty. The governments of El Salvador, Honduras, Guatemala, and Costa Rica had been suspicious of Nicaraguan intentions throughout the negotiating process.

This precipitous rush to finalize the process forced the four to reassess their positions and to examine more closely a document that they previously might have viewed as little more than a diplomatic exercise. The United States government, which had been advising the Salvadorans informally with regard to the negotiations, strongly recommended against signing the *acta,* citing its lack of adequate verification and enforcement provisions, its deferral of the issues of reductions in arms and foreign advisers, the freezing of United States military aid to El Salvador and Honduras, and the vagueness of the sections on democratization and internal reconciliation. Although Nicaragua's action had the effect of embarrassing the governments of the other four states and portraying Nicaragua before world public opinion as the only serious negotiator in the Contadora process, it ultimately succeeded in drawing the remaining four Central American states into closer consultation. This collaboration led to the October 1984 Act of Tegucigalpa in which the governments of El Salvador, Honduras, and Costa Rica emphasized their commitment to the establishment of pluralistic democratic systems and their belief that simultaneous and verifiable arms reductions were a necessary component of this process. The Guatemalan government was represented in the discussions in the Honduran capital but declined to sign the resultant document.

Although improved verification procedures were negotiated, the talks bogged down by mid-1985. The Nicaraguan delegates rejected discussion of democratization and internal reconciliation as an unwarranted intervention in their country's internal affairs. The other four states maintained that these provisions were necessary to ensure a lasting settlement. Another major sticking point was the cessation of aid to insurgent groups, particularly United States aid to the *contras.* Although the United States government was not a party to the Contadora negotiations, it was understood that the United States would sign a separate protocol agreeing to the terms of a final treaty in such areas as aid to insurgents, military aid and assistance to Central American governments, and joint military exercises in the region. The Nicaraguans demanded that any Contadora treaty call for an immediate end to *contra* aid, whereas the core four countries and the remaining Central American states, with the exception of Mexico, downplayed the importance of such a provision. In addition, the Nicaraguan government raised objections to specific cuts in its military force levels, citing the imperatives of the counterinsurgency campaign and defense against a potential United States invasion. In an effort to break this impasse, the governments of Argentina, Brazil, Peru, and Uruguay announced in July 1985 that they were joining the Contadora process as a "support group" in an effort to resolve the remaining points of contention and achieve a comprehensive agreement.

Despite the combined efforts of the core four and the "support group," the Contadora process unofficially came to a halt in June 1986, when the Central American countries still could not resolve their differences sufficiently to permit the signing of a final treaty draft. Later that month, the United States Congress approved US$100 million in aid to the *contras* in spite of numerous requests from the Contadora group to refrain from such unilateral action. Although the core four and support group countries vowed to continue their diplomatic efforts and did convene negotiating sessions subsequent to the unsuccessful June 6 meeting in Panama City, the Contadora process was clearly moribund. The Central American states, with the exception of Nicaragua, resolved to continue the negotiating process on their own without the benefit of outside mediation.

The Arias Plan

Throughout the Contadora negotiations, El Salvador's objectives included the preservation of its military aid and assistance relationship with the United States; the resolution of the civil conflict on terms consistent with the 1983 Constitution—that is, through incorporation of the rebels into the established system rather than through a power-sharing arrangement; and a verifiable termination of Nicaraguan military and logistical aid to the FMLN insurgents. On the final point, the Salvadorans felt, along with the Hondurans and Costa Ricans, that the liberalization of the Sandinista-dominated government in Nicaragua was the surest guarantor of success. Given the unanimity of opinion among these three governments and the less emphatic but still supportive response of the government of Guatemalan president Marco Vinicio Cerezo Arévalo, the regional consensus of opinion seemed to be that a streamlined, strictly Central American peace initiative stood a better chance of success than the by then unwieldy Contadora process.

The five Central American presidents had held a meeting in May 1986 in Esquipulas, Guatemala, in an effort to work out their differences over the revised Contadora draft treaty. This meeting was a precursor of the process that in early 1987 superseded Contadora. The leading proponent and architect of this process was the president of Costa Rica, Oscar Arias Sánchez. After consultations with representatives of El Salvador, Honduras, Guatemala, and the United States, Arias announced on February 15, 1987, that he had presented a peace proposal to representatives of the other Central

American states, with the exception of Nicaragua. The plan called for dialogue between governments and opposition groups, amnesty for political prisoners, cease-fires in ongoing insurgent conflicts, democratization, and free elections in all five regional states. The plan also called for renewed negotiations on arms reductions and an end to outside aid to insurgent forces.

The first formal negotiating session to include representatives of the Nicaraguan government was held in Tegucigalpa on July 31, 1987. At that meeting of foreign ministers, the Salvadoran delegation pressed the concept of simultaneous implementation of provisions such as the declaration of cease-fires and amnesties and the denial of support or safehaven for insurgent forces. This approach reportedly softened the attitude of the Nicaraguans, who had come to the meeting declaring opposition to any agreement that did not require a prior cutoff of foreign support to the *contras*.

The Tegucigalpa meeting paved the way for an August 6, 1987, gathering of the five Central American presidents in Esquipulas. The negotiations among the presidents reportedly were marked by blunt accusations and sharp exchanges, particularly between Duarte and Nicaraguan president Daniel Ortega Saavedra. Duarte's primary concern was Nicaraguan aid to the Salvadoran guerrillas, and he was reported to have pressed Ortega repeatedly on this issue. The Nicaraguan president's responses apparently reassured Duarte, who consented to sign the agreement. His decision to do so despite signals of disapproval from Washington reflected only in part the diminished influence of the Reagan administration in light of the Iran-Contra Affair; it was also a calculated move based on the Salvadoran president's belief that a more favorable treaty was not achievable. The final agreement, signed on August 7, called for the cessation of outside aid and support to insurgent forces but did not require the elimination or reduction of such aid to government forces. If they proved to be enforceable, these provisions would work to the benefit of the Salvadoran government and to the detriment of the FMLN, since the insurgents would be expected to forgo outside assistance while the government could continue to receive military aid from the United States. The agreement also urged dialogue with opposition groups "in accordance with the law" and was therefore compatible with the Duarte government's efforts and preconditions for negotiations with rebel forces. The Salvadorans were already in compliance with the sections calling for press freedom, political pluralism, and abolition of state-of-siege restrictions.

The Central American Peace Agreement, variously referred to as the "Guatemala Plan," "Esquipulas II," or the "Arias Plan," initially required the implementation by November 5, 1987, of certain conditions, including decrees of amnesty in those countries involved in insurgent conflicts; the initiation of dialogue between governments and unarmed political opposition groups or groups that had taken advantage of amnesty; the undertaking of efforts to negotiate cease-fires between governments and insurgent groups; the cessation of outside aid to insurgent forces as well as denying the use of each country's national territory to "groups trying to destabilize the governments of the countries of Central America;" and the assurance of conditions conducive to the development of a "pluralistic and participatory democratic process" in all the signatory states.

A meeting of the Central American foreign ministers held one week prior to November 5 effectively extended the deadline by interpreting that date as the requirement for initiation, not completion, of the agreement's provisions. The Salvadoran government, however, had already taken several steps by that time to comply with the agreement. Direct talks between the government and representatives of the FMLN–FDR held in October failed to reach agreement on terms for a cease-fire. The talks were broken off by the rebels, ostensibly in protest over the death squad-style murder of a Salvadoran human rights investigator. Duarte proceeded to declare a unilateral fifteen-day cease-fire to enable guerrilla combatants to take advantage of an amnesty program approved by the Legislative Assembly on October 27.

Overall compliance with the Arias Plan was uneven by late 1988, and the process appeared to be losing momentum. One round of talks took place between the Cerezo administration and representatives of the Guatemalan guerrilla front in Madrid, Spain, on October 6–7, 1987. President Cerezo discontinued this effort, however, claiming that the guerrilla representatives had taken an unrealistic and unreasonable bargaining position. The Nicaraguan government took a number of initial steps to comply with the treaty, such as allowing the independent daily *La Prensa* to reopen and the radio station of the Roman Catholic Church to resume broadcasting, establishing a national reconciliation committee that incorporated representatives of the unarmed opposition, and eventually undertaking cease-fire negotiations with representatives of the *contras*. The optimism engendered by the signature of a provisional cease-fire accord on March 23, 1988, at Sapoa, Nicaragua, however, had largely dissipated by July, when the government broke up a protest demonstration in the southern city of Nandaime, expelled the United States ambassador and seven other diplomats for alleged collaboration with the demonstrators, and again shut down *La Prensa* and the Catholic radio station. In El Salvador, although the FMLN–FDR had been persuaded by President Arias to accept the plan as the basis for negotiations with the Salvadoran government, neither side made any immediate effort to resume the direct talks broken off in October 1987. A definitive cease-fire, therefore, remained elusive. The Salvadoran government also maintained that the Sandinistas continued to provide aid and support to the FMLN. In January 1988, the Salvadorans protested before an international commission monitoring compliance with the treaty that the headquarters of the FMLN general command continued to function from a location near Managua, the Nicaraguan capital, that FMLN training and propaganda facilities continued to operate in Nicaragua, and that arms deliveries from Nicaragua to El Salvador persisted after the signing of the peace treaty on August 7. The effect of the PDC's political decline and Arena's higher government profile on the future course of the Arias Plan was unclear as the country approached the 1989 presidential elections.

El Salvador maintained normal bilateral diplomatic relations with the countries of Central America despite the strains of regional unrest, uncertainty over the intentions of the Sandinistas, and lingering disputes with Honduras. In the late 1980s, relations with Guatemala, governed by an ideologically compatible Christian democratic government, and with Costa Rica were stable. Differences with Nicaragua were rooted in basic ideological conflict, however, and appeared likely to persist. Although neighboring Honduras was experiencing a democratic transition not unlike that taking place in El Salvador, several points of contention prevented the full establishment of close and cooperative ties. The most intangible of these frictions was lingering ill will, especially between the two countries' respective military establishments, over the 1969 "Soccer War" (see The 1969 War with Honduras, ch. 1). Another dispute revolved around the future disposition of Salvadoran refugees residing in Honduras. In early 1988, there were an estimated 20,000 such refugees housed in a number of camps in Honduras, some of which were administered by the office of the United Nations High Commissioner for Refugees (see Migration, ch. 2). Despite ongoing security problems posed by the insurgency, a resettlement program initiated in 1986 by the Salvadoran government in cooperation with domestic and international relief agencies had assisted in the return of some 10,000 Salvadoran refugees. Complete repatriation from the camps, as advocated by the Honduran government, seemed to be contingent on a further winding down of the insurgency.

The main stumbling block in Salvadoran-Honduran relations, however, was the failure of the two countries to agree to a demarcation of their border. This dispute was another legacy of the 1969 war, although it also had deeper historical roots. Several agreements negotiated during the nineteenth century attempted to define the boundaries between the two states, but periodic disputes persisted. The 1969 war further complicated this situation, as Salvadoran troops pushed over a border that had never been firmly demarcated and briefly occupied Honduran territory. So contentious was the territorial dispute that a final peace treaty between the two countries was not signed until October 1980, and even then only 225 of the border's 343 kilometers were definitively delimited. The remaining disputed "pockets" (*bolsones*) along the border, along with island and maritime areas, were submitted to a joint border commission for resolution. At the end of its five-year mandate, the commission had not achieved agreement. Direct government-to-government talks also failed to resolve the issue. The dispute, therefore, was submitted to the International Court of Justice at The Hague, Netherlands, for adjudication. A decision was not expected until the late 1980s.

Relations with Other Nations

As the Salvadoran civil conflict continued during the 1980s, the imperative of maintaining support from the United States and the protracted diplomatic efforts to achieve a regional settlement in Central America consumed most of the country's foreign policy efforts. Although relations with other nations occupied a distinctly lower priority, the Duarte administration did make an effort to improve El Salvador's standing in Western Europe.

Duarte made an official trip to Western Europe in July 1984 with two major goals in mind: to secure foreign economic aid funds, some of which had been discontinued earlier in the decade as a result of his country's poor human rights record under military rule, and to convince West European leaders that real political and social reform was possible in El Salvador. The governments of most West European countries were on record as supporting the inclusion of the FDR or even the FMLN in a negotiated power-sharing government. The 1981 declaration by France and Mexico recognizing the FMLN–FDR as a "representative political force" was the most prominent product of this European foreign policy current. The FDR and its president, Ungo, maintained close ties with social democratic parties in Europe; the FDR also served as the Salvadoran representative to the Socialist International, the worldwide association of social democratic parties, and effectively used this forum to press its case against the existing government in El Salvador.

Duarte was received by the heads of state in the Federal Republic of Germany (West Germany), France, Portugal, Belgium, and Britain. The most productive meeting from the Salvadoran standpoint was that with Chancellor Helmut Kohl of West Germany. Kohl, a Christian Democrat, announced the resumption of German economic aid to El Salvador, aid that had been discontinued five years previously by the social democratic government of Helmut Schmidt. Duarte was also warmly received by British prime minister Margaret Thatcher, although no aid agreement resulted from his visit. The Salvadoran president failed to achieve one specific goal of his trip when French president François Mitterrand declined to modify or reject the 1981 Franco-Mexican declaration. Nevertheless, the French position vis-à-vis the Duarte government generally was perceived as more supportive after the July 1984 visit; in 1985 France shifted the residence of its ambassador from Belmopan, Belize, to San Salvador, partially in recognition of improved security conditions in the Salvadoran capital.

El Salvador received a limited amount of economic development assistance from Canada in the late 1980s. Canadian concerns over the increasing number of Salvadoran immigrants to that country as a result of more restrictive United States immigration laws, however, could prompt Canada to review the low priority of its dealings with El Salvador. In May 1988, the Salvadoran foreign minister paid the first official visit by a Salvadoran official to Japan. He returned with pledges of Japanese aid in the San Salvador reconstruction effort necessitated by the October 1986 earthquake, as well as very low-level commitments to fund or donate equipment for sanitation, agriculture, and sports and cultural projects. The Japanese government also promised to take steps to appoint a resident ambassador.

El Salvador did not maintain diplomatic relations with any communist countries in the late 1980s and did not recognize China. Its continued recognition of Taiwan reflected the historically conservative thrust of the country's foreign policy. In a similar vein, El Salvador was one of only two countries in the world (Costa Rica being the other) to maintain its embassy to Israel in Jerusalem rather than Tel Aviv.

*   *   *

Enrique A. Baloyra's *El Salvador in Transition* and numerous subsequent articles provide useful and objective insights into the workings of Salvadoran politics and foreign relations. Other authors, such as Kenneth E. Sharpe, Terry Lynn Karl, and José Z. García, have followed events in El Salvador closely and written informative articles as well. Because of the country's high profile in United States foreign policy, most major newspapers provide adequate coverage of developments; these reports can be supplemented, however, by publications with a regional focus, such as the *Latin American Weekly Report, Latin America Regional Reports: Mexico and Central America,* and *Latin American Monitor: Central America.*

With regard to the Contadora process and related diplomatic, political, and security developments in Central America, Susan Kaufman Purcell's "Demystifying Contadora" and "The Choice in Central America" provide accurate reporting of events while also attempting to explain the motivations of all actors involved. Bruce Michael Bagley's "Contadora: The Failure of Democracy" also provides a good overview of the process. (For further information and complete citations, see Bibliography.)

Chapter 5. National Security

Salvadoran Army recruit

IN THE POST-COLONIAL, PRE-COFFEE ERA of the early nineteenth century, incipient army and police forces emerged primarily for the purpose of protecting the expanding indigo plantations (*fincas*) and controlling the rural population. In return for these services, a large landowner would assume the role of quartermaster or patron (*patrón*) for his contingent of troops. Consequently, the interests of the military and paramilitary forces became closely identified with those of the economic elite.

The army developed gradually, aided in the late nineteenth century by the French military and in the first half of the twentieth century by other European and Chilean military influences. Spain played an important role in establishing the National Police and the National Guard in the World War I period.

After seizing power in 1931, the military continued to do the oligarchy's bidding, as exemplified by its brutal suppression of a communist-led peasant insurrection in 1932, an event that became known as *la matanza* (the massacre). For the next five decades, the military—in league with the large landholding interests—controlled El Salvador's political system through repression, rigged elections, and coups. The military allowed moderate social and economic reforms, however, depending on which of its liberal or conservative factions was in power. During the 1931–70 period, in which seven of nine military coup attempts succeeded, eight of the nine presidents were army officers. The one civilian president in that period served only four months before being replaced by an officer. The military presidents ruled with the tacit consent of the oligarchy. Although this informal alliance favored maintenance of the general status quo, it provided the country with four decades of comparative political stability and moderate social reforms.

Reformist military officers tried unsuccessfully on several occasions—such as in 1960 and 1972—to take control of the military and the government in order to end military corruption and repression, as well as to establish moderate reforms and democratic institutions. Hoping to avoid a Nicaraguan-style guerrilla war, reformist field-grade and junior officers (colonels, majors, captains, and lieutenants) deposed the repressive and corrupt regime of General Carlos Humberto Romero Mena on October 15, 1979, and established a civil-military government. Under United States prodding, the military eventually stepped aside and allowed a transition to democratic rule.

197

Until the 1980s, the army's primary mission had been to defend the nation from external aggression. By 1981, after El Salvador signed a peace agreement with Honduras formally ending the 1969 war and the newly organized Farabundo Martí National Liberation Front launched a large-scale guerrilla offensive, the army's mission focused primarily on counterinsurgency. The Salvadoran military had to reorient itself, changing from a conventional force that was organized, trained, and equipped to defend the country against a traditional foreign rival, Honduras, into a more aggressive military capable of waging a counterinsurgency war against elusive guerrillas supported by Cuba, Nicaragua, and other communist or radical states. For assistance in combating the insurgency, the military relied almost totally on the United States. Although massive United States military assistance had averted a victory by the rebels, the conflict remained stalemated in late 1988, and peace talks between the government and the rebels—numbering between 6,000 and 8,000 armed combatants—were still at an impasse. Right-wing death squad groups were not nearly as active as in the early 1980s, but they continued to make their presence known in 1988 by killing several dozen individuals involved in human rights groups or left-wing activism.

Although the Salvadoran military had a long record of intervening in governmental matters and being arbitrarily repressive, corrupt, and inefficient, by the late 1980s it had become a more pragmatic and professional entity that was more apolitical, more respectful of human rights, and much better equipped and trained for counterinsurgency. Whereas in the early 1980s the military often disregarded human rights considerations in its pursuit of the guerrillas, counterinsurgency operations conducted in the late 1980s under the purview of the civilian government of President José Napoleón Duarte Fuentes were characterized by a general commitment to respect the human rights of Salvadoran citizens and conduct the war in a more humanitarian manner. For example, in compliance with Duarte's directive regarding the use of aerial fire support, the Salvadoran Air Force was careful to avoid indiscriminate bombing. Whereas mass killings as a result of indiscriminate attacks by the military were frequent in the early 1980s, they were rarely reported in the late 1980s. Moreover, the military had made no attempt to stage a coup against the Duarte government as of the last quarter of 1988, despite its lack of enthusiasm for Duarte's policies in dealing with the guerrillas.

The political violence of the 1980s further debilitated El Salvador's historically weak criminal justice system. Politically motivated homicides, in particular, were rarely investigated or brought to trial. Although the Duarte government tried to uphold the rule of law and reform the system, acts of vengeance and vigilantism had become rampant because of a lack of public confidence in the court system.

Evolution of the Military's Role in Society and Government

The Oligarchy's Private Army, 1824–1931

The Salvadoran Army, like others in the region, developed from the city-based militia of the colonial period. Suppression of frequent Indian rebellions throughout the region and enforcement of tax, labor, and other obligations required of the Indians were principal functions of the militia and incipient armies during colonial times and carried over into the immediate postcolonial period. General Manuel José Arce, the first president of a regional federation called the United Provinces of Central America, which was established in 1823, created the first genuinely Salvadoran army in 1824 (see El Salvador and the United Provinces of Central America, ch. 1). He did this by consolidating a number of widely scattered cavalry units, which had fought against incursions by the army of the self-proclaimed Mexican emperor Agustín de Iturbide, and placing them under a central command. El Salvador's Armed Forces Day, called the Day of the Salvadoran Soldier, has been celebrated ever since on the date of the formal unification, May 7.

In 1825 two French military advisers helped to modernize Arce's militia, which saw considerable action in the internecine conflict between liberal and conservative forces. After the federation collapsed in 1840, newly independent El Salvador inherited most of Arce's troops. The resulting Salvadoran Army was basically a light cavalry with independent squadrons of dragoons. Unlike the region's other armies, most of which resembled bandit gangs during most of the nineteenth century, the Salvadoran Army had developed by the 1850s into a balanced and relatively disciplined force of infantry, cavalry, and artillery. Officers were almost exclusively criollos.

President Gerardo Barrios (1858–63) brought in another French military mission, which reorganized the militia into a European-style national army. Barrios also used Colombian advisers to improve the conduct, appearance, and discipline of the army and militia. In 1867 the French military mission assisted President Francisco Dueñas (1852–58 and 1863–67) in establishing an officer-training school that eventually became the Captain General Gerardo Barrios Military Academy (Escuela Militar Capitán General Gerardo Barrios).

The military supported the coffee oligarchy that emerged in the 1880s by functioning as an internal police force to suppress frequent peasant rebellions. In return, the landowners protected the military's interests and underwrote its expansion and professionalization, thereby laying the foundations of what became the most powerful institution in El Salvador in the twentieth century. President Carlos Erzeta (1890–94) founded the Military Hospital in San Salvador, opened the Noncommissioned Officers School (Escuela de Suboficiales), and employed a German military mission to reorganize and train artillery units.

During the first half of the twentieth century, the military had a primarily internal security function and was involved in active hostilities on only one occasion, a brief war with Guatemala in 1906. A number of Chilean officers participated directly in El Salvador's campaign against Guatemala, forging a strong link between their country and El Salvador. The Chilean military attaché, Carlos Ibáñez de Campo, who later became president of Chile, personally led a legendary charge of the Salvadoran cavalry in one of the major battles, at Platanar.

President Manuel Enrique Araujo (1911–13) implemented some army reforms that had a permanent effect on the security system. For example, he reduced its police functions. He also helped to professionalize the army by creating a general staff, an army educational corps, and a relatively efficient army reserve system. In 1922 El Salvador formed the Military Aviation Service (Servicio de Aviación Militar—SAM) by acquiring five Italian bomber-reconnaissance aircraft.

Beginning in 1929, the oligarchy relied increasingly on the military to suppress a series of major peasant rebellions in the coffee-growing areas of western El Salvador. President Arturo Araujo (March–December 1931) gave his vice president and minister of war, General Maximiliano Hernández Martínez, a free hand to suppress the revolts. At the same time, however, Araujo alienated the military by slashing its budget and refusing to revise its pay procedures.

The Military in Power, 1931–84

A group of young officers—angered by Araujo and concerned about the increasingly organized peasant activism—overthrew the democratically elected president in December 1931 and promptly turned over power to General Martínez. The cohesiveness of the regular conscript-based army was adversely affected by the coup, and army units therefore played little part in *la matanza* of January 1932, which was attributed to the security forces (see The Security

Forces, this ch.). Although the scale of the massacre would not be repeated, the use of indiscriminate violence as exemplified by *la matanza* nonetheless became part of Salvadoran military legend and was invoked by right-wing extremists in the late 1970s and early 1980s as a model for dealing with leftists.

By mid-1932 Martínez was in complete control of the army, the National Police (Policía Nacional—PN), and the National Guard (Guardia Nacional—GN). During his rule as absolute dictator (1932–44), the army remained subordinate to the more elite security services (the PN and GN). Under Martínez's system, the army answered to the minister of war, and the security services answered to the minister of government. After the 1944 coup, the minister of war assumed authority over all the security services, as well as the army.

Beginning with the Martínez regime, an almost unbroken succession of military governments ruled for five decades (see Repression and Reform under Military Rule, ch. 1). On December 14, 1948, a group of army majors belonging to the Military Youth (Juventud Militar) carried out what came to be known as the Revolution of 1948, also known as the "majors' coup." The young officers formed a corporate-style junta and forced all officers above the rank of lieutenant colonel to retire. After the coup, which was more concerned with establishing order than implementing reforms, the military established itself as a somewhat more independent force in politics by distancing itself from the oligarchy. The officers' movement also changed the army's own perception of its role in society by adopting new missions to uphold national law and safeguard the country's sovereignty. Thereafter, the military considered itself no longer merely the oligarchy's private army but rather the guardian of the people and the constitution. As such, it saw itself playing a legitimate role in virtually all aspects of government. It failed totally, however, to legitimize this role, because it did not challenge the oligarchy, implement reforms, or turn the control of the government over to civilians. Instead, it merely changed the pattern of military control of the political process by reaching a new accommodation with the oligarchy; establishing its own party, the Revolutionary Party of Democratic Unification (Partido Revolucionario de Unificación Democrática—PRUD); and ensuring that PRUD candidates took power, usually through fraudulent elections. The military's continuance in power appeared to violate the 1950 constitution, which stipulated that the armed forces were to be nonpolitical and obedient to the government in power.

By the mid-1960s, another major shift had occurred in the Salvadoran military's perception of its own role in society and its view of civilian involvement in the security system. Beginning in 1961, United States military and civilian law enforcement advisers had encouraged the Salvadoran military, not entirely successfully, to abandon the traditional concepts of military professionalism that had guided it since 1941 and to adopt some elements of a counterinsurgency doctrine. Whereas in the 1940s and 1950s the United States had taught Salvadoran Army officers to resist civilian attempts to interfere with military prerogatives, counterinsurgency doctrine in the 1960s encouraged the expansion of the traditional military role to include nonmilitary tasks, such as civic action projects, and the establishment of semiautonomous, politically oriented paramilitary organizations (see The Security Forces, this ch.). At the same time, a reformist Military Youth faction in the Salvadoran military led by Colonel Adolfo Arnoldo Majano Ramos also became increasingly critical of the old authoritarian model favored by the military traditionalists.

The surge of patriotic fervor aroused by the 1969 war with Honduras focused a new public attitude of respect and esteem on the Salvadoran armed forces, especially the ground forces, which performed well during the brief confrontation (see The 1969 War with Honduras, ch. 1). Salvadoran troops, supported by an overwhelming superiority in artillery, penetrated up to twenty-nine kilometers into Honduran territory during the five-day conflict, in which 2,000 to 4,000 soldiers and civilians were killed. The ill-equipped Salvadoran Air Force, however, was no match for the Honduran Air Force, Central America's best. Within months after the end of hostilities, therefore, the Salvadoran Air Force began to acquire new aircraft. El Salvador's seventeen-year-old navy, not having participated in the war with Honduras, benefited little from the postwar expansion and reequipment of the Salvadoran armed forces.

In the mid-1970s, as left-wing guerrilla and terrorist activities escalated, the military began to focus more on internal security than on political manipulation. Consequently, elements of the military adopted the doctrine of national security, emphasizing anticommunism, state autonomy, and limits on the exercise of civil liberties through heavy reliance on the state of siege and other security decree powers. Civil-military relations changed accordingly. In an attempt to reassert its control and protect its own institutional integrity from leftist subversion and rightist attempts to take power, the military tried to increase the distance between itself and civil society. The oligarchy encouraged the government's efforts to reinstate policies that characterized the traditional authoritarian model.

In 1979 a group of junior and field-grade military officers staged a successful coup and ousted the regime of General Romero. These officers quickly forced sixty senior officers to retire and temporarily exiled all of the generals and most of the colonels. Recognizing the need for social, political, and economic reforms, they formed the left-of-center, civilian-military Revolutionary Governing Junta (Junta Revolucionaria de Gobierno—JRG), which included two army officers: Colonel Jaime Abdul Gutiérrez and Colonel Majano. The JRG then formed a largely civilian cabinet that included, as defense minister, Colonel Guillermo García, a participant in the coup. The junior and field-grade officers who constituted the Military Youth also created the Permanent Council of the Armed Forces (Consejo Permanente de las Fuerzas Armadas—Copefa) to ensure that the proclaimed objectives of the reformist coup were not subverted and to serve as a policy consultative body for officers. The younger Copefa members distrusted the older commanders—particularly García and his deputy, Colonel Nicolás Carranza—whom they viewed as corrupt, reactionary, and more interested in the political loyalty of key military officers than their military competence. Nevertheless, it soon became apparent that the real power lay in the military High Command (Alto Mando), not in the governing Civil-Military Directorate (Directorio Cívico-Militar). García and the High Command consolidated power by purging the young reformist officers from Copefa on December 18, 1979, and replacing them with old-guard loyalists. After another junta reorganization in December 1980, which resulted in Majano's exile, Gutiérrez retained sole command of the armed forces, and junta member José Napoleón Duarte Fuentes became provisional president.

Before the 1982 election for the Constituent Assembly (see Glossary), Defense Minister García issued a public order requiring the military to defend the voting process. Thus, in an important break with the past, the military protected rather than manipulated an election. The High Command reportedly used its influence to prevent the right-wing Nationalist Republican Alliance (Alianza Republicana Nacionalista—Arena) from excluding the Christian Democratic Party (Partido Demócrata Cristiano—PDC) from the provisional government headed by Alvaro Magaña Borja, a political centrist, who succeeded Duarte as interim president. Nevertheless, the prospect of civilian government disturbed many in the military, including senior army officers. Although García forestalled a coup in early November 1982 by transferring or dismissing dissident senior army officers, criticism of him among the military hierarchy eventually turned into open rebellion.

García's most vocal military critic was Lieutenant Colonel Sigifredo Ochoa Pérez, military commander of Cabañas Department. On January 6, 1983, a day after being ordered by García to leave his command to serve as military attaché in Uruguay, Ochoa began a six-day mutiny, placing his troops on alert. Ochoa accused García of corruption and called for his resignation. Part of the conflict between Ochoa and García stemmed from differences over counterinsurgency strategy. Ochoa and his supporters advocated a more professional approach, emphasizing aggressive, small-unit actions and patrolling combined with political pacification (civic action projects). In response, the defense minister required all senior officers to sign a document condemning Ochoa's action as a violation of "the principles of discipline and obedience which men of the armed forces must observe at all times." Twenty-eight senior officers signed. Ochoa ended his rebellion after six days and accepted the president's offer of an assistant defense attaché post in Washington. Under increasing pressure from within the officer corps, García finally resigned on April 18, 1983, and was succeeded by General Carlos Eugenio Vides Casanova, the GN director general since October 1979. Ochoa eventually resigned from the army in June 1987, in part to protest what he viewed as interference in military affairs by the Duarte government and the United States but also to join Arena and serve as a deputy (*diputado*) in the Legislative Assembly.

In a major military reorganization in November 1983, Vides, the new minister of defense and public security, reassigned many commanders and reorganized the army in an effort to enhance its professionalism; his action also rendered the army's leadership more politically conservative. Until the reorganization, twenty-six separate commands had reported directly to the defense minister. The appointment of six brigade commanders reduced the number of subordinate commands significantly. One of Vides's key appointments was that of Colonel Adolfo Onecífero Blandón Mejía as army chief of staff. By the time the elected Constituent Assembly completed the new Constitution in late 1983, a military code of conduct had also been drafted (see Military Justice, this ch.).

The inauguration of Duarte as president on June 1, 1984, ushered in a new era of elected civilian rule. On taking office, Duarte promoted Blandón to brigadier general and made him chief of staff of the Joint General Staff (Estado Mayor Conjunto—EMC).

The Military under Democratic Rule, 1984–88

In the 1984–88 period, the military largely adhered to its new constitutional obligations to remain apolitical and obedient to

Army personnel in the field
Courtesy United States Department of Defense

civilian rule (see Mission and Organization, this ch.). It made no effort to influence the outcome of the elections that brought Duarte and the Legislative Assembly into office. The elected leadership determined the country's domestic and foreign policy, generally without discernible interference by the military. President Duarte normally made the basic decisions on how to deal with the guerrillas, and he set the rules of engagement, which the military obeyed. Military leaders spurned attempts by antidemocratic right-wing extremists to incite coups, and by late 1988 no military coup attempt had been made. Nevertheless, there were occasions when civil-military relations were seriously strained. For example, in October 1985 a group of army officers accused Duarte of endangering the national security by allowing 126 rebels to go free in exchange for the release of his kidnapped daughter. Although the officers asked the High Command to consider replacing the president, a day-long debate in that body defused the dissent.

The military reportedly also still set its own rules of conduct much of the time, despite Duarte's efforts to strengthen civilian control. For example, the military resisted civilian efforts to force it to make a public accounting of the involvement of some officers in a multimillion-dollar kidnapping ring, a corrupt arms deal, and the murder of several United States citizens. In addition, some army officers with records of human rights abuses continued to be promoted. Moreover, with the exceptions of Vides and Blandón, who became identified with Duarte and his administration, the military kept its distance from the PDC government and cultivated its own ties with political parties, the Roman Catholic Church, and business and labor groups.

Although the armed forces remained a powerful institution, exerting a strong, behind-the-scenes influence on national security affairs during the Duarte administration, usually through the High Command, the military's direct political involvement decreased. Observers cited three reasons why a consensus toward a professional, apolitical military institution gradually developed. First and foremost, the military understood that its submission to civilian authority was essential for obtaining United States support to carry out its primary national security mission, namely counterinsurgency. Second, a more apolitical stance by the military was necessary if the country wished to end its international isolation and improve economic, diplomatic, and perhaps even military cooperation with West European and Latin American democracies. And third, most military leaders understood that the political appeal of the insurgency could best be neutralized by setting up representative civilian institutions and the infrastructure of a democratic society, even though these were historically alien to the country. Thus, the military's role in Salvadoran political life changed dramatically during the Duarte administration. The military publicly supported the democratic process and remained neutral in it; military leaders stated repeatedly that civilian officials were responsible for determining El Salvador's political, economic, social, and foreign policies.

In 1987 the Duarte administration's relations with the military were strained, however, by the government's long-range plans to build up a police force independent of the army, by the release of guerrilla prisoners, and by a brief unilateral cease-fire declared by the president in order to comply with the Central American Peace Agreement that Duarte signed on behalf of El Salvador on August 7, 1987 (see The Crisis in Central America, ch. 4). Although the High Command approved peace talks with the guerrillas in September 1987, the military's public support for the dialogue seemed less than enthusiastic.

Two events in late November 1987 further strained civil-military relations. One was the temporary return from exile of two leaders of the political front of the Farabundo Martí National Liberation Front (Frente Farabundo Martí de Liberación Nacional—FMLN), the Revolutionary Democratic Front (Frente Democrático Revolucionario—FDR). Another was Duarte's release of new evidence purportedly linking Roberto D'Aubuisson Arrieta, the Arena leader, with the 1980 murder of Archbishop Oscar Arnulfo Romero y Galdámez. In response to these two events, Salvadoran right-wing political leaders, including D'Aubuisson and Ochoa, began appealing for "patriotic action" by their traditional ally, the army. Ochoa stressed the duty of the military commanders in the field to defend El Salvador from both the "terrorists" and the Christian democratic government. These rightist leaders also attempted to appeal to the nationalism of army officers who resented the United States embassy's influence over their actions. One target of the rightists was Colonel Carlos Reynaldo López Nuila, a senior army officer and the PN director general. López Nuila had strongly supported Duarte, had tried to loosen the army's control over police forces in San Salvador, and had actively investigated human rights abuses and other crimes by some senior army officers.

In mid-1988 the military, like the government, appeared to be in a transitional period. Reportedly disenchanted with the Christian democratic government over its handling of the economy and its efforts at dialogue with the guerrillas, and uneasy over the potential investigation of military officers accused of crimes, the military appeared receptive to the assumption of power by the right and by Arena. The military was particularly worried that after the 1989 presidential election the country would still have a weak civilian government. By mid-1988 Lieutenant Colonel René Emilio Ponce Torres, commander of the army's First Infantry Brigade in eastern San Miguel Department, had become publicly critical of civilians, saying bureaucratic infighting and the political parties' inability to resolve their differences were weakening the war effort. Ponce's renewed efforts to win over citizens in zones of conflict worried some in the civilian government, who felt that the powerful, more cohesive military was usurping their functions.

The High Command held a series of meetings to define its position and also met with politicians to discuss the electoral dispute that delayed the convening of the Legislative Assembly elected in March 1988. Defense Minister Vides publicly dismissed the possibility that a coup would result from the political crisis that had developed by June 1988, when Duarte left the country to receive medical treatment for what was reported to be terminal cancer. Meanwhile, members of the military academy's class of 1966 (the so-called *tandona,* or big class), led by Colonel Ponce, were beginning to move into positions of power (see Officer Corps Dynamics, this ch.). By mid-1988, after five years on the job, General Vides and General Blandón appeared to be losing influence as younger, more aggressive officers, some of whose attitudes toward the democratic process were unclear, anticipated the generals' approaching retirement.

The Armed Forces

Mission and Organization

Under Articles 211 and 212 of the 1983 Constitution, the army's missions and those of the armed forces in general are to defend the national territory and sovereignty; to maintain the public peace, tranquillity, and security; and to support democracy. Article 212 describes the armed forces more specifically as a fundamental institution for national security, of a permanent character, essentially apolitical, obedient to established civilian authority, and nondeliberative. It also charges the military with enforcing the no-reelection provision for the country's president, guaranteeing freedom of suffrage, ensuring respect for human rights, and collaborating with the agencies of the executive branch in promoting national development. In effect, the 1983 Constitution sought to change dramatically the political role of the military. Whereas military officers routinely served as president of the republic under the old constitutions, the 1983 Constitution does not permit any active-duty military officer to be president. Military personnel must resign from the service three years before the next presidential inauguration date in order to be eligible to run for that office.

Both the military organic law and Article 157 of the Constitution name the president as commander in chief of the armed forces, consisting of the army, air force, navy, and active reserve (see fig. 9). Article 168 empowers the president to organize and maintain the armed forces and confer military ranks in accordance with the law. The minister of defense and public security is in the chain of command and performs the president's command functions on a day-to-day basis. A deputy minister of defense and public security fulfills the purely administrative role assigned to the Ministry of Defense and Public Security. The EMC chief is the senior serving officer and also army commander and has operational control over the navy and air force chiefs. The vice minister of defense and public security oversees the Public Security Forces Joint Staff of the three security forces: the GN, PN, and the Treasury Police (Policía de Hacienda—PH), which together included some 12,600 personnel among their ranks in 1988. The regular armed forces (army, air force, and navy) totaled about 47,000 active members in 1988.

Colonel Juan Orlando Zepeda stated in a published interview in 1987 that the Salvadoran armed forces had two national-level intelligence organizations: the National Directorate of Intelligence (Dirección Nacional de Inteligencia—DNI) under the Ministry of Defense and Public Security; and the EMC's C-2, which Colonel Zepeda headed. Although the DNI was charged with providing strategic, political, and national intelligence, the demands of the war and a lack of training compelled it to develop mainly military operational intelligence at the strategic and tactical levels, duplicating the C-2's principal mission. The C-2 also used intelligence reports from agencies at the brigade and military unit levels.

Defense Budget

El Salvador's defense budgets traditionally were relatively modest, and the percentage of the national income devoted to the armed forces generally was conservative. Military expenditures in the post-World War II period to 1970 ranged from 9 to 11 percent of the national budget. The demands of counterinsurgency resulted, however, in large increases in the country's defense spending in the 1980s. The defense budget, which included the "public security sector," increased substantially from fiscal year (FY—see Glossary) 1982, when it totalled US$139 million, to FY 1988, when it reached US$204 million (see Foreign Military Influence and Assistance, this ch.). In 1986 army expenditures accounted for 71 percent of the total defense budget; air force, 23 percent; and navy, 4 percent. The 1986 defense budget constituted 4.7 percent of the gross national product (GNP—see Glossary). By the late 1980s, defense expenditures accounted for 25 percent of the national budget.

Military Service

Under Article 215 of the Constitution, military service for a minimum of two years is obligatory for all able-bodied male citizens between the ages of eighteen and thirty, although in practice youth from wealthy families avoided military service. In 1988 El Salvador had a manpower pool of 807,000 males fit for military service, and approximately 65,000 Salvadoran males reached military age (eighteen) annually. Prior to the guerrilla conflict and its attendant increase in military personnel, conscription was resorted to only rarely, and only one year of service was required. The services drew mainly young rural men whose lack of employment prospects made even low-paying, high-risk military service attractive. After 1979, however, the armed forces relied heavily on the draft. Conscripts (males only) were required initially to serve eighteen months at the age of eighteen or nineteen, but the period was soon increased to twenty-four months. On completion of their service, conscripts

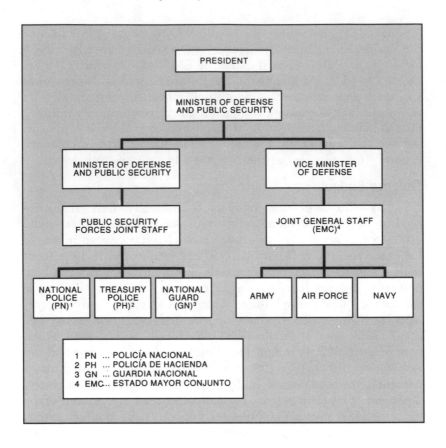

Figure 9. Armed Forces Chain of Command, 1988

reverted to "active reserve" status until the age of thirty, or they could choose to remain for a longer period of time at a higher salary. The army, however, limited reenlistment to 20 percent because a draftee was paid only US$80 per month, as compared with US$300 a month for a soldier who had completed two two-year tours. From the ages of thirty to sixty, reservists were assigned to the second-line Territorial Service, a part-time, volunteer security force that mainly provided reserve manpower for the army.

Recruitment to the regular armed forces was carried out nationally but was decentralized down to the township level. Conscript classes were called up biannually, and each individual reported to the military unit nearest his home. Local boards—consisting of officers, civilian officials, and medical personnel—examined prospective draftees and ruled on their qualifications and on requests for exemption or deferment. Each township received a quota of the vacancies in the regular service and filled them first with volunteers. After initial examinations, the local boards submitted a list of qualified volunteers to the departmental commander. Selections were made by lottery, in accordance with the choice of service indicated. Accepted candidates then reported to their new stations in the departmental regiment.

The army also frequently resorted to the impressment of young men into service, particularly in urban areas, in order to fulfill its manpower quotas. In the late 1980s, according to the *New York Times,* the armed forces were forcibly enlisting 12,000 youths a year. Those most affected by this press-gang system were usually from poor and rural families; often they were as young as fourteen. The military almost never forcibly recruited youths in wealthy neighborhoods. If recruited, they could generally buy their way out of the service with help from their families.

Historically, most women in the Salvadoran military served as nurses or were relegated to secretarial or domestic duties, such as cooking. In 1985 most of the 2,000 military nurses worked at the Military Hospital in San Salvador; few were assigned to field duty. At that time, the armed forces had six female officers, all of whom had received their commissions because of their foreign training. The highest ranking nurse was a captain, but none held any position in a chain of command.

In the early 1980s, thanks mainly to innovative commanders in the First Infantry Brigade in eastern El Salvador, the Ministry of Defense and Public Security allowed young women volunteers to begin basic combat training courses in San Miguel and Morazán departments. The initial seventy women recruits were organized into two all-women combat platoons. Most of the women recruits reportedly had either been displaced by the war or had had relatives kidnapped or murdered by the guerrillas. Although their basic training reportedly was rigorous and similar to that given male recruits, the women were not observed to be subjected to the same physical abuse. Those who successfully completed combat training qualified for the same pay as male privates, ¢450 (for value of the colón—see Glossary) a month, or about US$112. As of 1985, members of the two women's platoons reportedly were being integrated as replacements in previously all-male units.

Until the 1920s, officers were selected from the country's prominent families and constituted an elite caste. In time, the selection process became increasingly egalitarian, however, and by 1970 the officer corps was composed mostly of mestizos from farm communities. The officers came from segments of the population educated enough to qualify for the demanding officer training. All officers were career regulars, except for a small number of professional specialists, such as doctors.

In comparison with equivalent civilian standards, the conditions under which military personnel served were generally quite good. Officers, but not enlisted personnel, had separate family accommodations. Married noncommissioned officers (NCOs) received extra family allowances that were sufficient to enable them to procure local housing. Quarters, food, and pay were generally considerably better than the average campesino could find outside the service. Other benefits and advantages included medical care, accrued leave, retirement pay, and survivor benefits, although the latter were not always guaranteed. Special allowances were also available based on family size and the location of one's duty station; extra pay also was authorized for specialists and airborne and flight personnel. Retirement for disability, age, or length of service was either statutory or granted on request. Liberal leave policies allowed all ranks to accrue thirty days a year; there also were special provisions for emergency situations.

Ranks, Uniforms, and Insignia

The rank structure of the armed forces followed traditional lines and conformed to the pattern of the United States services, with minor variations reflecting the disparity in force levels. Army and air force ranks were identical, and the navy used conventional naval designations, although naval personnel generally were addressed by their equivalent army ranks. The only general officer rank was equivalent to a United States brigadier general.

Insignia of rank conformed to the designs adopted in 1968 by the Central American Defense Council (Consejo de Defensa Centroamericano—Condeca). Army and air force officer insignia were worn on shoulder straps and consisted of silver-colored stars for company-grade officers (second lieutenant, lieutenant, and captain), gold-colored stars for field-grade officers (major, lieutenant colonel, and colonel), and a laurel leaf for brigadier general. Naval officers displayed gold-colored metallic braid insignia of rank at the cuff or on shoulderboards, depending on the type of uniform worn. NCOs wore chevrons of gold braid or colored cloth. The grades of all enlisted personnel were indicated by cloth chevrons (gold-colored for army and air force and black for navy), worn on either the uniform coat or the shirt sleeves (see fig. 10; fig. 11).

Both army and air force wore dark-blue dress uniforms, whereas the navy wore traditional navy blue garb but donned standard whites for the hot-weather months. The army's service uniform consisted of a khaki shirt and beige trousers, with an overseas-type garrison cap. The air force's service uniform differed from the army's only in its light-blue color, and the navy used a khaki service uniform. Army and air force officers wore service uniforms in their respective colors. The army's basic garrison uniform consisted of olive-green shirt, trousers, and cap and a belt, socks, and shoes, all in black. The standard uniform became the combat uniform with the addition of short leggings, combat boots, a helmet, and field equipment. The air force's garrison uniform again differed from that of the army only in its blue color. Dress and service uniforms for female personnel were patterned after those for male personnel, but with skirts instead of trousers.

Capabilities

The Army

By far the dominant service in size and importance, the Salvadoran Army in 1988 had a total strength of 43,000 members, including conscripts. For territorial control, it divided the country into six military zones and fourteen subordinate military regions. The principal combat units consisted of twenty-two medium and fourteen light Antiterrorist Infantry Battalions (Batallones de Infantería Antiterrorista—BIATs) organized into six infantry brigades, nine cadre infantry regiments (up to forty battalions), one mechanized cavalry regiment (two battalions), one artillery brigade (three battalions), one engineer battalion, six independent immediate-reaction counterinsurgency battalions (1,100 to 1,400 men), and seven detachments (*destacamentos*). The army also had one paratrooper battalion and one antiaircraft artillery battalion that were under air force control. The usual service units—such as medical, military police, and ordnance—supported the combat forces. Each brigade also had a long-range reconnaissance patrol for small-unit reconnaissance and combat patrolling. Army equipment in the late 1980s included light tanks, armored personnel carriers, howitzers, mortars, and recoilless rifles (see table 7, Appendix).

Military Detachment Number Four (Destacamento Militar Número Cuatro-DM4), which was responsible for security in Morazán Department, typified the army's command organization. In 1987 DM4 consisted of four battalions, each of which was organized into four companies. A company had four platoons—actually called sections (*secciones*)—of about thirty-four members each. Its zone of responsibility was divided among its four platoons, each of which contained two patrols (*patrullas*). The patrols operated

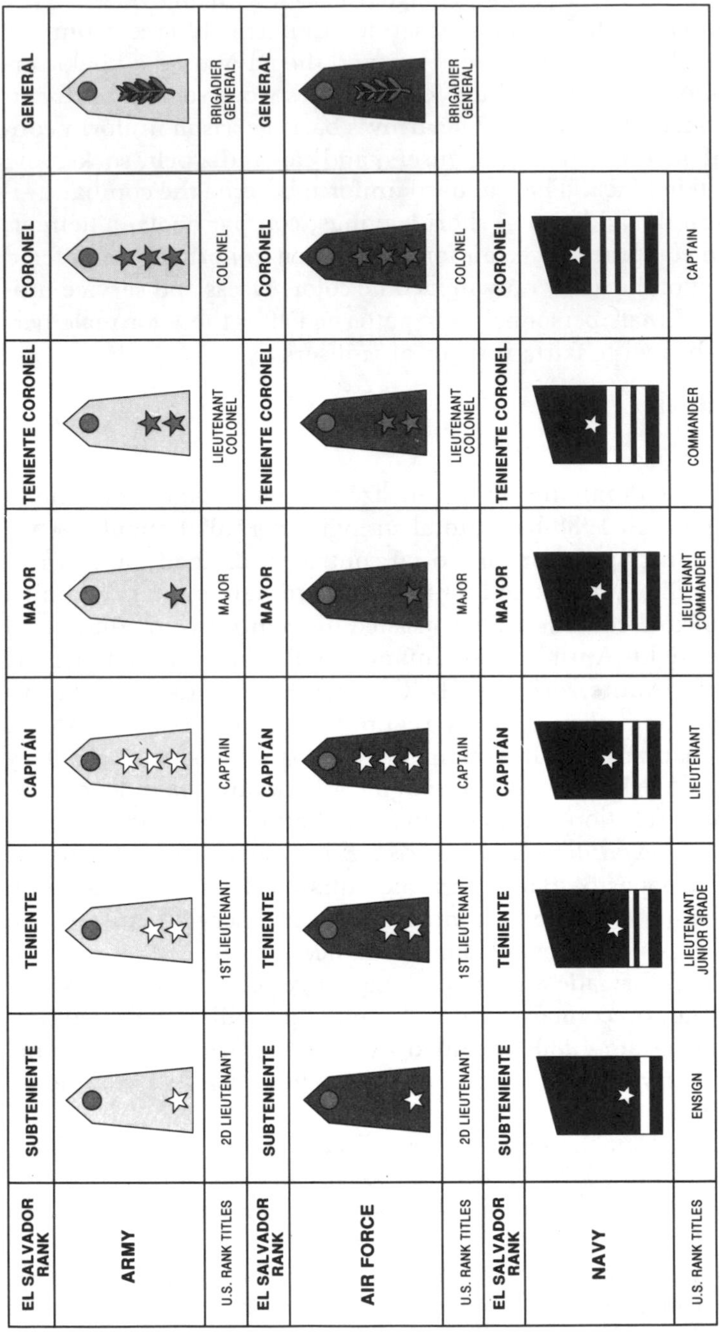

EL SALVADOR RANK	SUBTENIENTE	TENIENTE	CAPITÁN	MAYOR	TENIENTE CORONEL	CORONEL	GENERAL
ARMY							
U.S. RANK TITLES	2D LIEUTENANT	1ST LIEUTENANT	CAPTAIN	MAJOR	LIEUTENANT COLONEL	COLONEL	BRIGADIER GENERAL
EL SALVADOR RANK	SUBTENIENTE	TENIENTE	CAPITÁN	MAYOR	TENIENTE CORONEL	CORONEL	GENERAL
AIR FORCE							
U.S. RANK TITLES	2D LIEUTENANT	1ST LIEUTENANT	CAPTAIN	MAJOR	LIEUTENANT COLONEL	COLONEL	BRIGADIER GENERAL
EL SALVADOR RANK	SUBTENIENTE	TENIENTE	CAPITÁN	MAYOR	TENIENTE CORONEL	CORONEL	
NAVY							
U.S. RANK TITLES	ENSIGN	LIEUTENANT JUNIOR GRADE	LIEUTENANT	LIEUTENANT COMMANDER	COMMANDER	CAPTAIN	

Figure 10. Officer Ranks and Insignia, 1988

ARMY

EL SALVADOR RANK	SOLDADO	CABO	SUB-SARGENTO	SARGENTO
ARMY	NO INSIGNIA	(insignia)	(insignia)	(insignia)   
U.S. RANK TITLES	BASIC PRIVATE · PRIVATE 1ST CLASS	CORPORAL	SERGEANT · STAFF SERGEANT	SERGEANT 1ST CLASS · MASTER SERGEANT

AIR FORCE

EL SALVADOR RANK	SOLDADO	CABO	SUB-SARGENTO	SARGENTO
AIR FORCE	NO INSIGNIA	(insignia)	(insignia)	(insignia)   
U.S. RANK TITLES	AIRMAN BASIC · AIRMAN 1ST CLASS	SERGEANT	STAFF SERGEANT · TECHNICAL SERGEANT	MASTER SERGEANT · SENIOR MASTER SERGEANT

NAVY

EL SALVADOR RANK	MARINERO	CABO	SUBSARGENTO	SARGENTO	MAESTRE
NAVY	NO INSIGNIA	(insignia)	(insignia)	(insignia)	(insignia)    
U.S. RANK TITLES	SEAMAN RECRUIT · SEAMAN	PETTY OFFICER 3D CLASS	PETTY OFFICER 2D CLASS	PETTY OFFICER 1ST CLASS	CHIEF PETTY OFFICER · SENIOR CHIEF PETTY OFFICER

Figure 11. Enlisted Ranks and Insignia, 1988

independently, although two or more of the companies often cooperated in an operation.

The Air Force

In 1988 the Salvadoran Air Force had over 2,000 personnel, including an air defense unit, a security group, and some conscripts. The antiaircraft artillery battalion was equipped with twenty-four Yugoslav-made M–55 20mm guns and four self-propelled guns and was staffed with army personnel. From the mid-1970s to the late 1980s, the air force had acquired aircraft from Israel (French-made), France, Brazil, and the United States. Although the air force suffered a major setback on January 27, 1982, when guerrillas attacked Ilopango Air Base outside San Salvador and destroyed 75 percent of the air force's inventory, the United States delivered replacement aircraft within weeks. With additional United States assistance, the air force built up quickly in 1985 and by late 1986 had a large helicopter force and a variety of other aircraft (see table 8, Appendix). Attrition continued to be high in the late 1980s, with a number of helicopters and other aircraft downed by guerrilla forces or mechanical failure.

In the late 1980s, the Salvadoran Air Force was organized into the Military Aviation School (Escuela de Aviación Militar—EAM) and five squadrons: the Hunter Squadron (Escuadrilla de Caza), based in San Miguel; the Hunter Bomber Squadron (Escuadrilla de Caza Bombardeo), based at Ilopango Air Base; the Attack Squadron (Escuadrilla de Ataque) and the Transport Squadron (Escuadrilla de Transporte), also based at Ilopango; and the growing Helicopter Squadron (Escuadrilla de Helicóptero), with aircraft based at both Ilopango and San Miguel.

The Navy

In 1988 the Salvadoran Navy, with at least 1,300 members, included the 600-man Marine Infantry Battalion (Batallón de Infantería de Marina—BIM), a 330-man commando unit, and some conscripts. The principal naval base was located at La Unión. A naval school was located at Army Headquarters in San Salvador. In the late 1980s, the navy had acquired thirty patrol craft (see table 9, Appendix).

Revived in 1952, after a lapse of more than forty years without any naval vessels, the new navy assumed the functions of the established coast guard and expanded them to include coastal patrol and fishery protection. The navy also absorbed patrol craft from the coast guard; these craft, principally British vessels, were decommissioned by 1981 and replaced by United States-built boats.

The Naval Commandos force was established in August 1982 as a sixty-man unit intended to improve response to guerrilla operations in coastal areas. By mid-1985 the force numbered 330 men, among them 12 frogmen, 90 base security troops, and 110 men who regularly handled the weapons aboard their high-speed patrol boats. The Naval Commandos prowled mangroves, coconut forests, and beaches in eight- to fifteen-man teams, ambushing guerrilla columns and raiding rebel encampments.

Civic Action

The involvement of the armed forces in civic action projects began in the mid-1960s. A hierarchy of government officials at the highest levels supervised the national civic action program. The ranking official, the director of civic action, was attached to the Ministry of Defense and Public Security, directly under the minister. A committee composed of the ministers of defense and public security, agriculture and livestock, public health and social services, education, and public works served as an advisory group for the director. Regional committees supervised the various projects assigned to their localities. These national and regional committees prepared programs annually, with the national group deciding on the allocation of tasks, resources, and priorities. The army's engineer battalion generally supervised construction and public works projects. Other ministries represented on the national committee monitored literacy, health, and welfare activities.

Civic action programs had a significant impact on the economy and society. The army's civic action program was largely responsible for the country's good road system (see Transportation, ch. 3). Members of the military not only maintained and repaired roads but also built new ones, often in difficult terrain. Although highway maintenance was one of their primary activities, the army engineers also assisted in public works projects ranging from bridges to earthworks, airfields, and sewers. A particularly important facet of the civic action program was the literacy campaign. The army operated literacy centers for the public in rural communities throughout the country, as well as for recruits at military posts. The army's public health program, which included periodic immunization campaigns conducted nationwide, was also a great benefit to the public. The Army Medical Service maintained a number of clinics that served the local population as well as military personnel in the major barracks (*cuarteles*), and the service also operated mobile health centers in isolated areas. Beginning in 1983, the army combined civic action projects with its "pacification" campaigns (see Left-Wing Extremism, this ch.).

The navy and air force gradually began increasing their partici-pation in civic action in 1965, although their contribution was rela-tively small. The navy participated in search-and-rescue missions, particularly in the protection of fishing craft off the southern coast. The air force used its Cessna liaison aircraft extensively in civic action missions, especially in remote or isolated areas, where it transported medical teams to clinics and provided emergency evacuation.

Education, Training, and Rules of Conduct
Military Schools

Aspiring officers for all three services completed the four-year course of the Captain General Gerardo Barrios Military Academy, graduating with a bachelor's degree and being commissioned with the rank of second lieutenant. Located a few miles west of the cap-ital, the academy was the primary source of commissioned officers in the army, navy, and air force. In 1985 a shortage of officers forced the academy to begin operating on an emergency status that required the curriculum to be reduced to three years.

Enrollment was limited to unmarried males between the ages of seventeen and twenty-one who had graduated from high school and passed competitive entrance examinations. Students spent only their first year training at the academy. During the rest of the time, they were attached to various battalions throughout the country.

Most cadets came from lower-middle-class families; during the 1980s, many came from areas of heavy guerrilla activity. Fewer than 10 percent of the enrolled cadets were sons of military officers. The academy also trained cadets from other Central American countries. In the late 1980s, it usually had a student body of about 225 cadets, with about 100 to 125 candidates entering each year. Nevertheless, a tradition of strict, even brutal, discipline ensured a first-year drop-out rate of 35 to 40 percent, and only 10 to 20 percent of each class graduated. Under this system, loyalty to class-mates was particularly strong.

Academy graduates who elected to serve in the navy or air force received additional specialized training before being transferred to those services. For example, an officer who enlisted in the Salva-doran Air Force underwent flight training at the Military Avia-tion School (Escuela de Aviación Militar) or specialist training at the Specialists' School (Escuela de Especialización). Most officer personnel also pursued some additional training abroad, especially in the United States.

By law Salvadoran Army officers had to attend their own ser-vice schools, including the Command and General Staff School

(Escuela de Mando y Estado Mayor General). This war college provided courses in advanced military science for officers of the rank of lieutenant colonel and above and aspiring staff officers. Regular NCOs were trained at the Noncommissioned Officers School and at the Arms and Services School (Escuela de Armas y Servicios—EAS). The EAS provided specialist training for both officers and other ranks, as well as an advanced six-month course for field-grade officers. Basic and advanced officer training were offered at the Armed Forces Military Training Center (Centro de Entrenamiento Militar de las Fuerzas Armadas—CEMFA), which was established in La Unión in 1984. The military also had a human rights training program for officers and enlisted personnel. Most officers pursued additional postgraduate studies abroad. In the 1980s, many Salvadoran armed forces personnel received training in other Latin American countries, particularly Argentina and Chile; at the School of the Americas in Fort Benning, Georgia; and in Taiwan. In 1983 officers and cadets also began receiving scholarships from Britain, Belgium, Italy, Spain, and the Federal Republic of Germany (West Germany).

Officer Corps Dynamics

In the Salvadoran officer corps, personal ties and political orientation have traditionally been more important than military competence. The 1948 revolution institutionalized a caste-like "old-boy network" within the army by bringing to power a *tanda,* or military academy graduating class, for the first time. Henceforth, the members of each *tanda* traditionally were bound to lifelong loyalty to one another. A *tanda* formed a tight clique, with its members taking their first commands in the expectation that they would one day be running the country. A *tanda* was important throughout an officer's career, which by law could last thirty years. *Tanda* loyalty counted more than political or personal differences. The importance of a *tanda* increased with seniority, as its leaders moved up into positions of power and wealth. Members of one *tanda* often formed alliances with those of another, although, as Richard L. Millett has observed, not with the class one year ahead that had mistreated them during their first year, nor with the class one year behind that they had themselves harassed.

The 1963 *tanda* of D'Aubuisson, a former army and GN intelligence officer and an ultraconservative politician, dominated the army in the early 1980s. His *tanda* held eleven of the top twenty field commands, controlling four of the country's six infantry brigades, four of its seven regional garrisons, the artillery brigade, and the mechanized cavalry battalion. D'Aubuisson carefully cultivated this network. Merely having classmates in so many key positions did not mean, however, that he had their automatic support. Many of his classmates were opposed to his extreme political viewpoint. The importance of D'Aubuisson's *tanda* connections lay in the entrée they gave him into the *cuarteles* (barracks), where he also had the support of a number of junior officers.

Some observers believed that the *tanda* system was declining in importance by the mid-1980s because the much larger class sizes and the smaller amount of time that classmates were together were not conducive to developing strong bonds. The emergence in the late 1980s of the forty-six member *tandona* of 1966 appeared to contradict that view, however. The so-called reformist members of the *tandona* who played significant roles in the political system in the late 1970s and early 1980s included Defense Minister García, his deputy Carranza, and the PN head, Colonel López Nuila. These officers advocated a hard line against the opposition.

The promotion, transfer, or retirement of at least thirty senior officers in early July 1988 marked the start of the ascension of the *tandona* to command posts. As a result of the changes—in which younger, more conservative officers replaced those more closely identified with President Duarte—the *tandona* held five of the six prestigious infantry brigade commands; controlled five of the seven military detachments, the three security forces, and the intelligence, operations, and personnel posts in the High Command; and occupied numerous other key slots. The leading member of the *tandona*, Colonel Ponce, was promoted to the position of chief of the Joint General Staff in November 1988 and thus assumed the counterinsurgency command. Although most of the top hierarchy was expected to be replaced by March 1989, *tandona* members were moving into the top posts slowly because the traditional seniority rule did not allow them to displace officers who had graduated before them. The sweeping command changes, however, angered many younger officers, who viewed the colonels' unusual consolidation of control as a power grab that blocked others' chances for promotion. Officers above and below the *tandona* bitterly resented it because of its size and influence.

Military Justice

Military justice traditionally adhered to a standard Western pattern, providing for special and general courts martial. Unit or post commanders had considerable leeway to dispense punishment without resorting to formal trial; their disciplinary powers served the functions of a summary court. The average Salvadoran soldier traditionally respected authority and accepted discipline as a

Salvadoran Army officer and soldier
Courtesy United States Department of Defense

normal condition of military life. Although the officer corps had a history of staging coups against unpopular military leaders, military commanders rarely mutinied. Ochoa's rebellion in 1983 was a glaring exception (see The Military in Power, 1931–84, this ch.). Discipline was not usually a major problem in the armed forces, and most offenses and infractions were dealt with by administrative penalties.

The armed forces code of military justice, signed by Defense Minister Vides on May 13, 1983, was loosely enforced. It pertained only to military offenses and stressed the military's constitutional obligations, the proper treatment of civilians, respect for human rights, and the use of only the minimum force necessary to achieve an objective. A special section of the 1983 code of conduct was devoted to procedures for handling members of the armed forces arrested for criminal activities or human rights violations. Commanders of such personnel were required to notify the Joint General Staff immediately and to conduct a thorough investigation. Results of the investigation were then to be furnished to the general staff and the Ministry of Defense and Public Security. During the investigation, commanders were authorized to place the suspected service member under arrest. If sufficient proof of guilt was available, the suspect was to be turned over to the proper judicial authority.

Article 216 of the Constitution establishes military jurisdiction for special tribunals and proceedings (*procedimientos*) to try purely military felonies (*delitos*) and misdemeanors (*faltas*). The verdicts of these courts martial may be appealed in the ultimate instance to the general commander of the armed forces or to the respective chief of field operations. Civilian felonies (*delitos comunes*) committed by military personnel must be prosecuted in the civil judicial system, but intimidation and lack of cooperation have rendered military personnel essentially immune from prosecution in the civil courts. This reflected the generally accepted military ethos according to which one never subjected a fellow officer to punishment by civilians. Some army officers considered López Nuila's steps to investigate human rights abuses and other crimes by some senior army officers to have violated this unwritten code, the intent of which was to prevent any real or perceived loss of military power and influence.

In 1986 the directors of each of the three security forces created internal investigatory units responsible for inquiring into all accusations made against members of those forces. If the investigators found "probable cause" that a member of the military had committed a crime, the member was to be released from the force and turned over to the proper civilian judicial authorities for follow-up. If it was found that a crime had not been committed but that authority had been abused, the member was to be fined, disciplined, or released from the service. During the period from June 1985 to May 1986, over 200 members of the public security forces were remanded to the civilian courts for prosecution. Because of deficiencies in the Salvadoran judicial system's record-keeping, it was not known how many of those were convicted. Nevertheless, in 1987 the United States embassy in San Salvador conducted a study on the disposition of 905 cases of military and public security forces members who had been dismissed from the armed forces for misconduct and abuse of authority and whose cases had been remanded to the civilian courts for adjudication. The investigation found that few were convicted, a situation largely attributable to the inadequacies of the judicial system, although military intimidation was also presumed to be a strong factor.

Resistance to investigation was particularly strong within the officer corps, where *tanda* ties traditionally kept officers from being arrested or prosecuted for alleged crimes. For example, when Lieutenant Colonel Roberto Mauricio Staben Perla, a leading *tandona* member, was detained in 1987 under suspicion of being part of a kidnapping ring involving several military officers, his classmates demanded that Duarte permit him to return to duty. Consequently,

Staben was released without ever having to submit to a formal investigation of the charges made against him by two witnesses, and he resumed his post as commander of the Arce Battalion. By 1987 the government was known to have prosecuted only two cases involving abuses against Salvadoran citizens by members of the armed forces; no member of the regular officer corps had been convicted of involvement in the many murders of civilians since 1979.

Foreign Military Influence and Assistance

From 1901 until 1957, four different Chilean military missions directed El Salvador's military training and operations on an almost continuous basis. In 1941 the Chileans founded the first war college, called the Command and General Staff School, and they directed its activities until 1957, when the Salvadorans took over its administration.

Although Germany was El Salvador's first European supplier of military equipment in the 1920s, France and Denmark also provided weaponry in the 1920s and 1930s. Small groups of Italian specialists trained Salvadoran military personnel in the handling of military equipment acquired from Italy during the 1930s.

United States military assistance to El Salvador began in the 1930s with the provision of some aircraft and ground forces equipment. In the closing stages of World War II, the United States transferred a few additional aircraft to El Salvador. After signing the Inter-American Treaty of Reciprocal Assistance (the Rio Treaty) in 1947, El Salvador began benefiting from assistance provided by a United States air mission as well as from increased transfers of aircraft. The Salvadoran Air Force became equipped almost exclusively with United States aircraft.

Although the United States remained primarily responsible for El Salvador's foreign training assistance from 1957 through 1988, the aid program totaled less than US$17 million in equipment and training between 1950 and 1979. The US$7.4 million in Military Assistance Program (MAP) funds provided during that period was far less than that received by any other Central American country except Costa Rica. After the 1961 coup, the United States expanded its military mission, which by 1970 numbered sixteen personnel. In March 1977, after the United States administration of President Jimmy Carter criticized El Salvador for human rights violations, the country rejected further United States military aid.

El Salvador then turned to countries other than the United States for military matériel. Salvadoran land and air forces purchased modern counterinsurgency equipment primarily from Brazil, Israel, and France. In addition to acquiring numerous aircraft, El Salvador also completely reequipped its infantry with G3 rifles from West Germany, some of which were still in use in the late 1980s, and purchased quantities of West German wheeled armored personnel carriers (APCs). El Salvador also obtained some artillery pieces from Yugoslavia during the 1970s.

After reformist military officers overthrew the Romero regime in October 1979, the Carter administration, eager to improve contacts with the military, allocated to El Salvador a small amount of training funds and US$5.7 million in "nonlethal" foreign military sales (FMS) in FY 1980. Renewed United States military assistance began in November 1979 with the arrival of a six-man Mobile Training Team (MTT) to provide riot-control training. The Carter administration had hoped to use military aid to persuade the army to curb its human rights abuses, make basic reforms, and allow civilian rule. The murders of four churchwomen from the United States in December 1980, however, provoked the Carter White House into suspending US$5 million in military aid. After the FMLN guerrillas launched a major offensive in January 1981, United States military aid was renewed (see The United States Takes a Hand, ch. 1).

The new administration of President Ronald Reagan was alarmed by reports that military aid was being provided by the Soviet Union and East European countries to the guerrillas through Cuba and Nicaragua; the administration was also concerned about the prospect of "another Nicaragua" in Central America. Accordingly, in March 1981 it provided US$20 million in emergency funds and US$5 million in FMS credits for new equipment and supplies for the Salvadoran Army. A five-member United States advisory team helped the Salvadoran Army to reorganize its command structure, streamline planning, and develop intelligence and communications techniques. The United States also sent an additional 40 Special Forces trainers-advisers to El Salvador to train the first of four 1,000-man "rapid reaction" battalions, the Atlacatl Battalion. The United States military mission in El Salvador expanded in 1981 to include a naval element. That year the first group of 500 Salvadoran officer candidates participated in a general officer training course at Fort Benning, Georgia. The United States also began training Salvadoran NCOs in Panama. In 1982 Special Forces provided counterinsurgency training to the Belloso Battalion and the Atonal Battalion. By late 1983, the United States had trained 900 Salvadoran officers, or half the entire officer corps.

The United States also provided both indirect and direct war-related assistance to help El Salvador in its war against the FMLN. The indirect aid accounted for about 44 percent of the total United

Helicopters on alert status, Ilopango Air Base
Courtesy Donald C. Keffer

States assistance program up to the mid-1980s. This category included cash transfers to sustain the Salvadoran government and economy, aid to displaced people, and assistance to rebuild infrastructure damaged by guerrilla sabotage. Some 30 percent of the total program consisted of funds used to expand the army, train the soldiers, and provide the equipment and facilities needed to conduct the counterinsurgency efforts.

The provision of military aid to El Salvador was not without its critics in the United States government. By 1982, when the Reagan administration had more than doubled direct military assistance to El Salvador to US$82 million, the United States Congress required the president to certify semiannually that the Salvadoran government was making substantial progress in controlling the military, improving its human rights practices, and implementing economic and political reform. Failure to issue such a certification would trigger a suspension of United States military aid. In 1983 Congress passed a continuing resolution that withheld 30 percent of the military aid until Salvadoran authorities obtained a verdict in the trial of the members of the GN accused of murdering the churchwomen from the United States. In 1984 Congress passed another continuing resolution that made aid disbursements conditional on the Reagan administration's consultation with Congress. The resolution also called for substantial progress in the reduction of death squad activities, elimination of corruption, improvement in the military's performance, and progress toward a peaceful resolution of the conflict.

The Reagan administration sought to establish a domestic consensus on United States policy toward Central America by way of the National Bipartisan Commission on Central America (the Kissinger Commission). The commission concluded in January 1984 that the 37,500-man Salvadoran Army was too small to break the military stalemate with the 9,000 to 12,000 increasingly well-trained and well-armed FMLN guerrillas. It therefore recommended that the United States significantly and quickly increase military aid—conditioned on demonstrated progress in meeting specified human rights goals—to give the Salvadoran military the ability to carry out an effective and more humane counterinsurgency effort. The commission's recommendations were instrumental in securing increased levels of United States military aid for El Salvador. During the next four years, El Salvador received an average of US$100 million annually in United States military assistance. The assistance levels peaked at US$197 million in fiscal year (FY) 1984, then declined steadily, reaching US$89 million in FY 1988.

In 1983 and 1984, about 3,500 Salvadorans attended United States-taught training courses at the Regional Military Training Center (RMTC), operated by the United States forces at Puerto Castilla, Honduras, as an alternative to more costly training in the United States or an increase in the number of United States advisers in El Salvador. That September, however, the Honduran government banned Salvadoran troops from the facility, owing in part to a lack of progress in talks between Honduras and El Salvador over their longstanding border dispute. Honduras reportedly also was uneasy over the United States military training on Honduran territory of personnel from El Salvador, its adversary in the 1969 war. When Honduras and the United States failed to reach an accord over the training issue, the RMTC was closed in June 1985.

The United States began sending military advisers, officially designated "trainers," to El Salvador in 1983 to help instruct the army in basic skills and counterinsurgency tactics. The Reagan administration imposed a limit of fifty-five American advisers in El Salvador and adhered to that figure. In 1988 only half of the fifty-five reportedly were involved in training; the others performed administrative duties.

El Salvador also received military-related assistance from several other countries in the 1980s. In 1982 Argentina supplied a cadre of military advisers with a large order of Argentine-made infantry equipment. Israel reportedly provided assistance in the form of counterinsurgency training. Both Britain and Belgium offered military training to the Salvadoran Army after the Honduran decision to bar Salvadoran military personnel. By the mid-1980s, West Germany was a major supplier of military assistance.

The Security Forces

Historical Background

In the early post-colonial period, the primary function of police forces was to enforce, at the behest of local authorities of towns and communities, an 1825 law on vagrancy in order to ensure an adequate supply of labor for the large landowners. New regulations issued in 1855 established a state-subsidized regional "rural police" force, whose roving inspectors were to patrol the highways and countryside and to penalize offenders for minor offenses by fining or jailing them.

Salvadoran police structures, including the National Police (Policía Nacional—PN), which was founded in 1867, developed in the later part of the nineteenth century for the purpose of assuming most of the internal security functions that the urban-based militia or army had been performing. In 1883 San Salvador set up a permanent professional police corps of 100 men and 18 officers and administrators. As a result of the liberal government's measures to deprive the Indian population of their land, expanded police forces were needed to deal with the growing Indian unrest. An 1888 legislative decree authorized the formation of a rural mounted police corps for the prosperous coffee-growing areas of western El Salvador, principally the departments of Ahuachapán, Sonsonate, and Santa Ana.

A national urban police system developed concurrently with the rural National Guard (Guardia Nacional—GN). By the end of 1906, the full-time police forces of the other major cities were linked administratively to the San Salvador police. President Manuel Araujo established the basis of a professional law enforcement system in 1912 when he appointed a Spanish army captain as commander of all the permanent civil police organizations. The captain formed a national police corps of 1,200 officers and men and developed a training program.

The evolution of the rural police system culminated in 1912 when two Spanish officers formed a Salvadoran version of the Spanish Civil Guard called the GN. Placed under the operational control of the Ministry of Government and Development, the guard's black-helmeted troops were organized specifically to defend coffee and fruit plantations from thousands of peasants evicted from what had been communal properties. Although the main duty of the GN was to control the rural population, it also enforced petty agrarian provisions and kept records on personnel employed by plantations. Thus, many GN units—like their army counterparts—acted as private armies for the large landowners. The Treasury Police (Policía de Hacienda—PH), formed in 1926, functioned mainly as a frontier guard and customs force. Its initial mission was primarily to prevent campesinos from producing *chícha,* the local version of corn liquor.

In January 1932, a month after taking power, Martínez ordered his security forces to use indiscriminate violence to suppress a rural revolt in western El Salvador organized by the newly established Communist Party of El Salvador (Partido Comunista de El Salvador—PCES). The GN and Civic Guard (Guardia Cívica), a newly created civilian militia, thereupon massacred, by most historical accounts, approximately 30,000 peasants, trade unionists, and opposition members in *la matanza* and captured and executed the communist leader, Agustín Farabundo Martí (see The Coffee Republic, ch. 1).

The Martínez regime refined a system of stricter control of the rural population by developing the rural security forces, including the Civic Guard, with units in each of more than 2,000 local communities. After the rebellion, Civic Guard units functioned as a private militia for wealthy families and military commanders. The regime based its new security measures largely on existing legislation and the Agrarian Code, which it revised in 1941 in order to set down guidelines for law enforcement and the regimentation of rural life. The basic organization of the security system as established by Martínez operated with little modification until the 1980s. The Revolution of 1948, however, reversed the subordination of the army to the security services and disbanded the Civic Guard. The three police forces thereafter assumed primary responsibility for internal security.

In the early 1960s, some Salvadoran officers of an extreme rightist orientation formed paramilitary organizations to assist the army and GN in fighting subversion with unconventional and illegal methods (see Right-Wing Extremism, this ch.). The GN's Colonel José Alberto "Chele" Medrano helped found the Nationalist Democratic Organization (Organización Democrática Nacionalista—Orden). By the mid-1960s, Orden was a well-established, nationwide network of peasant informants and paramilitary forces, with a unit in most villages. Local army commanders supervised these units in coordination with GN commanders. Recruits came primarily from the army reserve system, and the GN provided most of their training. Orden units performed regular patrolling duties in their local areas, served as an informant network, and attempted to inculcate an anticommunist doctrine among the rural population. With the support of President Fidel Sánchez Hernández, its "supreme chief," and Medrano, its "executive director," the organization expanded its role in the late 1960s to include involvement in civic action and development projects. Because of the influence of some of the more zealous GN intelligence officers, however, Orden deteriorated into an undisciplined and even ruthless militia of between 50,000 and 100,000 members. After Medrano's removal from power in 1970, Orden's status was reduced from official to semiofficial by removing it from direct presidential control.

By the early 1970s, an extensive paramilitary organization utilizing the structure and personnel of Orden supplemented the traditional security system. Although the reformist coalition that seized power in October 1979 issued decrees to outlaw and disband Orden that November, the organization apparently was abolished in name only. In 1976 a new civil defense law had established a system to assist in national emergencies and to counter attempts at rural insurgency. The membership of the new civil defense units that were finally organized in 1981 reportedly tended to overlap with that of Orden. The main purpose of the new civil defense units was to serve as local self-defense militia and to repel guerrilla attacks on villages. By the late 1980s, the Salvadoran Army claimed to have organized 21,000 civil defense troops in 319 communities, with another 10,000 troops in training. Despite being lightly armed and poorly trained, the civil defense troops were an important supplement to the thinly stretched army.

Mission and Organization

In 1988, El Salvador's internal security forces, called the public security forces, consisted of the GN, with 4,200 members; the PN, with 6,000 members; and the PH, with about 2,400 members. These services were supported by the territorial Civil Defense (Defensa Civil—DC), with about 24,000 members. Although controlled by the minister of defense and public security, even in peacetime, and engaged in the counterinsurgency effort, the public security forces had primarily a police role. By mid-1988 the police forces had improved markedly in professionalism and performance, but they still lacked sufficient training and resources to deter or respond effectively to terrorist attacks.

The PN was responsible for urban security, the GN for rural security, and the PH—including customs and immigration personnel—for the prevention of smuggling, for border control, and for the enforcement of laws relating to alcohol production and associated tax matters. The GN was organized into fourteen companies, one for each of the fourteen departments. A tactical structure of five commands or battalions could replace the regular organization in an emergency. The PN was divided into the Line Police (Policía de Línea), which functioned as an urban police force; the Traffic Police (Policía de Tránsito), which handled traffic in urban areas; the Highway Patrol (Policía de Caminos); the Department of Investigations (Departamento de Investigaciones), or plainclothes detective force; and the Night Watchmen and Bank Guards Corps (Cuerpo de Vigilantes Nocturnos y Bancários).

Until the early 1980s, the security forces were among the most notorious violators of human rights in El Salvador. The PH, with an extensive network of rural informants, evolved into the most select and brutal of the three security forces during its first fifty years. Police and army units were involved in a number of bloody incidents when they attempted to break up large demonstrations (see The Reformist Coup of 1979, ch. 1).

After taking office as president in 1984, however, Duarte, in an effort to tighten discipline and centralize control over the traditionally semiautonomous security forces, created the new position of vice minister of defense and public security and named Colonel López Nuila to fill it. López Nuila thereupon reorganized all police forces and private guard organizations as he sought to clarify the ambiguous, overlapping responsibilities of the PN, PH, and GN. The reorganization gave the PN sole responsibility for urban law and order and restricted the GN's authority to rural areas. In addition, López Nuila merged the Customs Police (Policía de Aduana) with the PH, thus removing the latter from nationwide law-and-order duties and restricting it to handling border duties and supervising the defense of state property and customs. López Nuila also replaced the controversial PH director general, Carranza, with an ally, Colonel Rinaldo Golcher. Golcher placed all other paramilitary organizations—from the guard forces that defended electric companies and banks to the private guards that were hired by individuals or private firms—under the control and licensing of the PH. López Nuila also made an effort to purge the security services of disreputable personnel. He announced in December 1986 that 1,806 members of the public security forces had been dismissed between June 1985 and May 1986.

In November 1986, Duarte inaugurated a program under which the three security services would receive training. As a result, mandatory human rights instruction became part of police recruit training and officers' classes in the late 1980s. The security forces

Member of National Guard
Courtesy Donald C. Keffer

instituted a separate intensive human rights training program for all police. By early 1988, virtually all members of the PN had received the course, and the GN was in the process of receiving it.

Foreign Security Assistance

The United States provided some basic equipment and training to the public security forces. Between 1957 and 1974, the United States, under the auspices of the Public Safety Program of the Agency for International Development (AID), improved the law enforcement investigations, communications, and intelligence capabilities of the police services, including the GN. The US$2.1 million program assisted in the formation of two fifty-member, rapid-reaction, riot-control units based at the national police headquarters in the capital and similar units in national police quarters in San Miguel and Santa Ana. Program advisers also reorganized the Police Academy and implemented various measures to improve police antiterrorist capabilities. The GN's Special Investigations Section (Servicio de Investigaciones Especiales—SIE) received considerable United States assistance in the early 1970s. The Public Safety Program also aided in expanding and training personnel of the Customs Police, which grew from 250 members in 1967 to 527 in 1974. Until 1981 the Carter administration limited United States security assistance to El Salvador to "nonlethal" items, such

231

as bullet-proof vests, in an unsuccessful attempt to force the Salvadoran security forces to improve their human rights practices.

In late 1985, the Reagan administration, alarmed by several significant terrorist incidents in El Salvador, including the slaying of five Marine guards attached to the United States embassy, notified Congress that three United States military advisers in El Salvador would begin training 420 members of the PH, PN, and GN in antiterrorism techniques. The administration also intended to equip these forces with rifles, ammunition, patrol vehicles, and communications gear. The Foreign Assistance Act of 1974 prohibited the United States from providing financial support, training, or advice for the law enforcement forces of any foreign country. The United States Congress, however, passed an amendment to the act waiving the general police aid prohibition for El Salvador and Honduras for FY 1986 and FY 1987, contingent on biannual presidential certification of significant progress in reducing human rights violations in those countries. Under the waiver, the United States provided US$3.1 million in police training to El Salvador in FY 1986 and another US$14 million in FY 1987 through both the Antiterrorism Assistance Act and the Administration of Justice Program.

United States efforts to aid the counterterrorist capability of the Salvadoran armed forces included the formation in 1985 of a hostage-rescue unit called the Special Antiterrorist Command (Comando Especial Anti-Terrorista—CEAT). Although under the direct command of the army chief of staff, the CEAT reportedly consisted of PH members. Under the United States Law Enforcement Counterterrorism Assistance Program, El Salvador received several million dollars in police assistance. As a result of funding cutbacks, only three trainers were working with the public security forces on a national level in mid-1988. That year, the security forces also organized the Joint Intelligence Operations Center (Centro de Operaciones Conjuntos de Inteligencia—COCI), with a mission to collect, integrate, and analyze intelligence relating to terrorist activities in the San Salvador metropolitan area.

Threats to Internal Security

In the final quarter of 1988, El Salvador continued to suffer the effects of a nine-year-old insurgency by the FMLN, whose 6,000 to 8,000 armed combatants—a figure reduced by attrition and desertion from the estimated 12,000 guerrillas in the field in 1984—received varying degrees of support from Nicaragua, Cuba, and the Soviet Union. By most estimates, more than 63,000 people, or about 1.2 percent of the nation's total population, had died in political violence since 1979, victims of either leftist guerrillas, the military, or right-wing death squads. At the same time, 25 to 30 percent of the population had been displaced or had fled the country as a result of the conflict. Tutela Legal (Legal Aid—the human rights monitoring office of the archdiocese of San Salvador) and other human rights groups claimed that the rightist death squads had murdered more than 40,000 Salvadorans by 1985. During the Duarte government, military and right-wing death squad activity declined significantly, partially as a result of United States threats to withhold economic and military assistance.

In January 1987, constitutional rights were restored when the state of siege, instituted in 1980 and regularly renewed since that date, was allowed to lapse. Extraordinary legislation governing the prosecution of persons suspected of involvement with the insurgency (Decree 50) expired several weeks later. Although the military was concerned that the failure to renew these security decrees would adversely affect their ability to conduct the war, it complied nonetheless by reinstating due process procedures as set forth in the Constitution. The security forces followed presidential orders not to take coercive action to halt a series of violent demonstrations and strikes by guerrilla urban front groups, whose members vandalized and destroyed public and private property, in the May to August period of 1987.

Under the general amnesty law of November 1987, passed by the Legislative Assembly in an effort to comply with the Central American Peace Agreement, the government released about 470 suspected or convicted insurgents—including some involved in several major terrorist incidents—along with a few former military personnel involved in death squad murders. The amnesty covered "politically related crimes" and all common crimes committed in a group of more than twenty persons. It specifically excluded, however, the crime of kidnapping, the 1980 murder of Archbishop Romero, and the period after October 22, 1987. Interpreted broadly, the amnesty could prevent charges from being filed for massacres by the military and killings by the death squads and could require the release of soldiers convicted of human rights abuses. Both the left and the right criticized the law; the left objected to an effective pardon for thousands of death squad assassinations, and the far right condemned pardons for acts of terrorism and sabotage.

The government's leniency did little to alleviate political violence, however. The capital city was exposed almost daily to leftist-sponsored demonstrations, strikes, and economic sabotage, as well as bombings. According to the United States Department of State, in the first quarter of 1988 the capital suffered 213 incidents of sabotage against its telecommunications and electrical systems, as well as 49 acts of economic sabotage and 138 strikes or demonstrations.

Right-Wing Extremism

Background

The death squads that became active in the late 1970s had their historical roots in El Salvador's three security forces, which often functioned as a law unto themselves. Each security service had its own special unit charged with assassinating suspected ''subversives.'' The PH's intelligence section, the S-2, in particular was persistently linked to the political killings and kidnappings that became commonplace in the 1970s and early 1980s. Immediately after being appointed PH director general in 1984, Golcher disbanded the S-2 unit. Within six months, he had replaced it with a new forty-member police force trained by the PN in intelligence work.

The extreme right responded to the left-wing terrorism of the 1970s and the growing militancy of the popular (or mass) organizations in a violent fashion. Paramilitary forces—first Orden, later civil defense—supplemented the military establishment. Ultrarightists within the military, security forces, and oligarchy also organized death squads to eliminate leftist activists and sympathizers and to deter popular support through intimidation. Analysts generally agreed that right-wing death squads—often composed of active-duty military or security force personnel operating with the complicity of some senior officers of the armed forces—were responsible for thousands of murders in the 1970s and 1980s. At the same time, the regime's security forces themselves became increasingly violent.

Orden supplied recruits for the notorious White Hand (Mano Blanca), the death squad that Medrano organized in the late 1970s. Medrano's protégé, D'Aubuisson, reportedly helped organize the White Warriors Union (Unión de Guerreros Blancos—UGB), a group of death squads that emerged in early 1977 and became known for their terrorism against the Jesuit community working in El Salvador. Some military officers, particularly in the GN, privately supported and facilitated death squad killings during the Romero regime. The UGB reportedly was associated with the GN's intelligence branch (the G-2).

Extreme rightist political factions viewed the death squads as legitimate ''counterterrorists'' against the leftist guerrillas, and they did in fact do serious damage to the FMLN's urban base by 1982.

In 1983, however, the death squads were used to challenge directly the influence of the United States in El Salvador. They forced at least one American journalist out of the country, threatened a prominent labor leader supported by the United States embassy, and even threatened to assassinate United States ambassador Thomas Pickering. Other death squad victims included bureaucrats and office workers, labor organizers, professionals, politicians, priests, and even soldiers.

Right-wing terrorism crested during the 1980–82 period. At the peak of the violence in late 1980, the monthly toll of politically motivated murders ran between 700 and 800. In the most publicized political assassination of this period, suspected rightists shot Archbishop Romero—an outspoken advocate of dialogue with the popular organizations and a critic of military repression—while he was saying mass on March 24, 1980 (see The Role of Religion, ch. 2). An extreme right-wing group calling itself the Maximiliano Hernández Martínez Brigade claimed responsibility for several assassinations of Christian democratic and Marxist leaders in San Salvador in 1980. Four churchwomen from the United States were murdered in December 1980. Several army officers were linked to the submachine gun killings of two land reform advisers of the American Institute for Free Labor Development (AIFLD) in San Salvador's Sheraton Hotel on January 3, 1981, an act that was carried out by two GN corporals. After the cut-off of United States aid over the murders of the churchwomen, the Christian Democrats in the government were able to remove from command positions several key ultra-rightists, including Carranza, the deputy minister of defense and public security.

Curbing the Death Squads

In December 1983, the Reagan administration promised Magaña an additional US$100 million in military aid if his government took action against the death squads and dismissed from their official posts or transferred abroad at least eight armed forces officers and one civilian who had been identified as death squad leaders. Vice President George Bush personally visited San Salvador, however, to deliver the more decisive message that aid would be cut off if the abuses did not stop. The United States specifically asked for a halt to secret arrests by the three security forces and demonstrable progress in the court cases involving the murders of the churchwomen and the AIFLD advisers.

In response, senior Salvadoran officials and the armed forces leadership pledged a major crackdown on right-wing death squad activity and asked the United States for technical and investigative assistance in dealing with these groups. The Salvadoran Army also quietly dismissed or transferred abroad the officers whose names were on the United States list of suspects. In addition, the PN arrested a captain who had been linked to the murder of the two AIFLD advisers, but he was held on charges unrelated to the killings.

Despite these actions, the existence of the death squads remained a controversial issue in the United States in the late 1980s. In congressional testimony in February 1984, former United States ambassador to El Salvador Robert E. White identified six wealthy Salvadoran landowners, then living in exile in Miami, as the principal financiers of the death squads. Critics of the Reagan administration's Salvadoran policy also alleged that the United States had indirectly supported the death squads. After a six-month investigation, however, the United States Senate Select Committee on Intelligence reported in October 1984 that there was no evidence to support such allegations.

In 1984 and 1985, Duarte transferred to lesser positions several military officers with alleged links to death squads. During the 1984–88 period, the civilian government and armed forces reiterated their opposition to death squad activity and their commitment to dealing with the problem. As a result, death squad killings declined sharply. According to Tutela Legal, the annual totals of death squad killings were 225 in 1984, 136 in 1985, 45 in 1986, and 24 in 1987. Although violence continued to be endemic in El Salvador, the number of politically motivated deaths reported in the Salvadoran press averaged 28 per month during the first half of 1987, as compared with 64 in 1984 and 140 in 1983. These figures probably were inexact, but they indicated a general downward trend. Of the 183 political murders reported in the local press during the first nine months of 1987, most were attributed to the FMLN; only 2 were blamed on the extreme right and 5 on military personnel.

Death squad activities began to pick up, however, in late 1987 after the signing of the Central American Peace Agreement. The number of right-wing death squad killings reportedly continued to creep upward in 1988. According to Tutela Legal, suspected right-wing death squads killed thirty-two civilians during the first half of 1988.

Left-Wing Extremism

Background to the Insurgency

The FMLN insurgency was rooted in the 1960s when reform-minded groups emerged to challenge the alliance of the right-wing military and the landowning oligarchy. With the electoral option blocked by fraudulent presidential elections in 1972 and 1977, leftist groups resorted to militant demonstrations and terrorism to promote change. A pattern of mounting violence and polarization resulted (see The 1970s: The Road to Revolt, ch. 1). As in the early 1930s, the growing conflict had focused on the peasant population; most campesinos still lived at a subsistence level, and about two-fifths of rural families had no land at all (see Rural Life, ch. 2). The regime's token land reform of 1976 did little to address this longstanding problem. Political violence and the suspension of rights through the declaration of states of siege only served to further radicalize the left, including the Catholic groups increasingly influenced by liberation theology (see Glossary).

The Salvadoran guerrilla groups that emerged in the 1970s derived directly or indirectly from a 1969 split within the illegal, Moscow-line Communist Party of El Salvador (Partido Comunista de El Salvador—PCES) between the old-line Communists and a vocal minority faction of firebrand revolutionaries led by PCES secretary general Salvador Cayetano Carpio ("Marcial"). In April 1970, Carpio and his followers broke away from the PCES and founded the Popular Liberation Forces (Fuerzas Populares de Liberación—FPL). Under Carpio's leadership, the FPL advocated doctrinaire adherence to a Vietnamese-style "prolonged popular war" strategy against "imperialism" and the Salvadoran oligarchy. During the FPL's formative years, the National University in San Salvador was the largest urban center for recruiting and training members of the FPL and its mass organization, the Revolutionary Popular Bloc (Bloque Popular Revolucionario—BPR). With the aid of the clergy, the FPL recruited its cadres mostly from the National Association of Salvadoran Educators (Asociación Nacional de Educadores Salvadoreños—ANDES) and its rank-and-file mainly from the Federation of Salvadoran Christian Peasants (Federación de Campesinos Cristianos Salvadoreños—Feccas) and the Union of Farm Workers (Unión de Trabajadores del Campo—UTC).

In 1971 another group of PCES dissidents, disenchanted with the FPL's strategy of a prolonged popular war, left the party and joined with dissident students, religious activists, and PDC members to form the People's Revolutionary Army (Ejército Revolucionario del Pueblo—ERP). The ERP's "militarist" faction, headed by Joaquín Villalobos Hueso ("René Cruz"), contended that Sandinista-style popular insurrection could be sparked by dramatic armed attacks on the existing power structure. The ERP's "political" faction, led by Roque Dalton, a communist Salvadoran poet, emphasized the ideological preparation of the masses before undertaking major armed actions and the development of broad coalitions with other groups. After the Villalobos group passed death sentences on Dalton's followers, Villalobos reportedly murdered Dalton on May 10, 1975.

Under the leadership of Villalobos, the ERP advocated a strongly pro-Cuban, Marxist-Leninist ideology based on Ernesto "Che" Guevara's *foco*, or insurrectional center, theory of guerrilla warfare, as well as Maoist and West European revolutionary theories. Most of the ERP's cadres were of middle-class background, mainly university dropouts or professionals. They included considerably more women and foreigners than the other guerrilla groups. A leading ERP field commander, Ana Guadalupe Martínez, author of the propagandistic *El Salvador's Clandestine Prisons*, served as a main spokesperson on international affairs for the Revolutionary Democratic Front (Frente Democrático Revolucionario—FDR). Some cadres had radical Christian backgrounds. Rank-and-file elements generally were workers but also included some forcibly recruited peasants. Although the PCES and the other guerrilla groups that formed the FMLN in 1980 initially ostracized the ERP, Cuban leader Fidel Castro Ruz pressured the FMLN groups into including the ERP in the alliance.

Immediately after Dalton's murder, his followers broke away from the ERP and established the Armed Forces of National Resistance (Fuerzas Armadas de Resistencia Nacional—FARN). The FARN originated at the National University, and most of its cadres came from the middle class. Although led by a self-described Marxist, Eduardo Sancho Castañeda ("Fermán Cienfuegos"), the FARN developed close ties internationally with moderate social democrats and domestically with liberal members of the Salvadoran armed forces. On February 2, 1977, FARN and PCES dissidents, together with Salvadoran exiles living in Costa Rica, formed a Salvadoran branch of a Trotskyite regional organization called the Revolutionary Party of Central American Workers (Partido Revolucionario de Trabajadores Centroamericanos—PRTC). The PRTC recruited primarily from the National University in San Salvador, which PRTC leader Francisco Jovel ("Roberto Roca") had attended, and from the labor unions. Although the PRTC initially had a reputation for unpredictable radicalism and close ties to the Democratic People's Republic of Korea (North Korea), it moved toward more orthodox Marxism-Leninism after joining the FMLN in December 1980. Nevertheless, it continued to advocate a nonaligned international stance.

The PCES, under its new leader, Jorge Shafik Handal, followed the Moscow line in the 1970s, supporting reformist, noncommunist governments and an electoral strategy. At its April 1979 party congress, however, the PCES, which already had begun organizing its own guerrilla group, the Armed Forces of Liberation (Fuerzas Armadas de Liberación—FAL), adopted an "armed struggle" policy. While serving in the reformist government that came to power in a civil-military coup in October 1979, the PCES continued to prepare for guerrilla and terrorist activities by sending its recruits to training camps in the Soviet Union, Eastern Europe, Cuba, and Nicaragua. Although commanded exclusively by PCES cadres, FAL was made up mostly, not of party members, but of rural-based guerrillas who had been gradually indoctrinated into serving as PCES followers. By the late 1970s, the PCES consisted primarily of middle class elements and cadres of some workers' organizations. Although Handal espoused a "dialectical combination" of the ERP's insurrectional approach and the FPL's protracted popular war strategy, he remained more oriented toward the ERP.

During the 1977–79 period, the left-wing mass organizations conducted a campaign of civil disobedience, demonstrations, and takeovers of churches, government buildings, and foreign embassies. Much of this activity was perpetrated by the three largest mass organizations—the FPL's BPR, the FARN's United Popular Action Front (Frente de Acción Popular Unidad—FAPU), and the ERP's 28th of February Popular Leagues (Ligas Populares 28 de Febrero—LP–28). At the same time, the extreme left engaged in numerous significant acts of terrorism, such as the kidnapping of foreign businessmen for fund-raising purposes, political kidnappings, assassinations, and bombings. The FARN specialized in kidnapping and claimed to have raised US$60 million in ransoms in the late 1970s.

Most of the mass organizations rejected talks with the reformist junta that took power in January 1980. Instead, they consolidated their forces by forming the Revolutionary Coordinator of the Masses (Coordinadora Revolucionaria de las Masas—CRM) at the same time that the armed left increased its own efforts at greater coordination. In April 1980, the CRM allied itself with the Democratic Front (Frente Democrático)—an alliance consisting of disaffected Christian Democrats, Social Democrats led by Guillermo Manuel Ungo Revelo, and a small association of professionals. The merger of these two umbrella organizations created the FDR, which recognized the guerrilla movement as its "vanguard." Although the Romero assassination enabled the FDR, through the mass organizations, to mobilize tens of thousands of demonstrators in the spring of 1980, the overall movement was hampered by a lack of arms, poor coordination between guerrilla and noncombatant forces, continued infighting, and severe repression by the security forces.

In May 1980, the guerrilla leaders met in Havana and formed a political-military command, the Unified Revolutionary Directorate (Dirección Revolucionaria Unificada—DRU), as their central executive arm for political and military planning. Unification of forces reportedly was a precondition for Cuban aid to the Salvadoran insurgents. The DRU established its headquarters near Managua and helped to direct planning and operations and coordinate logistical support for its forces in El Salvador. The fifteen-member DRU included three leaders from each of the five guerrilla groups: the ERP, FPL, FARN, FAL/PCES, and, beginning in late 1980, the PRTC. The DRU also included a five-member executive directorate, known as the General Command, consisting of the principal leaders of the five guerrilla groups: the ERP's Villalobos (the first among equals of the FMLN commanders), the FPL's Leonel González, the FARN's Sancho, the PRTC's Francisco Jovel, and the FAL/PCES's Handal.

The guerrilla groups took a step toward closer unity in October 1980 by forming the Farabundo Martí National Liberation Front (Frente Farabundo Martí de Liberación Nacional-Frente Democrático Revolucionario—FMLN–FDR), which constituted an umbrella entity or alliance for operational and strategic coordination among the insurgent forces and their popular fronts. The FMLN had a leadership structure (DRU), a regional military organization (five guerrilla fronts), and a political-diplomatic front (the FDR). A self-described Marxist-Leninist movement with a generally pro-Soviet and pro-Cuban orientation, the FMLN–FDR committed itself to seizing power through a two-pronged military strategy of economic sabotage and a prolonged guerrilla war of attrition based on a combination of Maoist, Vietnamese, and Guevarist principles. It sought to entrench its rural guerrilla forces while developing urban support bases in preparation for an eventual general insurrection. During the 1980–82 period, politically related violence in El Salvador increased dramatically as the former terrorist groups completed their transition to primarily guerrilla organizations.

In preparation for the FMLN's "final offensive" of January 1981 (the name of which seemed to contradict the FPL's long-term strategy), tons of modern weapons, primarily United States-made arms from captured stockpiles in Vietnam, were delivered covertly to guerrilla forces in El Salvador, mostly through Cuba and Nicaragua. Despite the substantial weapons deliveries, the 1981 offensive failed in its effort to incite a countrywide insurrection; the FMLN had greatly overestimated its popular support and the efficiency of its outside supply system. Salvadoran military and security forces, operating with minimal United States assistance (military aid had been suspended until then), beat back the offensive after about ten days of combat. The vast majority of Salvadorans ignored the FMLN's call for an uprising, much to the chagrin of guerrilla strategists. The FMLN tried and failed again to defeat the army in a general offensive in early 1982. After these setbacks, however, the five FMLN groups worked to increase their strategic and tactical coordination and made substantial progress during 1982 in overcoming logistical and communications problems. They began to equip their forces increasingly with United States-made weapons and equipment captured from the army or purchased in the international gray arms market. In addition, United States officials maintained that Nicaraguan supplies for the FMLN continued to be sent by sea, air, and land to El Salvador almost daily.

The FMLN overcame major factional disputes during 1983. At a January 1983 meeting of the FPL's Central Committee, the doctrinaire line of Carpio, a long-time opponent of close cooperation with other FMLN groups, reportedly was voted down in favor of greater FMLN unity of action, as advocated by another senior FPL leader, Ana Melinda Montes ("Ana María"). Nevertheless, the existence of a continuing deep division over policy within the guerrilla forces was revealed in April 1983 by the bizarre murder and suicide, respectively, in Managua of Carpio and Montes. The deaths weakened the FPL's influence in the FMLN in favor of the ERP, whose leader, Villalobos, had long advocated greater operational cooperation. In September 1983, however, the long-standing policy dispute within the FPL eased substantially with the consolidation of a position emphasizing unity with other FMLN groups and openness toward cooperation with outside groups. The FPL's policy shift reduced friction with the FMLN's four other military factions and with Nicaragua's ruling Sandinista National Liberation Front (Frente Sandinista de Liberación Nacional—FSLN). Furthermore, the FPL, which previously had operated largely independently of other FMLN groups, formally agreed to cooperate in a centralized military command (the DRU).

The relatively united FMLN again went on the offensive that September and decisively escalated the war from company- to battalion-level guerrilla combat, involving as many as 500 guerrillas in an offensive. Over the next five years, the conflict remained a military stalemate. The FMLN established a sophisticated internal communications system linking its fronts and became—

241

allegedly with Cuban and Nicaraguan assistance—better trained and armed. The organization, which by 1984 reportedly was receiving mostly ammunition, not weapons, from Nicaragua, also achieved important military tactical successes. By early 1984, the Salvadoran Army held less than a four-to-one advantage over a guerrilla force of at least 9,000 combatants, down from 10,000 to 12,000 in 1983 (military tacticians usually consider a ten-to-one advantage the minimum necessary to defeat a guerrilla insurgency).

Some commentators opined that the insurgents had failed decisively by the end of 1984 and that the war was winding down. The FMLN was put on the defensive in 1984 and 1985 when substantial United States military aid was rushed in and the Salvadoran Army expanded rapidly. Under heavy pressure in the rural area it once dominated, the FMLN committed itself to a new long-term strategy and began rebuilding its political bases—peasant, labor, and student militant groups—in cities and towns. Many guerrillas hid their weapons and moved into San Salvador. By mid-1985 the FMLN had adapted to the army's new tactics and capabilities by breaking down its large guerrilla columns into smaller squads assigned to ambush and sabotage government targets. By late December 1985, the number of guerrillas dropped to between 5,000 and 7,000, of which at least 2,000 remained active in the rural areas.

The FMLN also reverted to classic guerrilla tactics and increased its use of land mines, which it called "popular armament." In mid-1985 the FMLN, in addition to kidnapping or assassinating numerous military and government officials, began kidnapping and assassinating mayors and burning their offices. It also targeted United States military personnel for assassination. In June 1985, PRTC terrorists assassinated four off-duty United States embassy Marine guards at a sidewalk café in San Salvador in a massacre that also left nine civilians, including two United States businessmen, dead and fifteen others wounded. According to the FMLN high command, the chief purpose of its raid on the army's basic training center in eastern La Unión Department in October 1985 was to kill or capture United States soldiers serving there.

Insurgent Organization

Although the FMLN continued to suffer from long-standing sectarian rivalries, the FMLN groups—with Cuban training and other assistance—reorganized during 1983. The FMLN divided the country into five war fronts: the Feliciano Amo Western Front (covering Ahuachapán, La Libertad, Santa Ana, and Sonsonate departments), Modesto Ramírez Central Front (including Cuscatlán, San Salvador, and parts of Cabañas and La Paz departments),

Damage to Fourth Infantry Brigade compound from guerrilla attack,
El Paraíso, Chalatenango Department, December 1983
Courtesy United States Department of Defense

Anastasio Aquino Paracentral Front (comprising parts of Cabañas and La Paz departments, as well as San Vicente Department), Francisco Sánchez Eastern Front (covering La Unión, Morazán, San Miguel, and Usulután departments), and Apolinario Serrano Northern Front (consisting of Chalatenango Department).

The individual FMLN groups each claimed traditional areas of operation and influence within the five FMLN fronts and were organized on Marxist-Leninist structures. The ERP, which had a Marxist-Leninist political front, the Party of the Salvadoran Revolution (Partido de la Revolución Salvadoreña—PRS), was a particularly well-organized group. Directed by its nine-member general command, the ERP's principal force was the Rafael Arce Zablah Brigade (Brigada Rafael Arce Zablah—BRAZ), which operated on the Francisco Sánchez Eastern Front. The BRAZ was subdivided into two groups consisting of several battalions. The FPL operated on the northern, central, and western fronts. Directed by a general command, composed of more than twenty-five commanders, the FPL's leadership structure also included a revolutionary council, a central committee, and a political commission. The FPL's complex military structure was also collectively known as the Popular Army of Liberation (Ejército Popular de Liberación—EPL). Virtually indistinguishable from the FPL, the

243

EPL was composed of elite "vanguard units," less skilled "guerrilla columns," and the "urban front" commando groups in the cities.

Based primarily in the area of Guazapa Volcano, the FARN served as the military apparatus of the National Resistance (Resistencia Nacional—RN) party, a Marxist-Leninist political front whose secretary general and second in command constituted the FARN's general military command. The PRTC operated with other FMLN groups through its armed wing, the Revolutionary Armed Forces of Popular Liberation (Fuerzas Armadas Revolucionarias de Liberación Popular—FARLP). In addition to its rural forces, the PRTC had a San Salvador-based terrorist apparatus called the Mardoqueo Cruz Urban Guerrilla Commando. The PCES military wing, the FAL, also reportedly was based at Guazapa Volcano, but its principal rural guerrilla force operated mainly in northern and central El Salvador. Although Handal commanded the FAL, it also had an operational commander.

In the late 1980s, the rebels were still operating in small units, avoiding confrontations with the army except on their own terms, and emphasizing hit-and-run attacks mainly against economic targets. In 1986 FMLN attacks on the economy increased by 29 percent. The eastern region of El Salvador, the FMLN's main area of operations, suffered the brunt of the sabotage campaign. The FMLN facilitated its operations in El Salvador by using as sanctuaries demilitarized border zones (*bolsones*), such as north of the Torola-Jocoaitique line in northern Morazán Department.

One of the FMLN's prime objectives was to sabotage the country's economic infrastructure by attacking systematically such targets as bridges, the power grid, and communications equipment. Guerrilla forces also disrupted the transportation system by paralyzing road traffic every month or two. The intimidation of private investors through threats, "war taxes," kidnapping, and armed attacks on their business premises was another aspect of this strategy, as was the infiltration of labor unions in an effort to promote unrest. Guerrilla sabotage and indirect economic losses caused by the war amounted to nearly US$2 billion during 1979–88, more than the total amount of United States economic assistance provided the country during the same period. Salvadoran officials reported that 2,477 attacks on the country's energy grid in the 1980–87 period destroyed 654 primary and secondary distribution lines, costing US$51 million to repair.

Peace Talks

In 1983 the interim government, led by Magaña, created a Peace Commission and began meeting privately with FMLN–FDR representatives. Continued military stalemate led to direct public talks for the first time between the government and the FMLN–FDR in the town of La Palma on October 15, 1984. Duarte and Vides, representing the government at the talks, offered an amnesty to any guerrillas who laid down their arms and urged them to participate in the elections that year. The two parties reached some agreements on the conduct of the war and the evacuation of guerrilla prisoners, but they made no progress toward achieving a negotiated solution to the insurgency. The FMLN–FDR restated its longstanding demands. It wanted a power-sharing arrangement whereby a certain number of its representatives would be included in an interim government to be established before the holding of elections, and it wanted to maintain its own armed forces after the cessation of active hostilities. The guerrilla representatives insisted that these were nonnegotiable elements of their position.

The Duarte government lost the initiative in the war in part as a result of the FMLN's kidnapping in September 1985 of the president's daughter, Inés Guadalupe Duarte Durán, an action that totally preoccupied Duarte and virtually paralyzed his government for almost two months. Duarte lost considerable influence and credibility with the military and the public by ignoring El Salvador's policy against complying with the demands of kidnappers and releasing 126 FMLN prisoners in exchange for his daughter and 33 municipal officials (mainly mayors) previously taken hostage by the guerrillas. The agreement did not include a monetary ransom. Although the FMLN pledged as part of the agreement not to kidnap relatives of government officials, it verbally reneged on this promise a few months later.

The FMLN–FDR took advantage of Duarte's political weakness by rejecting his amnesty offer at the second meeting, held at Ayagualo, on November 30, 1985. The rebels countered with a tough three-phase peace plan calling for the creation of a new, transitional government of national consensus, with FMLN–FDR participation, that would hold national elections. Bitter over his daughter's kidnapping, Duarte postponed the scheduled third round of talks and rejected the FMLN proposal as contrary to the 1983 Constitution.

The FMLN boycotted the session scheduled for September 1986 in the Salvadoran town of Sesori after the government refused an FMLN demand that army troops be cleared out of a 650-square-kilometer area around the meeting place. Between the breakdown of the Sesori dialogue and the signing of the Central American Peace Agreement in August 1987, no formal talks were held for the purpose of achieving a negotiated solution between the FMLN and the government.

Some observers characterized the FMLN–FDR's proposals made in May 1987 as a formula for the "Cubanization" of El Salvador, citing the rebels' demands for nonalignment; formation of an extraconstitutional transitional government, without elections, to include members of the FMLN–FDR; maintenance of guerrilla armed forces until the government was reorganized; imposition of a socialist economy; dismantling of the police forces; and nonintervention of foreign governments. Duarte rejected the proposal in a May 1987 speech, calling it a formula to weaken the government militarily and politically.

There was no further movement on dialogue until the five Central American presidents, at the initiative of Costa Rican president Oscar Arias Sánchez, met in Guatemala in early August 1987 and signed the Central American Peace Agreement, charting a peaceful resolution of regional conflicts through national reconciliation, cease-fires, democratization, and free elections (see The Crisis in Central America, ch. 4). Although the so-called Arias plan did not require dialogue with armed insurgent groups unless they accepted amnesty, the Duarte government called on the FMLN–FDR leaders to accept the peace plan as the framework for negotiations and dialogue. Duarte also persuaded the military High Command to endorse the Central American peace document, although several officers voiced doubts about it. Guided by the agreement, Duarte reopened a dialogue with the guerrillas, promulgated a broad amnesty, ordered the military to undertake a unilateral cease-fire after the FMLN broke off cease-fire talks, and permitted the self-exiled FDR leaders—Rubén Zamora Rivas and Ungo—to return to El Salvador.

In early October 1987, two days of talks were held between government and rebel leaders. The representatives—who included President Duarte, four FMLN military commanders, and four FDR leaders—agreed to establish two commissions that would include government and rebel leaders, one commission responsible for negotiating a cease-fire, the other for addressing other measures of the peace plan. A second round of talks, held in Caracas on October 22, became deadlocked, with the participants merely pledging to continue the dialogue in Mexico City. The FMLN subsequently suspended the Mexico City dialogue, however, and unilateral cease-fires in November 1987 were unsuccessful. The guerrillas continued to demand a power-sharing arrangement and the maintenance of their own military force as conditions for a settlement. Rejecting a cease-fire, the FMLN–FDR proposed a "moratorium" on arms deliveries, an end to recruitment on both sides, and the withdrawal of foreign military advisers. According to United States press reports, however, the FMLN agreed at top-level FMLN–FDR meetings held in Managua in July 1988 not to oppose the FDR's participation in the 1989 presidential elections. The FMLN escalated its military and terrorist activities in the San Salvador area in the fall of 1988 and commenced a policy of seeking to cause civilian casualties by these actions. The FMLN also embarked on a campaign to assassinate democratically elected mayors. The guerrillas executed seven serving mayors, one former mayor, and one government official between March and November 1988. They threatened to kill more than twenty others.

Counterinsurgency Tactics

Initially, the army used conventional warfare tactics against the insurgents. It typically would rely on massive frontal assaults or sweeps against guerrilla positions. These operations were less risky than the small-unit tactics urged by United States advisers but were ineffective against the more mobile guerrilla units, which easily evaded the army forces. At nightfall, the army invariably returned to the safety of its garrisons instead of pursuing the insurgents. Although army troops sometimes retook towns previously held by guerrillas, the army usually withdrew after a short stay, and FMLN forces returned.

United States military assistance helped to transform the army into a more capable force. During the second part of 1982, the Salvadoran government began deploying United States-trained and United States-equipped "hunter" counterinsurgency battalions, consisting of 220 members. "Hunter" tactics called for operations in highly mobile small units, carrying out night patrolling and night attacks in place of the army's ineffective massed assaults.

The army was slow to adopt these new tactics and largely continued to conduct the war in a lackadaisical manner. It responded to attacks by much larger FMLN units in 1983 by abandoning the United States-inspired concept of the "hunter" battalions. It replaced them with the 580-man Antiterrorist Infantry Battalions (Batallones de Infantería Antiterrorista—BIAT) and 390-man Countersubversion Infantry Battalions (Batallones de Infantería para Contrasubversión—BIC). Again, the guerrillas easily evaded these slow-moving forces in the field.

Badly needed organizational changes resulted from the May 1983 replacement of General García by Vides. Within weeks, Vides's new chief of staff of the armed forces, Colonel Blandón, implemented United States-style organization and tactics in key combat

247

units, adopting new counterinsurgency objectives of denying the guerrillas sanctuary, movement, and supplies. He also announced a 20 percent increase in troop strength for 1984 to bring the army's force level to 30,000. Blandón adopted more aggressive actions using small, air-mobile combat units. These moves turned the war in the army's favor, but subsequent adjustments by the FMLN frustrated government forces and again stalemated the conflict.

In mid-1983 the army also launched a United States-designed and United States-funded pacification program consisting of military sweeps followed by civic action programs designed to reduce political violence. The army plan was to coordinate military operations in two eastern departments with government-sponsored economic development of the area and to establish local civil defense and social improvement programs. The persistent army presence, it was thought, would keep the guerrillas on the move and isolate them from the civilian population. The first phase of the program, called Operation Well-Being (Operación Bienestar), focused on San Vicente and Usulután departments, where guerrilla forces were particularly active. The program called for the organization of paramilitary networks and their integration into the counterinsurgency operations of the regular army and security forces. The army stationed 4,000 troops in central San Vicente Department with the objectives of forcing guerrilla units out of their bases in the northern sector and then establishing a buffer zone defended mainly by civil defense units.

In September 1984, Colonel Ochoa, then commander of the Fourth Infantry Brigade in Chalatenango Department, attempted a similar campaign to clear guerrillas from the two northern departments of Chalatenango and Cabañas. Villagers, however, believing their safety depended on remaining neutral, were uncooperative. By the end of 1985, the campaign had failed, largely because the guerrilla forces easily evaded the army troops and then frustrated implementation of civic action programs.

Frustrated at its failure to defeat the FMLN after five years of fighting, the army reportedly turned increasingly to the forced relocation of the rebels' civilian supporters, particularly in the Guazapa Volcano area some twenty kilometers north of San Salvador, in northern Chalatenango Department, and in the eastern departments. The Ministry of Interior's National Commission to Assist the Displaced Persons of El Salvador (Comisión Nacional de Asistencia a los Desplazadas de El Salvador—Conades) reported in July 1985 that 412,000 of El Salvador's population of about 5 million had been displaced from their homes by the war since 1981. According to some estimates, an additional 500,000 had left the

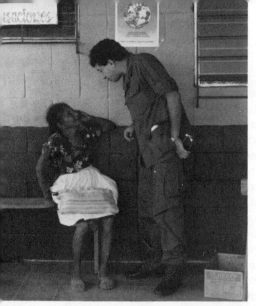
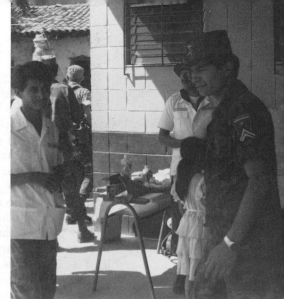

Army civic action program, El Paisnal, San Salvador Department
Courtesy Ana B. Montes

country altogether. Although army officers suggested that the government's main concern was to deprive the rebels of political and logistical support, Duarte claimed that the new policy was designed to ensure the safety of civilians.

In October 1986, Blandón introduced a second United States-financed pacification plan, United to Rebuild (Unidos para Reconstruir). In addition to giving the military control over repopulation and reconstruction programs nationwide, it contained a public relations element that gave the military the potential to build a popular support base of its own. Although intended to reassert army control and begin economic recuperation in war-torn areas, it too failed as a result of a lack of resources, incompetence in its implementation, and insufficient cooperation from the population.

By mid-1988, according to some observers, the army had become burdened by conventional tactics, mediocre officers, overreliance on air power, and the need to defend against economic sabotage. For example, fully a third of the government's troops were tied down guarding bridges, electrical plants, and other economic targets.

That fall Colonel Ponce launched a new counterinsurgency campaign in rebel territory. Designed without the assistance of United States military advisers, it relied heavily on night patrols by fifteen-man groups of highly trained commandos. It also took a new approach to civic action efforts. Instead of merely handing out supplies to villagers, the new campaign, called United to Work (Unidos para Trabajar), put greater emphasis on forcibly evicting left-wing community groups and replacing them with new organizations responsible for allocating army donations of food and medicine. The army imposed two main conditions for this aid: that the village establish a civil defense unit and that it make its young men available for conscription. The army's civic action efforts were not reassuring, however, to more than 7,000 Salvadoran refugees who had returned from Honduran camps since the previous October to abandoned villages in northern El Salvador. Suspicious of the returning Salvadorans, the army prevented church and other outside relief workers from delivering supplies to them.

Crime and Punishment
The Criminal Justice System
Judicial Ineffectiveness

El Salvador's criminal justice system, which is derived from nineteenth-century Spanish jurisprudence, extends customary procedural safeguards to accused persons. Under Article 12 of the 1983 Constitution, any person accused of a crime shall be presumed innocent until proven guilty in conformance with the law and in a public trial. A person who is detained must be immediately informed of his or her rights, including the right to an attorney, and the reasons for the detention. Forced confession is prohibited. Article 13 prohibits any governmental organ, authority, or functionary from dictating orders for the unlawful arrest or imprisonment of any individual. Furthermore, arrest orders must always be in writing. The Constitution also provides that the periods for administrative or investigative detention not exceed seventy-two hours, during which time the detainee's case must be assigned to a competent judge. The United States Department of State reported that this requirement was followed in the great majority of cases in 1987. Americas Watch, however, charged in late 1987 that both the security forces and the army had violated this constitutional provision.

In the event of war, invasion, rebellion, sedition, catastrophe, epidemic, or other general calamity, the constitutional guarantees provided by Articles 12 and 13 may be suspended under Article 29 for a period not to exceed thirty days if at least three-fourths of the deputies in the Legislative Assembly vote to do so (see The Constitution of 1983, ch. 4). For example, the 1986 state of siege allowed fifteen days of incommunicado detention for prisoners detained for political reasons.

The constitutional guarantees notwithstanding, El Salvador's criminal judicial system historically has been weak. For years the courts acquitted the few politically powerful individuals who were accused of crimes and held dissidents and poor prisoners in jail without trial indefinitely. The great majority of offenders nationwide traditionally were laborers, agricultural workers, unemployed individuals, and skilled workers. Well-to-do professional and technical personnel were rarely charged with, much less prosecuted for, crimes. The acquittal rate in court trials also traditionally was high, not only in the lower tribunals but even in the courts of first instance, which try felonies.

A Department of State study noted that the criminal justice system was characterized by consistent underfunding; unwieldy laws of evidence that created an overreliance on confessions to obtain convictions; the intimidation of judges, prosecutors, jurors, and witnesses; a lack of modern investigative and forensic equipment and expertise; judges and court officers who worked only half-days; and antiquated and wholly inadequate administrative systems and office equipment. Political violence in the 1970s and 1980s further crippled the judicial system. Virtually no attempt was made to investigate the many thousands of murders perpetrated between

1979 and 1983 or to punish those responsible. By 1985 the homicide conviction rate, which in 1978 was 25 percent, had dropped to 13 percent. It was as low as 4 percent in rural areas by 1988. The number of homicide cases brought before the courts also declined steadily in the 1980s. Although the reported homicide rate reached a record high of 6,145 in 1980, only 812 cases were brought to trial, and only 109 convictions were obtained.

According to the Ministry of Justice, only about 10 percent of those in prison had been sentenced; the rest were detained suspects awaiting trial. Investigations of crimes dragged on long past the legal time limits, and the accused often spent years in prison awaiting trial.

Because the courts could not be relied on to prosecute the perpetrators of crimes nor to provide those arrested with speedy and fair trials, citizens had little confidence in obtaining redress of grievances through the courts. In the absence of a functional criminal justice system, acts of vengeance and vigilantism were rampant. Even in civil cases, attorneys rarely risked confronting powerful interests or wealthy families for fear of physical retribution.

The judiciary also suffered from the political polarization and extremism that gripped the country during the 1980s. Unidentified terrorists killed a military court judge in May 1988. That June FMLN terrorists assassinated an alternate justice of the peace and threatened two prosecuting attorneys. Right-wing obstructionists in the courts and the Salvadoran attorney general's office also repeatedly delayed highly publicized cases such as the murder of Archbishop Romero. The Romero case was shelved in December 1984 by judicial authorities claiming insufficient evidence. In August 1985, however, a Salvadoran court ordered the reopening of an investigation into the archbishop's murder. Duarte publicly presented new evidence in December 1987 that he said strongly implicated D'Aubuisson. Nevertheless, the government announced in December 1988 that the Romero killing would remain unresolved because of a Supreme Court ruling that the testimony of a key witness was invalid.

Some military personnel reportedly also resorted to kidnapping to intimidate lawyers and witnesses. A lawyer assigned to defend the five Salvadoran members of the GN accused of murdering the United States churchwomen said he was forced to take part in a "conspiracy" aimed at preventing higher ranking military officers from being implicated in the case. After refusing to cooperate, the lawyer charged that he was abducted by members of the GN, tortured, and imprisoned at GN headquarters.

Prior to January 1987, suspected FMLN members were charged with violations of Articles 373 to 411 of the Penal Code (the articles dealing with crimes against the state) but were processed under Decree 50, a special state-of-emergency law that established a military court system to try such cases. As a result of the Legislative Assembly's January 1987 decision not to renew the state of emergency, all terrorism-related cases had to be tried under normal Salvadoran law. New FMLN suspects were therefore remanded to the regular courts, although the previous cases continued to be tried under Decree 50 provisions. By mid-1987 the Decree 50 courts had cleared more than half of their backlog of pending cases, acquitting some defendants, convicting some, and sending others to the regular courts for trial for common crimes. Judges in the regular courts tended to follow the Penal Code strictly and often released suspects despite evidence of their membership in the FMLN. The continuous threat of FMLN violence was a principal reason that court personnel avoided making decisions that might draw retaliation.

In the late 1980s, several developments suggested that the principle of military accountability to the judicial system was slowly being established. First, two military officers were jailed in 1987 for their involvement with a kidnap-for-profit ring. In addition, an army lieutenant was arrested and turned over to the courts in connection with the murders of three civilians in August 1987; and third, a jury in May 1987 determined that four policemen were guilty of the January 1983 murders of two students. As of late 1988, however, the courts had never convicted any military officer of a crime.

Two high-profile cases involving United States citizens were included under the 1987 amnesty program. In the first case, the Military Court of First Instance ruled in November 1987 that three PRTC terrorists jailed for killing four United States Marines, two American technicians, and seven Latin Americans in the 1985 sidewalk-café attack were covered by the amnesty decreed by Duarte because theirs was a "political" crime with a military objective. None of the three PRTC terrorists was ever tried for the crimes. The Military Appeals Court upheld the decision on January 26, 1988. That February, however, the United States attorney general, supported by the United States embassy, appealed to Duarte to reverse the court's decision in his capacity as commander in chief of the armed forces. In a decision made public on April 11, 1988, Duarte, knowing that United States aid to El Salvador was at stake, ruled that the three men charged in the killings could not be freed under the amnesty law. Duarte argued that the four United States

Marines who were slain had diplomatic status as provided by the Convention on the Prevention and Punishment of Crimes Against Internationally Protected Persons, which El Salvador ratified in 1980.

In the second case, a Salvadoran chamber of second instance (appeals court) decided in December 1987 to free the two convicted killers of the three agrarian reform officials. As a result, the case then pending against former Lieutenant Roberto I. López Síbrian, who had ordered the killings, was expected to be closed, although he remained in jail in late 1988. A similar attempt to secure the release of three of the five national guardsmen sentenced to thirty-year terms in 1984 for the killing of four United States church-women in 1980 was unsuccessful.

Judicial Reform

With the enactment of enabling legislation by the Legislative Assembly in the summer of 1985, the Salvadoran government initiated a judicial reform effort in collaboration with AID, which provided US$9.2 million in assistance. The program called for in-stitutionalizing due process and the rule of law, including the speedy and fair trial of persons accused of crimes. Another important objective was to bring to justice the perpetrators of particularly notorious crimes, such as political assassinations.

The Salvadoran government's reform effort included establish-ing a study commission that drafted changes in the military justice and penal codes and proposed steps to reduce the prison popula-tion, create a judicial career system, and implement merit selec-tion of judges. Progress in reforming the judicial institution continued to be slow, however, and encountered many problems in 1988. Under the judicial administration and training portion of the program, the government established four new courts in order to reduce case backlogs, completed a management assessment of the judiciary, inaugurated three new law libraries, and trained judicial personnel both locally and abroad. The government also drafted legislation aimed at improving the administrative efficiency of the judiciary.

According to the Department of State, the judicial reform pro-gram comprised a legal revisory commission, a judicial protection unit, a commission for investigations, and a judicial training pro-gram. The first component was created by decree in June 1985 and called the Revisory Commission for Salvadoran Legislation. It consisted of ten presidential appointees representing three minis-tries, the Supreme Court, law faculties, and attorney associations. Its purpose was to coordinate the overall judicial reform effort, to study the Salvadoran judicial system, and to develop the resulting draft legislation for the Legislative Assembly. The commission focused its efforts initially on revising procedures and laws to improve such facets of the existing criminal law system as rules of evidence and procedures, the jury system, and legal defense and detention. The commission also planned to explore the possibility of a new Decree 50-style code to prosecute crimes against the government. In addition, it envisioned longer term and costlier reforms such as merit selection of judges and a judicial career service.

The second component, the Judical Protection Unit (Unidad de Protección Judicial—UPJ), was initiated in 1984 (formally created by decree in September 1985) to provide security for judges, jurors, prosecutors, and witnesses in politically controversial criminal cases. In the UPJ's first assignments, a group of sixty prison guards who had received training in the United States provided security for participants in the churchwomen's murder trial in the summer of 1984 and the Sheraton case trial in February 1986. The initial concept of the unit was found unworkable, however, owing to the high costs of maintaining a sufficiently large and well-trained force. In early 1988, the government was considering a new proposal to establish the unit as a professional risk-assessment team that would plan and organize protection in appropriate cases; protective personnel would then be drawn from law enforcement units or private contractors.

The third component, the Investigations Commission (Comisión para Investigaciones—CI), was created by decree in July 1985 to develop criminal investigation capabilities, supported by forensic laboratories. The members of this civilian-controlled agency were appointed by the president. Chaired by the minister of justice, it included the vice minister of interior and a representative of the president. Reporting to the commission was an executive-branch office responsible for managing the twenty-seven-member Special Investigative Unit, the eight-member Forensic Unit, and a legal and administrative support unit. The SIU was formed in 1985 to investigate politically important crimes and consisted of Salvadoran soldiers or officials trained by the United States Federal Bureau of Investigation (FBI). Required by law to be drawn from the security forces, SIU members remained salaried employees of those forces. The Forensic Unit was inaugurated in mid-1987 and by early 1988 was approaching full operational capacity. The SIU and the Forensic Unit, which were almost fully equipped and trained, had made valuable contributions to the investigations of several key cases, including the Romero assassination. The investigative and forensic expertise of the two units was unprecedented in El

Salvador and represented a significant step in the professionalization of the country's criminal justice system.

The fourth component, the Judicial Training Program, was designed to improve the court system's administrative management, human resources, and physical facilities. Under this project, the government established two new courts to deal with a serious backlog of cases, assessed court equipment needs, set up a new administrative unit for the court system to release judges from administrative tasks, and provided short-term training for judges and justices of the peace.

Penal and Procedural Codes

El Salvador's penal and procedural codes are derived from the established precedents of nineteenth-century Spanish jurisprudence and therefore follow the standard Latin American pattern. Although adopted early in the twentieth century, both documents have been revised and updated periodically since then. Changes in the Penal Code of 1904 have been enacted through supplementary legislation in the form of laws or decrees. El Salvador published a revised Penal Code in 1980. The code recognizes three distinct levels of offenses: felonies (*delitos*), misdemeanors (*faltas*), and infractions (*contravenciones*). The major categories of offenses distinguish among crimes against the state, crimes against persons or property, and threats to public order or safety. The Penal Code contains statutes prohibiting crimes against the state (Articles 373 to 411), subversion (Articles 376 to 380), treason (Article 381), terrorism (Articles 400, 402, and 403), and other actions against the stability of the state. Crimes against persons or property cover the more conventional types of lawbreaking, including such offenses as homicide, assault, robbery, and fraud. The code takes into account possible extenuations and mitigating factors, such as self-defense. Ignorance of the law is not considered an excuse, however, and an unsuccessful attempted crime is punishable as though perpetrated. Provisions allow for increased penalties in cases considered aggravated or grossly malicious.

The code carefully defines penalties and their range in considerable detail. Recognized punishments include fines, imprisonment, banishment, loss of civil rights, and death. Article 27 of the Constitution, however, allows the death penalty only in cases established by military laws during a state of international war. The code also prohibits imprisonment for debt, perpetual and dishonorable sentences, banishment, and all kinds of mental or physical torment. Persons arrested for crimes against the state have the same legal protection as common criminals. Holding views opposed to the government is not justification for arrest if the suspect does not advocate violence. Thus, the courts have held that membership in a front organization controlled by the insurgents is not by itself sufficient reason to hold an arrestee, although membership in a guerrilla group is.

In the Salvadoran system, the courts become involved in the case almost immediately after the crime is committed because the judge oversees the investigation. If the police conduct a preliminary investigation, they must submit the result to the courts within seventy-two hours. A justice of the peace handles minor crimes, but must forward major cases to a judge in a court of first instance within fifteen days. In cases involving death, a judge—usually a justice of the peace—goes to the scene of the crime and "recognizes" the death judicially; a medical examiner determines the cause of death Arrest regulations require that the security forces register detainees and have them examined by a doctor or nurse on entry into police facilities. In insurgency-related cases, the authorities must promptly notify the family of the detainee or one of the human rights offices of the arrest. Mistreatment of prisoners is prohibited. The judge has seventy-two hours to determine if the evidence shows sufficient cause to hold the suspect and, if so, orders pretrial detention. After being turned over to the courts within seventy-two hours, an arrestee has the right to have a defense attorney present.

The judge then begins the investigation (*instrucción*) phase, actually conducting an in-depth investigation into the crime. The judge lists all of the elements of proof needed in order to determine the guilt or innocence of the accused, then presides over each step of the investigation, issuing orders for witnesses to come to testify, visiting the scene of the crime, and ordering the police to perform forensic tests. While the judge is conducting the investigation, suspects accused of major crimes often remain in pretrial confinement, even though the investigation phase may take years to complete.

Once the judge is satisfied that all the available information has been collected, the case may be dismissed or moved to the plenary phase of the trial, in which the judge, the defense, and the prosecution prepare in writing their explanations of what the evidence shows. In murder cases, the final step of the plenary phase is the jury stage, in which the court clerk reads to a panel of five jurors a summary of the evidence and the statements by the judge, defense, and prosecution. Extensive procedural safeguards protecting the rights of the defendant and rigid rules of evidence under the civilian Penal Code severely limit the capabilities of the prosecution. This

257

is one reason why only about 15 percent of jury trials resulted in convictions in the mid-1980s.

The accused has the right to file an *amparo* petition (a claim that a constitutional right has been violated) with the Supreme Court at any time during the process, as well as one habeas corpus petition per phase of the process, starting from the time the accused becomes aware that the judge may issue a warrant for his or her arrest. When any petition is filed with the Supreme Court, all work on the case by the judge in the court of first instance ceases, and the entire case record is sent to the Supreme Court. The defense may also file appeals to the chambers of second instance at certain times in the process, and this too causes the judge in the court of first instance to cease work on the case. Finally, a type of appeal known as a cassation may be filed with the Supreme Court, also causing a halt in work on the case. Some time limits set down in the laws for consideration of these appeals have been followed rigorously, whereas others were ignored in the late 1980s.

The Penal System

The 1983 Constitution reaffirms that the penal system shall be designed to rehabilitate prisoners rather than solely to punish them. Article 28 prescribes that "the state shall organize the penitentiaries with the aim of reforming offenders, educating them, and teaching them industrious habits, seeking their rehabilitation and the prevention of crime." Overall direction and administration of the prison system is under the jurisdiction of the director general of penal and rehabilitation centers, under the minister of justice.

As of the late 1980s, the prison system was composed of three national penitentiaries and at least thirty jails or preventive detention facilities distributed throughout the country. The federal government operated the penitentiaries, located in Ahuachapán, Santa Ana, and San Vicente. The penitentiaries were the principal incarceration institutions, housing approximately half of the total prison population. Other than the penitentiaries, the prison system was loosely organized and received little centralized guidance or control. The government published few statistics on prisons. Local authorities supervised subordinate facilities and had few restrictions on their authority over methods and procedures. Each of the country's departments had at least one jail or detention facility, with at least one in every departmental capital, although San Salvador had no facility for men. The two women's prisons were located at the town of Ilopango and Santa Ana; their inmates consisted mainly of prostitutes serving six-month terms. Prison facilities ranged from simple frame enclosures with little security and few amenities to well-built, professionally planned buildings with good protection and adequate accommodations.

In late 1988, El Salvador's security situation worsened. The FMLN, armed for the first time with some Soviet-made AK–47 assault rifles, actually had brought the war to its bloodiest level in two or three years by launching another countrywide guerrilla and terrorist offensive, which once again included assassinating mayors. FMLN guerrillas inflicted disproportionately high casualties on the army in attacks on installations such as the Fourth Infantry Brigade garrison at El Paraíso in Chalatenango Department and in a mortar barrage on a GN facility in San Salvador. Other FMLN actions in San Salvador included breaking criminals out of a jail and carrying out nightly terrorist bombings. FMLN leaders, including Villalobos, also opened an unusual diplomatic offensive by visiting several Latin American capitals. The army, for its part, was widely reported to have perpetrated a massacre, the first in three years, of ten peasants in the hamlet of San Sebastián in San Vicente Department, after accusing them of collaborating with the guerrillas. Under increasing criticism for its conduct of the war, the military underwent another orderly shakeup, with General Blandón being replaced as armed forces chief of staff by Colonel Ponce, a strong advocate of promoting economic development in the areas affected by the war. Under Ponce's command, the military was expected to become a more aggressive, offensive-minded force, but one placing greater emphasis on the "hearts and minds" campaign.

*   *   *

As of mid-1988, no book devoted exclusively to Salvadoran national security topics was available. Relevant data can be derived mainly from disparate publications other than books, such as United States government or congressional reports, journal articles, newsletters, and newspaper reports, as well as Salvadoran legal documents. A few books prove to be useful. A good source for historical information on the Salvadoran military establishment, despite its strongly anti-United States policy bias, is Michael McClintock's *The American Connection.* Adrian J. English's *Armed Forces of Latin America* contains other useful historical and military data on the Salvadoran armed forces. More recent military data are provided in *The Military Balance,* an annual published by the International Institute for Strategic Studies. Informative 1988 reports prepared by the United States Department of State include *The Situation in El Salvador.* Discussions of El Salvador's human rights record are found in the Department of State's *Country Reports on Human Rights Practices for 1987* and publications of Americas Watch. The Committee on Foreign Affairs of the United States Congress has published the transcripts of numerous hearings on El Salvador since 1981, including *Human Rights and Political Developments in El Salvador, 1987*. (For further information and complete citations, see Bibliography.)

Appendix

Table 1. Metric Conversion Coefficients and Factors

When you know	Multiply by	To find
Millimeters	0.04	inches
Centimeters	0.39	inches
Meters	3.3	feet
Kilometers	0.62	miles
Hectares (10,000 m²)	2.47	acres
Square kilometers	0.39	square miles
Cubic meters	35.3	cubic feet
Liters	0.26	gallons
Kilograms	2.2	pounds
Metric tons	0.98	long tons
....	1.1	short tons
....	2,204	pounds
Degrees Celsius	9	degrees Fahrenheit
(Centigrade)	divide by 5 and add 32	

Table 2. Population Trends, 1970–2000

Period	Population at Beginning of Period (in thousands)	Crude Birth Rate	Crude Death Rate
1970–75	3,516	42.2	11.1
1975–80	4,108	41.1	9.5
1980–85	4,813	40.0	8.2
1985–90	5,643	38.3	7.2
1990–95	6,595	36.1	6.3
1995–2000	7,654	33.5	5.6
2000	8,803		

Source: Based on information from Robert W. Fox and Jerrold W. Huguet, *Population and Urban Trends in Central America and Panama*, Washington, 1977, 97.

Table 3. Causes of Death, 1983

Cause of Death	Number of Deaths	Percentage of Total Deaths	Rate per 100,000 Inhabitants
Perinatal conditions and diseases	3,552	11.2	75.2 *
Intestinal infections	2,206	6.9	46.7
Homicides and other purposeful injuries	2,198	6.9	46.5
Pulmonary circulation and other forms of heart disease	1,102	3.5	23.3
Cancer	966	3.0	20.4
Bronchitis, emphysema, and asthma	945	3.0	20.0
Cerebrovascular disease	886	2.8	18.7
Ischemic heart disease	876	2.7	18.5
Motor vehicle accidents	685	2.2	14.5
Pneumonia	611	1.9	12.9
Other	17,799	55.9	n.a.
TOTAL	31,826	100.0	n.a.

n.a. = not available
* Rate per 1,000 live births was 20.1.

Source: Based on information from Pan American Health Organization, *Health Conditions in the Americas, 1981–1984,* Washington, 1986, 113.

Table 4. *Gross Domestic Product (GDP) at Constant 1962 Prices, Including and Excluding Coffee, 1981–86* (value in millions of Salvadoran colones [1]; annual growth rate in percentage)

	1981		1982		1983		1984		1985		1986 [2]	
	Value	Growth	Value	Growth	Value	Growth	Value	Growth	Value	Growth	Value	Growth
GDP (including coffee)	3,016.7	−8.3	2,847.7	−5.6	2,870.4	−0.8	2,935.6	2.3	2,993.6	2.0	3,012.5	0.6
Coffee (value added)	273.2	−6.6	271.1	−0.8	242.3	−10.6	231.8	−4.3	231.1	−0.3	214.6	−7.1
GDP (excluding coffee)	2,743.5	−8.5	2,576 6	−6.1	2,628.1	2.0	2,703.8	2.9	2,762.5	2.2	2,797.9	1.3

[1] For value of the colón—see Glossary.
[2] Preliminary.

Source: Based on information from Banco Central de Reserva de El Salvador, *Revista Trimestral: Octubre-Diciembre, 1987*, San Salvador, 1988, 103.

Table 5. Economically Active Population by Age-Group, Selected Years, 1970–2000

Age-Group	1970	1975	1980	1985	1990	1995	2000
10–14	85,096	92,461	98,293	105,177	113,973	119,581	123,234
15–19	177,997	212,409	242,219	272,356	312,064	359,281	402,666
20–24	188,143	230,976	282,746	331,980	368,711	457,213	540,490
25–29	151,307	179,984	223,073	276,755	333,276	393,473	466,673
30–34	123,763	144,544	172,684	216,146	274,694	332,191	393,833
35–39	110,753	117,806	138,017	166,378	213,942	272,791	330,944
40–44	96,818	105,088	111,703	131,908	163,704	210,901	269,365
45–49	73,946	90,347	98,233	105,056	128,363	159,943	206,871
50–54	56,578	67,613	82,888	90,632	100,005	122,445	152,868
55–59	47,444	49,894	59,651	73,778	83,112	91,822	112,517
60–64	34,902	39,861	41,758	50,346	64,329	72,440	79,995
65–69	22,640	26,753	30,513	32,001	39,801	50,776	57,092
70–74	13,477	15,298	17,982	20,506	21,984	27,176	34,449
75–79	5,979	7,395	8,347	9,830	11,463	12,216	15,002
80 and over	2,214	2,565	3,129	3,731	4,643	5,661	6,521
TOTAL	1,191,057	1,382,994	1,611,236	1,886,580	2,254,064	2,687,910	3,192,520

Source: Based on information from James W. Wilkie and David Lorey (eds.), *Statistical Abstract of Latin America*, 25, Los Angeles, 1987, 241.

Table 6. *Imports, Exports, and Current Account Balance, 1983–87*
(in millions of United States dollars)

	1983	1984	1985	1986	1987 *
Imports	831	915	895	772	911
Exports	735	726	679	713	573
Current account balance ..	-37	-54	-29	64	-110

* Estimate.

Source: Based on information from Economist Intelligence Unit, *Country Report: Guatemala, El Salvador, Honduras,* London, 1988, 3; and International Monetary Fund, *International Financial Statistics,* 41, No. 1, Washington, December 1988, 214–16.

Table 7. *Major Army Equipment, 1988*

Description	Country of Origin	Inventory
Tanks		
AMS–13 (light)	United States	12
Armored personnel carriers		
M–3A1	do–	5
M–113	–do–	20
AML–90	–do–	10
UR–416 (armored repair vehicle)	West Germany	8
M–37B1	United States	66
Field artillery		
105mm Howitzer	–do–	50
105mm M–101	–do–	30
105mm M–102	–do–	6
M–56	Yugoslavia	14
155mm M–114	United States	6
Mortars		
81mm	–do–	300
120mm UB–M52	–do–	60
Recoilless rifles		
90mm M–67	–do–	400
Antiaircraft		
20mm M–55	–do–	24

Source: Based on information from *The Military Balance, 1988–1989,* London, 1988, 196; and *Jane's Defence Weekly* [London], June 28, 1986, 1243, 1261.

Table 8. *Major Air Force Equipment, 1988*

Description	Country of Origin	Inventory
Fixed-wing aircraft		
Arava transport	Israel	25
AC–47D Skytrain gunship	United States	7
Beech AT–11 and T–34	–do–	2
C–123 Provider transport	–do–	2
Cessna 337 0–2A Super Skymaster	–do–	5 to 9
Cessna T–41	–do–	7
Cessna A–37B Dragonfly light attack jet ...	–do–	10
C–47D transport	–do–	6
Dassault MD–450 Ouragan fighter-bomber (obsolete)	France	8
DC–6B transport	United States	1
Fairchild-Hiller FH–1100	–do–	1
Fouga CM–170 Magister trainer/light strike (obsolete)	France	6
Helicopters		
Aérospatiale SA–315 Lama	–do–	3
Alouette-3 transport	–do–	3
Bell UH–1M Iroquois gunship	United States	Over 14
Bell UH–1H Iroquois transport	–do–	Over 40
Hughes 500D gunship	–do–	9

Source: Based on information from *The Military Balance, 1988–1989,* London, 1988, 196; *Military Technology,* 10, No. 13, 1986, 97; and *Jane's Defence Weekly* [London], June 28, 1986, 1261.

Table 9. *Major Navy Equipment, 1988*

Description	Country of Origin	Inventory
Patrol craft		
31m GC–6 Camcraft	United States	3
20m Sewart	–do–	1
20m Swiftship	–do–	1
26m Swiftship (*Libertad*)	–do–	1
32m craft	–do–	3
Patrol launches		
13m coast guard utility	–do–	2
11m craft	–do–	4
11m Latana	–do–	11
8m river patrol	–do–	6

Source: Based on information from *The Military Balance 1988–1989,* London, 1988, 196; *Military Technology,* 10, No. 13, 1986, 97; and *Jane's Defence Weekly* [London], June 28, 1986, 1261.

Bibliography

Chapter 1

Anderson, Charles W. "El Salvador: The Army as Reformer." Pages 70–91 in Martin C. Needler (ed.), *Political Systems of Latin America.* New York: Van Nostrand Reinhold, 1970.

Anderson, Thomas P. *Matanza: El Salvador's Communist Revolt of 1932.* Lincoln: University of Nebraska Press, 1971.

Baloyra, Enrique A. *El Salvador in Transition.* Chapel Hill: University of North Carolina Press, 1982.

Caldera T., Hilda. *Historia del Partido Demócrata Cristiano.* Tegucigalpa, Honduras: Instituto Centroamericano de Estudios Políticos, 1983.

Christian, Shirley. "The Other Side: El Salvador's Fractious, Frenzied Left," *New Republic,* 189, No. 3, October 24, 1983, 13–15, 18–19.

Dickey, Christopher. "Expected Certification for El Salvador Based on Mixed Record," *Washington Post,* January 21, 1983, A19.

Duarte, José Napoleón. *Duarte: My Story.* New York: G.P. Putnam's Sons, 1986.

Feinberg, Richard E. "Central America: No Easy Answers," *Foreign Affairs,* 59, No. 5, Summer 1981, 1121–46.

Findling, John E. *Close Neighbors, Distant Friends.* (Contributions in American History, No. 122.) New York: Greenwood Press, 1987.

Flemion, Philip F. *Historical Dictionary of El Salvador.* (Latin American Historical Dictionaries, No. 5.) Metuchen, New Jersey: Scarecrow Press, 1972.

Harris, Kevin, and Mario Espinosa. "Reform, Repression, and Revolution in El Salvador," *Fletcher Forum,* 5, No. 2, Summer 1981, 295–319.

Karnes, Thomas L. *The Failure of Union: Central America, 1824–1960.* Chapel Hill: University of North Carolina Press, 1961.

Kincaid, A. Douglas. "Peasants into Rebels: Community and Class in Rural El Salvador," *Comparative Studies in Society and History,* 29, No. 3, July 1987, 466–94.

Leiken, Robert S. "The Salvadoran Left." Pages 111–30 in Robert S. Leiken (ed.), *Central America: Anatomy of Conflict.* New York: Pergamon Press, 1984.

Leiken, Robert S., and Barry Rubin (eds.). *The Central American Crisis Reader.* New York: Summit Books, 1987.

LeoGrande, William M., and Carla Anne Robbins. "Oligarchs and Officers: The Crisis in El Salvador," *Foreign Affairs,* 58, No. 5, Summer 1980, 1084–1103.

McColm, R. Bruce. "El Salvador's Guerrillas: Structure, Strategy, and . . . Success?" *Freedom at Issue,* No. 74, September–October 1983, 3–16.

McDonald, Ronald H. "El Salvador: The Politics of Revolution." Pages 528–44 in Howard J. Wiarda and Harvey F. Kline (eds.), *Latin American Politics and Development.* (2d ed.) Boulder, Colorado: Westview Press, 1985.

Montgomery, Tommie Sue. *Revolution in El Salvador: Origins and Evolution.* Boulder, Colorado: Westview Press, 1982.

North, Liisa. *Bitter Grounds: Roots of Revolt in El Salvador.* Westport, Connecticut: Lawrence Hill, 1985.

Rodríguez, Mario. *Central America.* Englewood Cliffs, New Jersey: Prentice-Hall, 1965.

Schmidt, Steffen. *El Salvador: America's Next Vietnam?* Salisbury, North Carolina: Documentary, 1983.

Schulz, Donald E. "El Salvador: Revolution and Counterrevolution in the Living Museum." Pages 189–268 in Donald E. Schulz and Douglas H. Graham (eds.), *Revolution and Counterrevolution in Central America and the Caribbean.* Boulder, Colorado: Westview Press, 1984.

Simpson, Lesley Bird. *The Encomienda in New Spain.* (University of California Publications in History Series.) Berkeley and Los Angeles: University of California Press, 1929.

United States. Congress. 97th, 2d Session. Senate. Committee on Foreign Relations. *Report of the U.S. Official Observer Mission to the El Salvador Constituent Assembly Elections of March 28, 1982.* Washington: GPO, 1982.

_____. Department of State. *Communist Interference in El Salvador: Documents Demonstrating Communist Support of the Salvadoran Insurgency.* Washington: February 23, 1981.

Webre, Stephen. *José Napoleón Duarte and the Christian Democratic Party in Salvadoran Politics, 1960–1972.* Baton Rouge: Louisiana State University Press, 1979.

White, Alastair. *El Salvador.* (Nations of the Modern World Series.) Boulder, Colorado: Westview Press, 1982.

Woodward, Ralph Lee, Jr. *Central America: A Nation Divided.* (Latin American Histories Series.) New York: Oxford University Press, 1985.

Chapter 2

Adams, Richard N. *Cultural Surveys of Panama-Nicaragua-Guatemala-El Salvador-Honduras.* (Scientific Publications Series.) Washington: Pan American Sanitary Bureau, 1977.

Anderson, Thomas P. *The War of the Dispossessed: Honduras and El Salvador, 1969.* Lincoln: University of Nebraska Press, 1981.

Armstrong, Robert. "El Salvador—Beyond Elections," *NACLA Report on the Americas,* 16, No. 2, March–April 1982, 2–31.

Armstrong, Robert, and Janet Shenk. *El Salvador: The Face of Revolution.* Boston: South End Press, 1982.

Baloyra, Enrique A. *El Salvador in Transition.* Chapel Hill: University of North Carolina Press, 1982.

Berryman, Phillip. *The Religious Roots of Rebellion.* Maryknoll, New York: Orbis Books, 1984.

Browning, David. "Agrarian Reform in El Salvador," *Journal of Latin American Studies* [London], 15, November 1983, 399–426.

Capa, Cornell, and J. Mayone Stycos. *Margin of Life: Population and Poverty in the Americas.* New York: Grossman, 1974.

Constable, George (ed.). *Planet Earth: Continents in Collision.* (Planet Earth Series.) Alexandria, Virginia: Time-Life Books, 1983.

Dhanji, Farid. *El Salvador: Demographic Issues and Prospects.* (World Bank Country Study.) Washington: World Bank, 1979.

Dominguez, Enrique, and Deborah Huntington. "The Salvation Brokers: Conservative Evangelicals in Central America," *NACLA Report on the Americas,* 18, No. 1, January–February 1984, 2–36.

Durham, William H. *Scarcity and Survival in Central America.* Stanford: Stanford University Press, 1979.

El Salvador. Instituto Salvadoreño de Administración Municipal. *Primer Seminario de Coordinación Interinstitucional del Saneamiento Ambiental en El Salvador, Ilopango, El Salvador, 11–15 Noviembre 1985.* San Salvador: 1985.

_____. Ministerio de Educación. Centro Regional de Construcciones Escolares para América Latina y El Caribe. *La Participación Comunal en el Proceso de Construcciones Educativas.* San Salvador: 1975.

_____. Ministerio de Planificación y Coordinación del Desarrollo Económico y Social. *Estudios de Población.* San Salvador: 1979.

"El Salvador." Pages 731–32 in *Encyclopedia Britannica,* 6. Chicago: William Benton, 1976.

"El Salvador." Page 124 in Graham Hancock (ed.), *Latin America and the Caribbean, 1981–1982.* Saffron Walden, Essex, United Kingdom: World of Information, 1981.

"El Salvador." Pages 81–82 in *Lands and Peoples: Central and South America,* 6. Danbury, Connecticut: Grolier, 1981.

"El Salvador, 1984," *NACLA Report on the Americas,* 18, No. 2, March–April 1984, 13–47.

Fox, Robert W., and Jerrold W. Huguet. *Population and Urban Trends in Central America and Panama.* Washington: Inter-American Development Bank, 1977.

Huezo Selva, Rafael. *Agenda Demográfica de El Salvador.* San Salvador: Asociación Demográfica Salvadoreña, 1980.

Huntington, Deborah. "Visions of the Kingdom: The Latin American Church in Conflict," *NACLA Report on the Americas,* 19, No. 5, September–October 1985, 13–45.

La Iglesia en El Salvador. San Salvador: UCA Editores, 1982.

Kincaid, A. Douglas. "Peasants into Rebels: Community and Class in Rural El Salvador," *Comparative Studies in Society and History,* 29, No. 3, July 1987, 466–94.

North, Liisa. *Bitter Grounds: Roots of Revolt in El Salvador.* Westport, Connecticut: Lawrence Hill, 1985.

Pan American Health Organization. *AIDS in the Americas: The Situation.* Washington: February 16, 1988.

_____. "El Salvador." Pages 127–29 in *Evaluation of the Strategy for Health for All by the Year 2000.* Washington: 1986.

_____. "El Salvador." Pages 371–73 in *Program Budget, 1988–89.* Washington: May 1987.

_____. *Health Conditions in the Americas, 1981–1984.* (Scientific Publication No. 500.) Washington: 1986.

Rodríguez, Luis Angel. *Quince Años de Labor en Población y Planificación Familiar.* San Salvador: Asociación Demográfica Salvadoreña, 1979.

Russell, Philip L. *El Salvador in Crisis.* Austin, Texas: Colorado River Press, 1984.

Shenk, Janet. "El Salvador: The New and the Old War," *NACLA Report on the Americas,* 19, No. 3, May–June 1985, 9–11.

Simon, Laurence R., and James C. Stephens, Jr. *El Salvador Land Reform, 1980–1981: Impact Audit.* Boston: OXFAM America, 1981.

Steel, R.W. (ed.). *Latin America: A Regional Geography,* London: Longmans, Green, 1960.

Stephen, David, and Phillip Wearne. *Central America's Indians.* (Report No. 62.) London: Minority Rights Group, 1984.

United States. Central Intelligence Agency. "El Salvador." Pages 69–70 in *World Factbook.* Washington: 1988.

_____. Department of Health and Human Services. Social Security Administration. *Social Security Programs Throughout the World, 1985.* (Research Report No. 60.) Washington: GPO, 1986.

West, Robert C., and John P. Augelli (eds.). *Middle America: Its Lands and Peoples.* Englewood Cliffs, New Jersey: Prentice-Hall, 1966.

White, Alastair. *El Salvador.* (Nations of the Modern World Series.) Boulder, Colorado: Westview Press, 1982.

————. *Squatter Settlements, Politics, and Class Conflict.* (Occasional Papers, No. 17.) Glasgow: Institute of Latin American Studies, University of Glasgow, 1975.

Williams, Robert G. *Export Agriculture and the Crisis in Central America.* Chapel Hill: University of North Carolina Press, 1986.

Women's International Resource Exchange. *Women and War: El Salvador.* New York: 1980.

Chapter 3

Banco Central de Reserva de El Salvador. *Revista Trimestral: Octubre–Diciembre, 1987.* San Salvador: 1988.

Browning, David. *El Salvador: Landscape and Society.* London: Oxford University Press, 1971.

Centro América, 1988. Guatemala City: Inforpress Centroamericana, 1988.

Comisión Económica para América Latina (CEPAL). *El Desarrollo de América Latina y sus Repercusiones en la Educación: Alfabetismo y Escolaridad Básica.* Santiago, Chile: 1982.

————. *Estudio Económico de América Latina y El Caribe, 1981: El Salvador.* Santiago, Chile: 1982.

————. *Estudio Económico de América Latina y El Caribe, 1986: El Salvador.* Santiago, Chile: 1987.

Direction of Trade Statistics Yearbook, 1988. Washington: International Monetary Fund, 1988.

Economist Intelligence Unit. *Country Profile: Guatemala, El Salvador, Honduras.* London: 1987.

————. *Country Profile: Guatemala, El Salvador, Honduras.* London: 1988.

————. *Country Report: Guatemala, El Salvador, Honduras,* No. 3. London: 1988.

————. *Country Report: Guatemala, El Salvador, Honduras,* No. 4. London: 1988.

El Salvador. Ministerio de Planificación y Coordinación del Desarrollo Económico y Social. *Estado Actual del Programa de Reconstrucción por Fuente Financiera.* San Salvador: 1987.

————. Ministerio de Planificación y Coordinación del Desarrollo Económico y Social. *Evaluación General del Programa Económico de 1988.* San Salvador: 1987.

————. Ministerio de Planificación y Coordinación del Desarrollo Económico y Social. *Indicadores Económicos y Sociales, Enero–Diciembre 1984.* San Salvador: 1985.

_____. Ministerio de Planificación y Coordinación del Desarrollo Económico y Social. *Memoria de Labores.* San Salvador: 1982.

García G., Rigoberto. *Un País Pequeño con Problemas Gigantes: El Salvador.* (Occasional Papers Series.) Stockholm: Institute of Latin American Studies, November 1981.

Government Finance Statistics Yearbook, 1986. Washington: International Monetary Fund, 1986.

Herold, Marc W. "Finanzekapital in El Salvador, 1900–80," *Economic Forum,* 14, No. 1, Summer 1983, 79–94.

Ink, Dwight A. "Statement Before the Subcommittee on Foreign Relations." United States. Congress. 100th, 2d Session. House of Representatives. Committee on Appropriations. (Hearings April 21, 1987.) Washington: GPO, 1987.

Inter-American Development Bank. *Economic and Social Progress in Latin America, 1971.* Washington: 1972.

_____. *Economic and Social Progress in Latin America, 1973.* Washington: 1974.

_____. *Economic and Social Progress in Latin America, 1979.* Washington: 1980.

_____. *Economic and Social Progress in Latin America, 1985.* Washington: 1986.

_____. *Economic and Social Progress in Latin America, 1986.* Washington: 1987.

_____. *Economic and Social Progress in Latin America, 1987.* Washington: 1988.

International Monetary Fund. *Balance of Payments Statistics,* 38. Washington: 1987.

_____. *El Salvador: Recent Economic Developments.* Washington: November 6, 1984.

_____. *Exchange Arrangements and Exchange Restrictions.* Washington: 1987.

_____. *International Financial Statistics,* 41, No. 4. Washington: April 1988.

_____. *International Financial Statistics,* 41, No. 12. Washington: December 1988.

North, Liisa. *Bitter Grounds: Roots of Revolt in El Salvador.* Westport, Connecticut: Lawrence Hill, 1985.

Russell, Philip L. *El Salvador in Crisis.* Austin, Texas: Colorado River Press, 1984.

Siri, Gabriel. *El Salvador and Economic Integration in Central America.* Lexington, Massachusetts: Lexington Books, 1984.

United Nations. Food and Agriculture Organization. *FAO Production Yearbook,* 40. Rome: 1986.

_____. *Fishery Country Profile: El Salvador.* Rome: January 1986.

_____. *Food Aid in Figures*. Rome: 1986.

United States. Central Intelligence Agency. *Economic and Energy Indicators*. Washington: June 3, 1988.

_____. Central Intelligence Agency. "El Salvador." Pages 69–70 in *World Factbook*. Washington: 1988.

_____. Department of Commerce. *Foreign Economic Trends: El Salvador*. (Report 87–51.) Washington: GPO, July 1987.

_____. Department of Commerce. National Oceanic and Atmospheric Administration. National Marine Fisheries Service. *Capture and Aquaculture Fisheries: Impact on U.S. Seafood Markets*. Washington: GPO, 1988.

_____. Department of Health and Human Services. Social Security Administration. *Social Security Programs Throughout the World, 1985*. (Research Report No. 60.) Washington: GPO, 1986.

_____. Department of State, Bureau of Public Affairs. *Background Notes: El Salvador*. (Department of State Publication, 7794.) Washington: GPO, November 1987.

Wharton Econometric Forecasting Associates. *Latin American Economic Outlook*. Philadelphia: Spring 1987.

Wilkie, James W., and David Lorey (eds.). *Statistical Abstract of Latin America*, 25. Los Angeles: UCLA Latin American Center, 1987.

World Bank. *World Debt Tables, 1987–88*. Washington: 1988.

_____. *World Development Indicators, 1988*. Washington: 1988.

Yearbook of International Trade Statistics, 1985. New York: United Nations, 1986.

Year-Book of Labour Statistics. (47th ed.) Geneva: International Labour Organisation, 1987.

(Various issues of the following publications were also used in the preparation of this chapter: *Central America Report* [Guatemala City], March 1987–January 1988; *Christian Science Monitor*, March 1988; *Latin American Monitor* [London], February 1986; *Latin America Regional Reports: Mexico and Central America* [London], July 1987; *Newsweek*, June 1982; *New York Times*, January 1986– March 1988; *Wall Street Journal*, March 1982–February 1988; and *Washington Post*, May 1982–February 1988.)

Chapter 4

Arana, Ana. "Real News in El Salvador," *Columbia Journalism Review*, 26, No. 6, March–April 1988, 10, 12.

Bagley, Bruce Michael. "Contadora: The Failure of Diplomacy," *Journal of Interamerican Studies and World Affairs,* 28, No. 3, Fall 1986, 1–32.

Bakhtiari, Bahman. "Revolution and the Church in Nicaragua and El Salvador," *Journal of Church and State,* 28, No. 1, Winter 1986, 15–42.

Baloyra, Enrique A. *El Salvador in Transition.* Chapel Hill: University of North Carolina Press, 1982.

————. "Negotiating War in El Salvador: The Politics of End-game," *Journal of Interamerican Studies and World Affairs,* 28, No. 2, Spring 1986, 123–47.

————. "Political Change in El Salvador?" *Current History,* 83, No. 490, February 1984, 54–58, 85–87.

————. "The Seven Plagues of El Salvador," *Current History,* 86, No. 524, December 1987, 413–16, 433–34.

Bell, Judith. "El Salvador-Honduras." Pages 372–74 in Alan J. Day (ed.), *Border and Territorial Disputes.* Detroit: Gale Research, 1982.

Blaustein, Albert P., and Gisbert H. Flanz (eds.). *Constitutions of the Countries of the World.* Dobbs Ferry, New York: Oceana, 1984.

"Central America: New Peace Efforts." Pages 203–12 in *Strategic Survey, 1987–88.* London: International Institute for Strategic Studies, 1988.

Chitnis, Pratap C. "Observing El Salvador: The 1984 Elections," *Third World Quarterly,* 6, No. 4, October 1984, 963–80.

El Salvador. "Código Electoral," *Diario Official* [San Salvador], 298, No. 12, January 19, 1988, 3–35.

————. Secretaria de Información de la Presidencia de la República. *El Salvador de Hoy, 1979.* San Salvador: 1979.

"El Salvador: Introductory Survey." Pages 975–89 in *The Europa Year Book, 1987: A World Survey.* London: Europa, 1987.

Farer, Tom J. "Contadora: The Hidden Agenda," *Foreign Policy,* No. 59, Summer 1985, 59–72.

García, José Z. "El Salvador: A Glimmer of Hope," *Current History,* 85, No. 515, December 1986, 409–12.

————. "El Salvador: Legitimizing the Government," *Current History,* 84, No. 500, March 1985, 101–4, 135–36.

Gastil, Raymond D., and R. Bruce McColm. "The 1984 Presidential Elections in El Salvador," *Freedom at Issue,* No. 79, July–August 1984, 16–20.

Haglund, David G. "The Missing Link: Canada's Security Interests and the Central American Crisis," *International Journal* [Toronto], 42, No. 4, Autumn 1987, 789–820.

Hammer, Michael A. "President Reagan's Policy Toward El Salvador: Success or Failure?" *Fletcher Forum,* 12, No. 1, Winter 1988, 89–109.

Heberle, Jack. "Marxist-Leninist Unions in El Salvador," *Freedom at Issue,* No. 91, July–August 1986, 24–29.

Jessup, David. "El Salvador Unions—The Real Story," *Dissent,* 33, No. 4, Fall 1986, 514–18.

Karl, Terry Lynn. "After La Palma: The Prospects for Democratization in El Salvador," *World Policy Journal,* 2, Spring 1985, 305–30.

_____. "Exporting Democracy: The Unanticipated Effects of U.S. Electoral Policy in El Salvador." Pages 173–91 in Nora Hamilton, Jeffry A. Frieden, Linda Fuller, and Manuel Pastor, Jr. (eds.), *Crisis in Central America: Regional Dynamics and U.S. Policy in the 1980s.* Boulder, Colorado: Westview Press, 1988.

Mason, T. David. "Land Reform and the Breakdown of Clientelist Politics in El Salvador," *Comparative Political Studies,* 18, No. 4, January 1986, 407–516.

Mujal-León, Eusebio. "European Socialism and the Crisis in Central America," *Orbis,* 28, No. 1, Spring 1984, 53–81.

Nichols, John Spicer, and Charles T. Salmon. "El Salvador." Pages 317–24 in George Thomas Kurian (ed.), *World Press Encyclopedia,* 1. New York: Facts on File, 1982.

Purcell, Susan Kaufman. "The Choice in Central America," *Foreign Affairs,* 66, No. 1, 1987, 109–28.

_____. "Demystifying Contadora," *Foreign Affairs,* 64, No. 1, Fall 1985, 74–95.

Robinson, Linda. "Peace in Central America?" *Foreign Affairs,* 66, No. 3, 1988, 591–613.

Sanford, Jonathan E. "Major Trends in U.S. Foreign Assistance to Central America, 1978–1986." (Library of Congress, Congressional Research Service, Report No. 86–88F.) Washington: April 8, 1986.

Serafino, Nina M. "Central American Compliance with the August 5, 1987, Peace Agreement as of November 5, 1987." (Library of Congress, Congressional Research Service, Report No. 87–916F.) Washington: November 16, 1987.

Sharpe, Kenneth E. "El Salvador Revisited: Why Duarte Is in Trouble," *World Policy Journal,* 3, No. 3, Summer 1986, 473–94.

Smyth, Frank. "Don't Put El Salvador in the Win Column Yet," *SAIS Review,* 6, No. 2, Summer–Fall 1986, 59–68.

Sol, Ricardo. *El Salvador: Medios Masivos y Comunicación Popular.* San José, Costa Rica: Editorial Porvenir, 1984.

Stein, Ricardo. "Civil War, Reform, and Reaction in El Salvador." Pages 193–205 in Nora Hamilton, Jeffry A. Frieden, Linda Fuller, and Manuel Pastor, Jr. (eds.), *Crisis in Central*

America: Regional Dynamics and U.S. Policy in the 1980s. Boulder, Colorado: Westview Press, 1988.

Storrs, K. Larry. "El Salvador Aid: Congressional Action, 1981–1986, on President Reagan's Requests for Economic and Military Assistance for El Salvador." (Library of Congress, Congressional Research Service, Report No. 87–230F.) Washington: March 18, 1987.

_____. "El Salvador, 1982–1984: A Chronology of a Period of Transition Resulting from the 1982 and 1984 Elections." (Library of Congress, Congressional Research Service, Report No. 87–656F.) Washington: August 7, 1987.

_____. "Land Reform in El Salvador since Promulgation of a New Salvadoran Constitution in December 1983." (Library of Congress, Congressional Research Service, Report No. 84–534F.) Washington: February 10, 1984.

United States. Congress. 97th, 2d Session. Senate. Committee on Foreign Relations. *Report of the U.S. Official Observer Mission to the El Salvador Constituent Assembly Elections of March 28, 1982.* Washington: GPO, 1982.

_____. Congress. 100th, 1st Session. House of Representatives. Committee on Foreign Affairs. Arms Control and Foreign Policy Caucus. *Bankrolling Failure: United States Policy in El Salvador and the Urgent Need for Reform.* (Report submitted to Arms Control and Foreign Policy Caucus by Senator Mark O. Hatfield, Representative Jim Leach, and Representative George Miller, November 1987.) Washington: 1987.

_____. Congress. 100th, 1st Session. House of Representatives. Committee on Foreign Affairs. Subcommittee on Human Rights and International Organizations and Subcommittee on Western Hemisphere Affairs. *Human Rights and Political Developments in El Salvador, 1987.* Washington: GPO, 1988.

_____. Department of State. Bureau of Public Affairs. "El Salvador," *Gist,* June 1982.

_____. Department of State. Bureau of Public Affairs. "El Salvador: Revolution or Reform?" *Current Policy,* No. 546, February 1984.

Weiner, Lauren. "The Contadora Process: Something for Everyone, Solving Nothing," *National Interest,* No. 4, Summer 1986, 65–73.

(Various issues of the following publications were also used in the preparation of this chapter: *Christian Science Monitor,* July 1984–December 1987; *Latin American Monitor: Central America,* [London], May–June 1985; *Latin American Weekly Report* [London], June 1985–May 1988; *Latin America Regional Reports: Mexico and Central America,* May 1985–June 1988; *New York Times,* June 1983–June 1988 and *Washington Post,* March 1987–July 1988.)

Chapter 5

Americas Watch. *The Civilian Toll, 1986–1987: Ninth Supplement to the Report on Human Rights in El Salvador.* New York: 1987.

Anderson, Thomas P. *Matanza: El Salvador's Communist Revolt of 1932.* Lincoln: University of Nebraska Press, 1971.

Arbucle, Tammy. "Same Hardware, Same Tactics, Same Conclusion in El Salvador?" *Armed Forces Journal International,* 123, December 1985, 46, 48, 52, 56, 58.

Baloyra, Enrique A. *El Salvador in Transition.* Chapel Hill: University of North Carolina Press, 1982.

———. "Negotiating War in El Salvador: The Politics of Endgame," *Journal of Interamerican Studies and World Affairs,* 28, No. 2, Spring 1986, 123–47.

Boyd, Larry. "El Salvador's Armed Forces," *Jane's Defence Weekly* [London], 4, June 28, 1986, 1260–61.

Breene, Robert G., Jr. "Salvador Sitrep," *Soldier of Fortune,* 12, September 1987, 40–44.

Christian, Shirley. "El Salvador's Divided Military," *Atlantic Monthly,* 251, June 1983, 50–53, 57–60.

Devine, Frank. *El Salvador: Embassy under Attack.* New York: Vantage Press, 1981.

DeWind, Adrian W., and Stephen L. Kass. "Justice in El Salvador: A Report of a Mission of Inquiry of the Association of the Bar of the City," *Record of the Association of the Bar of the City of New York,* 38, March 1983, 112–39.

DeYoung, Karen. "White Hand: How the Peace was Lost in El Salvador," *Mother Jones,* 6, June 1981, 26–36, 45–48.

Dickey, Christopher. "Behind the Death Squads: Who They Are, How They Work, and Why No One Can Stop Them," *New Republic,* 189, December 26, 1983, 16–21.

Diskin, Martin. *The Impact of U.S. Policy in El Salvador, 1979–1985.* Berkeley: Institute of International Studies, University of California, 1986.

El Salvador. Ministerio de Justicia. *Código Penal.* San Salvador: 1980.

"El Salvador," *Military Technology,* 10, No. 12, December 1986, 97.

El Salvador: Background to the Crisis. Cambridge, Massachusetts: Central America Information Office, 1982.

El Salvador under General Romero. London: Latin America Bureau, 1979.

English, Andrian J. *Armed Forces of Latin America: Their Histories, Development, Present Strength, and Military Potential.* London: Jane's, 1984.

_____. "Central American Navies," *Navy International* [London], 89, No. 9, September 1984, 532–35.

Gettleman, Marvin E., Patrick Lacefield, Louis Menashe, and David Mermelstein (eds.). *El Salvador: Central America in the New Cold War.* New York: Grove Press, 1986.

Guidos Vejar, Rafael. *El Ascenso del Militarismo en El Salvador.* San Salvador: UCA Editores, 1980.

Hutson, Heyward G. "Are the Salvadoran Armed Forces Ready to Fold?" *World Affairs,* 146, Winter 1983–84, 263–71.

Jane's Defence Weekly [London], June 28, 1986, 1243.

Kapuscinski, Ryszard. "The Soccer War: Design for a Central American Battlefield," *Harper's Magazine,* 272, June 1986, 17.

Kelly, Ross. "Special Operations in El Salvador," *Defense and Foreign Affairs,* 14, August–September 1986, 56–57, 60.

Krulak, Victor H. "Strategic Implications of the Little War," *Strategic Review,* 13, Spring 1985, 31–36.

Leiken, Robert S. "Anatomy of Resistance, El Salvador: Who Are the Rebels and What Do They Want?" *Worldview,* 26, June 1983, 5–9.

Lungo, Mario. *El Salvador, 1981–1984.* San Salvador: UCA Editores, 1986.

McClintock, Michael. *The American Connection: State Terror and Popular Resistance in El Salvador,* 1. London: Zed Books, 1985.

_____. "US Military Assistance to El Salvador: From Indirect to Direct Intervention," *Race and Class,* 26, No. 3, Winter 1985, 63–82.

McColm, R. Bruce. *El Salvador.* New York: Freedom House, 1982.

_____. "El Salvador's Guerrillas: Structure, Strategy, and . . . Success?" *Freedom at Issue,* No. 74, September–October 1983, 3–16.

McDonald, Ronald H. "El Salvador: The Politics of Revolution." Pages 528–44 in Howard J. Wiarda and Harvey F. Kline (eds.), *Latin American Politics and Development.* Boulder, Colorado: Westview Press, 1979.

Maitre, H. Joachim. "The Dying War in El Salvador." Pages 121–35 in Walter F. Hahn (ed.), *Central America and the Reagan Doctrine.* Boston: United States Strategic Institute, 1987.

_____. "The Subsiding War in El Salvador," *Strategic Review,* 13, Winter 1985, 22–29.

Manwaring, Max G., and Court Prisk (eds.). *El Salvador at War: An Oral History.* Washington: National Defense University Press, 1988.

The Military Balance, 1987–1988. London: International Institute for Strategic Studies, 1987.

The Military Balance, 1988–1989. London: International Institute for Strategic Studies, 1988.

Millett, Richard L. "The Politics of Violence: Guatemala and El Salvador," *Current History*, 80, No. 463, February 1981, 70–74, 80.

_____. "Praetorians or Patriots." Pages 326–30 in Robert S. Leiken and Barry Rubin (eds.), *The Central American Crisis Reader*. New York: Summit Books, 1987.

Pena Kampy, Alberto. *El General Martínez: Un Patriarchal Presidente Dictador*. Santa Anita, Mexico: Editorial Tip. Ramírez, 1976.

Radu, Michael S. "Insurgent and Terrorist Groups in Latin America." (Research paper, No. MDA908–83–C–1980.) Philadelphia: Foreign Policy Research Institute, 1984.

_____. "The Structure of the Salvadoran Left," *Orbis*, 28, Winter 1985, 673–84.

Sanford, Jonathan E. "Major Trends in U.S. Foreign Assistance to Central America, 1978–1986." (Library of Congress, Congressional Research Service, Report No. 86–88F.) Washington: April 8, 1986.

Schulz, Donald E. "El Salvador: Revolution and Counterrevolution in the Living Museum." Pages 189–268 in Donald E. Schulz and Douglas H. Graham (eds.), *Revolution and Counterrevolution in Central America and the Caribbean*. Boulder, Colorado: Westview Press, 1984.

Sharpe, Kenneth E., and Martin Diskin. "Facing Facts in El Salvador: Reconciliation or War," *World Policy Journal*, 1, Spring 1984, 517–47.

Storrs, K. Larry. "El Salvador Aid: Congressional Action, 1981–1986, on President Reagan's Requests for Economic and Military Assistance for El Salvador." (Library of Congress, Congressional Research Service, Report No. 87–230F.) Washington: March 18, 1987.

Storrs, K. Larry, and Mark P. Sullivan. "El Salvador: U.S. Foreign Assistance Facts." (Library of Congress, Congressional Research Service, Major Issues System, IB 85113.) Washington: August 26, 1987.

Thomas, Marilyn. *Women of El Salvador*. Philadelphia: Institute for the Study of Human Issues, 1986.

United States. Congress. 97th, 1st Session. House of Representatives. Committee on Foreign Affairs. *U.S. Policy Options in El Salvador*. Washington: GPO, 1981.

_____. Congress. 97th, 1st Session. House of Representatives. Committee on Foreign Affairs. *U.S. Policy Toward El Salvador.* Washington: GPO, 1981.

_____. Congress. 97th, 1st Session. Senate. Committee on Foreign Relations. *The Situation in El Salvador.* Washington: GPO, 1981.

_____. Congress. 97th, 2d Session. Senate. Committee on Foreign Relations. *Certification Concerning Military Aid to El Salvador.* Washington: GPO, 1982.

_____. Congress. 98th, 1st Session. House of Representatives. Committee on Foreign Affairs. *Human Rights in El Salvador.* Washington: GPO, 1983.

_____. Congress. 98th, 1st Session. Senate. Committee on Foreign Relations. *Presidential Certification on Progress in El Salvador.* Washington: GPO, 1983.

_____. Congress. 98th, 2d Session. Senate. Select Committee on Intelligence. *Recent Political Violence in El Salvador.* (98–659.) Washington: GPO, 1984.

_____. Congress. 99th, 1st Session. House of Representatives. Committee on Foreign Affairs. *Developments in El Salvador.* Washington: GPO, 1985.

_____. Congress. 99th, 2d Session. House of Representatives. Committee on Foreign Affairs. *The Air War and Political Developments in El Salvador.* Washington: GPO, 1986.

_____. Congress. 100th, 1st Session. House of Representatives. Committee on Foreign Affairs. Subcommittee on Human Rights and International Organizations and Subcommittee on Western Hemisphere Affairs. *Human Rights and Political Development in El Salvador, 1987.* Washington: GPO, 1988.

_____. Department of State. "Communist Interference in El Salvador." Washington: GPO, 1981.

_____. Department of State. "Report on the Situation in El Salvador." Washington: April 1, 1988.

_____. Department of State. Bureau of Public Affairs. *The Situation in El Salvador.* (Special Report No. 144.) Washington: April 1986.

_____. Department of State. Office of Public Diplomacy for Latin America and the Caribbean. "Victims of Guerrilla Land Mines in El Salvador," *Latin America Dispatch,* July 1987, 8.

_____. Department of State and Department of Defense. "Nicaragua's Military Build-up and Support for Central American Subversion." (Background paper.) Washington: GPO, 1984.

Villalobos Hueso, Joaquin. *Why Is the FMLN Fighting?* San Salvador: S.I., Sistema Radio Venceremos, 1984.

Welson, Linda, et al. *DMS International Defense Budget Forecast.* Greenwich, Connecticut : Defense Marketing Services, 1986.

Wilkie, James W., et al. *Statistical Abstract of Latin America.* Los Angeles: UCLA Latin American Center, 1988.

"World Air Forces," *Flight International* [London], 130, November 29, 1986, 51–52.

Zaid, Gabriel. "Enemy Colleagues: A Reading of the Salvadoran Tragedy," *Dissent,* 29, Winter 1982, 13–40.

(Various issues of the following publications were also used in the preparation of this chapter: *Christian Science Monitor; Financial Times;* Foreign Broadcast Information Service, *Daily Report: Latin America; Jane's Defence Weekly* [London]; *Latinamerica Press; Latin American Monitor* [London]; *Latin American Weekly Report* [London]; *Latin America Regional Reports: Mexico and Central America* [London]; *Los Angeles Times; New York Times; Philadelphia Inquirer; Wall Street Journal; Washington Post;* and *Washington Times.*)

Glossary

Central America—Region between Mexico and Panama including present-day Belize, Guatemala, Honduras, El Salvador, Nicaragua, and Costa Rica.

Central American Common Market (CACM)—The CACM was established by the Organization of Central American States under the General Treaty of Central American Economic Integration signed in Managua, Nicaragua, on December 15, 1960. Its members include Costa Rica, El Salvador, Guatemala, Honduras, and Nicaragua. Its original goals included the establishment of a Central American regional free-trade area, a customs union, and the integration of the industrialization efforts of its member countries. Its efforts were curtailed following the 1969 war between El Salvador and Honduras, when the Hondurans reestablished import duties on CACM products. Despite the continued existence of the organization, most intraregional economic relations have been handled on a bilateral basis since 1970.

colón—El Salvador's monetary unit, divided into 100 centavos. The colón was pegged by the government at US$1 = ¢2.50 until November 1986, when it was officially devalued to US$1 = ¢5 as part of an overall economic austerity package. As of late 1988, there was no parallel exchange market, but dollars could be traded at a higher rate on the black market.

Constituent Assembly—A deliberative body made up of elected delegates who are charged with the responsibility of drafting a new constitution and, in some instances, electing a new president. Traditionally, after it has completed its work a Constituent Assembly reverts to a Legislative Assembly (traditional title of Salvadoran legislatures), which then serves as the country's legislative body until the next scheduled elections.

encomienda—A fiduciary grant of tribute collection rights over Indians conferred by the Spanish crown on individual colonists, who in turn undertook to maintain order and propagate Christianity.

fiscal year (FY)—El Salvador's fiscal year is the calendar year. Where reference is made to United States aid appropriations or disbursements, the United States government's fiscal year is used, which runs from October 1 to September 30, with the date of reference drawn from the year in which the period ends.

For example, FY 1987 began on October 1, 1986, and ended on September 30, 1987.

Gross domestic product (GDP)—A measure of the total value of goods and services produced by the domestic economy during a given period, usually one year. Obtained by adding the value contributed by each sector of the economy in the form of profits, compensation to employees, and depreciation (consumption of capital). Only domestic production is included, not income arising from investments and possessions owned abroad, hence the use of the word *domestic* to distinguish GDP from gross national product (*q.v.*).

gross national product (GNP)—The total market value of all final goods and services produced by an economy during a year. Obtained by adding the gross domestic product (*q.v.*) and the income received from abroad by residents and subtracting payments remitted abroad to nonresidents.

import substitution industrialization—An economic development strategy that emphasizes the growth of domestic industries, often by import protection using tariff and nontariff measures. Proponents favor the export of industrial goods over primary products.

International Monetary Fund (IMF)—Established along with the World Bank (*q.v.*) in 1945, the IMF is a specialized agency affiliated with the United Nations that takes responsibility for stabilizing international exchange rates and payments. The main business of the IMF is the provision of loans to its members when they experience balance of payments difficulties. These loans often carry conditions that require substantial internal economic adjustments by the recipients.

Legislative Assembly—See Constituent Assembly.

liberation theology—An activist movement led by Roman Catholic clergy who trace their inspiration to Vatican Council II (1965), where some church procedures were liberalized, and the Second Latin American Bishops' Conference in Medellín, Colombia (1968), which endorsed greater direct efforts to improve the lot of the poor. Advocates of liberation theology—sometimes referred to as "liberationists"—work mainly through Christian Base Communities (Comunidades Eclesiásticas de Base—CEBs). Members of CEBs meet in small groups to reflect on scripture and discuss its meaning in their lives. They are introduced to a radical interpretation of the Bible, one that employs Marxist terminology to analyze and condemn the wide disparities between the wealthy elite and the impoverished masses in most underdeveloped countries. This reflection often leads members to organize to improve their living standards through cooperatives and civic improvement projects.

repartimiento—Derived from Spanish verb *repartir* (to divide up); a loosely regulated system under which Spanish colonial authorities were empowered to impose and regulate the labor of Indians.

terms of trade—Number of units that must be given up for one unit of goods received by each party, e.g., nation, to a transaction. The terms of trade are said to move in favor of the party that gives up fewer units of goods than it did previously for one unit of goods received, and against the party that gives up more units of goods for one unit of goods received. In international economics, the concept plays an important role in evaluating exchange relationships between nations.

World Bank—Informal name used to designate a group of three affiliated international institutions: the International Bank for Reconstruction and Development (IBRD), the International Development Association (IDA), and the International Finance Corporation (IFC). The IBRD, established in 1945, has the primary purpose of providing loans to developing countries for productive projects. The IDA, a legally separate loan fund administered by the staff of the IBRD, was set up in 1960 to furnish credits to the poorest developing countries on much easier terms than those of conventional IBRD loans. The IFC, founded in 1956, supplements the activities of the IBRD through loans and assistance designed specifically to encourage the growth of productive private enterprises in less-developed countries. The president and certain senior officers of the IBRD hold the same positions in the IFC. The three institutions are owned by the governments of the countries that subscribe their capital. To participate in the World Bank group, member states must first belong to the IMF (*q.v.*).

Index

Published Country Studies

(Area Handbook Series)

550–65	Afghanistan		550–153	Ghana
550–98	Albania		550–87	Greece
550–44	Algeria		550–78	Guatemala
550–59	Angola		550–174	Guinea
550–73	Argentina		550–82	Guyana
550–169	Australia		550–151	Honduras
550–176	Austria		550–165	Hungary
550–175	Bangladesh		550–21	India
550–170	Belgium		550–154	Indian Ocean
550–66	Bolivia		550–39	Indonesia
550–20	Brazil		550–68	Iran
550–168	Bulgaria		550–31	Iraq
550–61	Burma		550–25	Israel
550–37	Burundi/Rwanda		550–182	Italy
550–50	Cambodia		550–30	Japan
550–166	Cameroon		550–34	Jordan
550–159	Chad		550–56	Kenya
550–77	Chile		550–81	Korea, North
550–60	China		550–41	Korea, South
550–26	Colombia		550–58	Laos
550–33	Commonwealth Caribbean, Islands of the		550–24	Lebanon
550–91	Congo		550–38	Liberia
550–90	Costa Rica		550 85	Libya
550–69	Côte d'Ivoire (Ivory Coast)		550–172	Malawi
550–152	Cuba		550–45	Malaysia
550–22	Cyprus		550–161	Mauritania
550–158	Czechoslovakia		550–79	Mexico
550–36	Dominican Republic/Haiti		550–76	Mongolia
550–52	Ecuador		550–49	Morocco
550–43	Egypt		550–64	Mozambique
550–150	El Salvador		550–88	Nicaragua
550–28	Ethiopia		550–157	Nigeria
550–167	Finland		550–94	Oceania
550–155	Germany, East		550–48	Pakistan
550–173	Germany, Fed. Rep. of		550–46	Panama

305